Bulletin of the Philosophical Society of Washington

Vol. V

Also from Westphalia Press

westphaliapress.org

Bulletin of the Philosophical Society of Washington

Vol. V

From The Philosophical Society of Washington Minutes

1881-1882

WESTPHALIA PRESS
An imprint of Policy Studies Organization

Bulletin of the Philosophical Society of Washington, Vol. IV
All Rights Reserved © 2015 by Policy Studies Organization

Westphalia Press
An imprint of Policy Studies Organization
1527 New Hampshire Ave., NW
Washington, D.C. 20036
info@ipsonet.org

ISBN-13: 978-1-63391-183-3
ISBN-10: 1633911837
Cover design by Taillefer Long at Illuminated Stories:
www.illuminatedstories.com

Daniel Gutierrez-Sandoval, Executive Director
PSO and Westphalia Press

Devin Proctor, Director of Media and Publications
PSO and Westphalia Press

Updated material and comments on this edition
can be found at the Westphalia Press website:
www.westphaliapress.org

SMITHSONIAN MISCELLANEOUS COLLECTIONS.

—— 503 ——

BULLETIN

OF THE

PHILOSOPHICAL SOCIETY

OF

WASHINGTON.

VOL. V.

OCTOBER 8, 1881—DEC. 16, 1882.

WASHINGTON:

SMITHSONIAN INSTITUTION.

1883.

BULLETIN

OF THE

PHILOSOPHICAL SOCIETY

OF

WASHINGTON.

VOL. V.

Containing the Minutes of the Society from the 203d Meeting, October 8, 1881, to the 226th Meeting, Dec. 16, 1882.

PUBLISHED BY THE CO-OPERATION OF THE SMITHSONIAN INSTITUTION.

WASHINGTON:
1883.

CONTENTS.

Constitution, March, 1871 ------ ---- ----- ----- ---- ----- ---- -----   6

Standing Rules for the government of the Philosophical Society of Washington, January, 1881 ---- ----- -- --- ---- ----- ---- ----   7

Standing Rules of the General Committee, January, 1881 ---- ----   10

Rules for the Publication of the Bulletin, January, 1881 ----- -----   13

Officers elected December, 1881 --- ---- ---- ---- ---- ---- ----   14

List of Members corrected to May, 1882 ----- ----- ----- -----   15

Bulletin of the regular Meetings ---------------------- ----   21

Officers elected December, 1882 --- ----- ---- --- ---- ---- ----   175

Annual Report of the Treasurer- ------------ ----- ----   176

Index of Names --- ----- ---- ---- ----- ---- ---- ----   183

Index of Subjects ---- ----- ---- ---- ----- ---- -----   187

CONSTITUTION, STANDING RULES,

AND

LIST OF OFFICERS AND MEMBERS

OF

THE PHILOSOPHICAL SOCIETY

OF

WASHINGTON.

CONSTITUTION

OF

THE PHILOSOPHICAL SOCIETY OF WASHINGTON.

ARLICLE I. The name of this Society shall be THE PHILOSOPHICAL SOCIETY OF WASHINGTON.

ARTICLE II. The officers of the Society shall be a President, four Vice-Presidents, a Treasurer, and two Secretaries.

ARTICLE III. There shall be a General Committee, consisting of the officers of the Society and nine other members.

ARTICLE IV. The officers of the Society and the other members of the General Committee shall be elected annually by ballot; they shall hold office until their successors are elected, and shall have power to fill vacancies.

ARTICLE V. It shall be the duty of the General Committee to make rules for the government of the Society, and to transact all its business.

ARTICLE VI. This constitution shall not be amended except by a three-fourths vote of those present at an annual meeting for the election of officers, and after notice of the proposed change shall have been given in writing at a stated meeting of the Society at least four weeks previously.

STANDING RULES

PHILOSOPHICAL SOCIETY OF WASHINGTON.

JANUARY, 1881.

---

1. The Stated Meetings of the Society shall be held at 8 o'clock P. M. on every alternate Saturday; the place of meeting to be designated by the General Committee.

2. Notice of the time and place of meeting shall be sent to each member by one of the Secretaries.

When necessary, Special Meetings may be called by the President.

3. The Annual Meeting for the election of officers shall be the last stated meeting in the month of December.

The order of proceedings (which shall be announced by the Chair) shall be as follows:

First, the reading of the minutes of the last Annual Meeting.

Second, the presentation of the annual reports of the Secretaries, including the announcement of the names of members elected since the last annual meeting.

Third, the presentation of the annual report of the Treasurer.

Fourth, the announcement of the names of members who having complied with Section 12 of the Standing Rules, are entitled to vote on the election of officers.

Fifth, the election of President.

Sixth, the election of four Vice-Presidents.

Seventh, the election of Treasurer.

Eighth, the election of two Secretaries.

Ninth, the election of nine members of the General Committee.

Tenth, the consideration of Amendments to the Constitution of the Society, if any such shall have been proposed in accordance with Article VI of the Constitution.

Eleventh, the reading of the rough minutes of the meeting.

4. Elections of officers are to be held as follows:

In each case nominations shall be made by means of an informal ballot, the result of which shall be announced by the Secretary; after which the first formal ballot shall be taken.

In the ballot for Vice-Presidents, Secretaries, and Members of the General Committee, each voter shall write on one ballot as many names as there are officers to be elected, viz., four on the first ballot for Vice-Presidents, two on the first for Secretaries, and nine on the first for Members of the General Committee; and on each subsequent ballot as many names as there are persons yet to be elected; and those persons who receive a majority of the votes cast shall be declared elected.

If in any case the informal ballot result in giving a majority for any one, it may be declared formal by a majority vote.

5. The Stated Meetings, with the exception of the annual meeting, shall be devoted to the consideration and discussion of scientific subjects.

The Stated Meeting next preceding the Annual Meeting shall be set apart for the delivery of the President's Annual Address.

6. Sections representing special branches of science may be formed by the General Committee upon the written recommendation of twenty members of the Society.

7. Persons interested in science, who are not residents of the District of Columbia, may be present at any meeting of the Society, except the annual meeting, upon invitation of a member.

8. Similar invitations to residents of the District of Columbia, not members of the Society, must be submitted through one of the Secretaries to the General Committee for approval.

9. Invitations to attend during three months the meetings of the Society and participate in the discussion of papers, may, by a vote of nine members of the General Committee, be issued to persons nominated by two members.

10. Communications intended for publication under the auspices of the Society shall be submitted in writing to the General Committee for approval.

11. New members may be proposed in writing by three members of the Society for election by the General Committee: but no person shall be admitted to the privileges of membership unless he signifies his acceptance thereof in writing within two months after notification of his election.

12. Each member shall pay annually to the Treasurer the sum of five dollars, and no member whose dues are unpaid shall vote at the annual meeting for the election of officers, or be entitled to a copy of the Bulletin.

In the absence of the Treasurer, the Secretary is authorized to receive the dues of members.

The names of those two years in arrears shall be dropped from the list of members.

Notice of resignation of membership shall be given in writing to the General Committee through the President or one of the Secretaries.

13. The fiscal year shall terminate with the Annual Meeting.

14. Members who are absent from the District of Columbia for more than twelve months may be excused from payment of the annual assessments, in which case their names shall be dropped from the list of members. They can, however, resume their membership by giving notice to the President of their wish to do so.

15. Any member not in arrears may, by the payment of one hundred dollars at any one time, become a life member, and be relieved from all further annual dues and other assessments.

All moneys received in payment of life membership shall be invested as portions of a permanent fund, which shall be directed solely to the furtherance of such special scientific work as may be ordered by the General Committee.

STANDING RULES

OF THE

GENERAL COMMITTEE OF THE PHILOSOPHICAL SOCIETY OF WASHINGTON.

JANUARY, 1881.

1. The President, Vice-Presidents, and Secretaries of the Society shall hold like offices in the General Committee.

2. The President shall have power to call special meetings of the Committee, and to appoint Sub-Committees.

3. The Sub-Committees shall prepare business for the General Committee, and perform such other duties as may be entrusted to them.

4. There shall be two Standing Sub-Committees; one on Communications for the Stated Meetings of the Society, and another on Publications.

5. The General Committee shall meet at half-past seven' o'clock on the evening of each Stated Meeting, and by adjournment at other times.

6. For all purposes except for the amendment of the Standing Rules of the Committee or of the Society, and the election of members, six members of the Committee shall constitute a quorum.

7. The names of proposed new members recommended in conformity with Section 11 of the Standing Rules of the Society, may be presented at any meeting of the General Committee, but shall lie over for at least four weeks before final action, and the concur-

(11)

rence of twelve members of the Committee shall be necessary to election.

The Secretary of the General Committee shall keep a chronological register of the elections and acceptances of members.

8. These Standing Rules, and those for the government of the Society, shall be modified only with the consent of a majority of the members of the General Committee.

RULES

FOR THE

PUBLICATION OF THE BULLETIN

OF THE

PHILOSOPHICAL SOCIETY OF WASHINGTON.

JANUARY, 1881.

---

1. The President's annual address shall be published in full.

2. The annual reports of the Secretaries and of the Treasurer shall be published in full.

3. When directed by the General Committee, any communication may be published in full.

4. Abstracts of papers and remarks on the same will be published, when presented to the Secretary by the author in writing within two weeks of the evening of their delivery, and approved by the Committee on Publications. Brief abstracts prepared by one of the Secretaries and approved by the Committee on Publications may also be published.

5. Communications which have been published elsewhere, so as to be generally accessible, will appear in the Bulletin by title only, but with a reference to the place of publication, if made known in season to the Committee on Publications.

NOTE. *The attention of members to the above rules is specially requested.*

(13)

OFFICERS

OF THE

PHILOSOPHICAL SOCIETY OF WASHINGTON.

ELECTED DECEMBER 17, 1881.

President _____ WILLIAM B. TAYLOR.

Vice Presidents _____ J. K. BARNES,   J. E. HILGARD,
                                  J. C. WELLING,   J. J. WOODWARD.

Treasurer _____ CLEVELAND ABBE.

Secretaries _____ MARCUS BAKER,   T. N. GILL.

MEMBERS AT LARGE OF THE GENERAL COMMITTEE.

J. S. BILLINGS,	WILLIAM HARKNESS,
C. E. DUTTON,	GARRICK MALLERY,
J. R. EASTMAN,	SIMON NEWCOMB,
E. B. ELLIOTT,	J. W. POWELL,
C. A. SCHOTT.	

STANDING COMMITTEES.

On Communications :

MARCUS BAKER, *Chairman.*   C. E. DUTTON,   T. N. GILL.

On Publications :

T. N. GILL, *Chairman.*   CLEVELAND ABBE,   S. F. BAIRD,*   MARCUS BAKER.

* As Secretary of the Smithsonian Institution.

LIST OF MEMBERS

OF THE

PHILOSOPHICAL SOCIETY OF WASHINGTON.

Corrected to May, 1882.

(a) indicates a *founder* of the Society.

(b) indicates *deceased.*

(c) indicates *absent* from the District of Columbia and excused from payment of dues until announcing their return.

(d) indicates *resigned.*

(e) indicates *dropped* for non-payment or nothing known of him.

NAME.	P. O. Address and Residence.	Date of Admission.
Abbe, Cleveland..............................	Army Signal Office. 2017 I St. N. W.	1871, Oct. 29
Abert, Sylvanus Thayer.................	Engineer's Office, War Department. 1724 Penn. Ave. N.W.	1875, Jan. 30
Adams, Henry	1605 H St................	1831, Feb. —
Aldis, Asa Owen.............................	1617 Rhode Island Ave. N. W...	1873, Mar. 1
Allen, James	Army Signal Office. 1707 G St. N. W.	1882, Feb. 25
Alvord, Benjamin	1207 Q St. N. W.............................	1872, Mar. 23
Antisell, Thomas (a)	Patent Office. 1311 Q St. N. W......	1871, Mar. 13
Avery, Robert Stanton...................	Coast and Geodetic Survey Office. 320 A St. S. E.	1879, Oct. 11
Babcock, Orville Elias...................	2024 G St. N. W............................	1871, June 9
Bailey, Theodorus (b)	....	1873, Mar. 1
Baird, Spencer Fullerton (a)	Smithsonian Institution. 1445 Mass. Ave. N. W.	1871, Mar. 13
Baker, Frank..............................	326 C St. N. W...............................	1881, May 14
Baker, Marcus.......	Coast and Geodetic Survey Office. 1205 Rhode Island Ave. N. W.	1876, Mar. 11
Bancroft, George...........................	1623 H St. N. W...............................	1875, Jan. 16
Barnes, Joseph K (a)	Surg. Genl's Office. 1723 H St. N. W.	1871, Mar. 13
Bartley, Thomas Welles	Office, 1343 F St. N.W. Res., 1016 13th St. N. W.	1873, Mar. 29
Bates, Henry Hobart....................	Patent Office. 1313 R St. N. W............	1871, Nov. 4
Beardslee, Lester Anthony (c)........	Navy Department.	1875, Feb. 27
Bell, Alexander Graham	1221 Conn. Ave. N.W. Res., 1302 Conn. Ave. N. W.	1879, Mar. 29
Bell, Chichester Alexander..........	1221 Conn. Ave. N.W. Res., 2023 Mass. Ave. N. W.	1881, Oct. 8
Benét, Stephen Vincent (a)	Ordnance Office, War Department. 1717 I St. N. W.	1871, Mar. 13
Bessels, Emil.................................	Smithsonian Institution. 1441 Mass. Ave. N. W.	1875, Jan. 16
Billings, John Shaw (a)	Surg. Génl's Office. 3027 N St. N. W.	1871, Mar. 13
Birney, William................................	330 4½ St. N.W. Res., 1901 Harewood Ave., Le Droit Park.	1879, Mar. 29
Birnie, Rogers (c)...........................	Cold Spring, Putnam Co., N. Y.	1876, Mar. 11
Burchard, Horatio Chapin.............	Director of the Mint, Treasury Dept. Res., Riggs House.	1879, May 10
Burnett, Swan Moses.....................	1215 I St. N. W.............................	1879, Mar. 29
Busey, Samuel Clagett...................	1525 I St. N. W.............................	1874, Jan. 17
Capron, Horace (a)	The Portland.................................	1871, Mar. 13
Case, Augustus Ludlow (c)............	Navy Department. Bristol, R. I.........	1872, Nov. 16
Casey, Thomas Lincoln (a)	Engineer Bureau, War Department. 1419 K St. N. W.	1871, Mar. 13

15

NAME.	P. O. ADDRESS AND RESIDENCE.	DATE OF ADMISSION.
Caziarc, Louis Vasmer	Army Signal Office. 1446 N St. N. W.	1882, Feb. 25
Chase, Salmon Portland (a b)		1871, Mar. 13
Chickering, John White, Jr.	Deaf Mute College, Kendall Green	1874, Apr. 11
Christie, Alexander Smyth	Coast and Geodetic Survey Office. 1102 14th St. N. W.	1880, Dec. 4
Clapp, William Henry	Army Signal Office. 806 18th St. N.W.	1882, Feb. 25
Clark, Edward	Architect's Office, Capitol. 417 4th St. N. W.	1877, Feb. 24
Clark, Ezra Westcott	Revenue Marine Bureau, Treasury Department. Res., Woodley road.	1882, Mar. 25
Clarke, Frank Wigglesworth (c)	University of Cincinnati. Albion Place, Cincinnati, Ohio.	1874, Apr. 11
Coffin, John Huntington Crane (a)	1901 I St. N. W.	1871, Mar. 13
Collins, Frederick (b)		1879, Oct. 21
Comstock, John Henry	Cornell University, Ithaca, N. Y	1880, Feb. 14
Coues, Elliott	Smithsonian Inst. 1321 N St. N. W	1874, Jan. 17
Craig, Benjamin Faneuil (a b)		1871, Mar. 13
Craig, Robert	Army Signal Office. 1008 I St. N. W.	1873, Jan. 4
Craig, Thomas	Johns Hopkins Univ., Baltimore, Md.	1879, Nov. 22
Crane, Charles Henry (a)	Surg. Genl's Office. 1909 F St. N. W.	1871, Mar. 13
Curtis, Josiah	428 7th street N. W. Riggs House.	1874, Mar. 28
Cutts, Richard Dominicus	Coast and Geodetic Survey Office. 1725 H St. N. W.	1871, Apr. 29
Dall, William Healey (a)	P. O. Box 406. 1119 12th St. N. W	1871, Mar. 13
Davis, Charles Henry (b)		1874, Jan. 17
Davis, Charles Henry	Navy Department. 1705 Rhode Island Ave. N. W.	1880, June 19
Dean, Richard Crain (b)		1872, Apr. 23
De Caindry, William Augustin	Commissary General's Office. 924 19th St. N. W.	1881, Apr. 30
De Land, Theodore Louis	Treasury Dept. 126 7th St. N. E	1880, Dec. 18
Dewey, George (d)	Light House Board. 826 14th St. N.W.	1879, Feb. 15
Doolittle, Myrick Hascall	Coast and Geodetic Survey Office. 1925 I St. N. W.	1876, Feb. 12
Dorr, Fredric William (b)		1874, Jan. 17
Dunwoody, Henry Harrison Chase	Army Signal Office. 1412 G St. N. W.	1873, Dec. 20
Dutton, Clarence Edward	Geological Survey	1872, Jan. 27
Dyer, Alexander B. (a b)		1871, Mar. 13
Eastman, John Robie	Naval Observatory. 2721 N St. N. W.	1871, May 27
Eaton, Amos Beebe (a b)		1871, Mar. 13
Eaton, John	Bureau of Education, Interior Dept. 712 East Capitol St.	1874, May 8
Eldredge, Stewart (c)		1871, June 9
Elliot, George Henry (a d)	Engineer Bureau, War Department	1871, Mar. 13
Elliott, Ezekiel Brown (a)	Mint Bureau, Treasury Department. 607 I St. N. W.	1871, Mar. 13
Endlich, Frederic Miller	Smithsonian Institution	1873, Mar. 1
Ewing, Charles (e)		1874, Jan. 17
Ewing, Hugh (c)	Lancaster, Ohio	1874, Jan. 17
Farquhar, Edward Jessop	Patent Office Library. 1915 H St. N.W.	1876, Feb. 12
Farquhar, Henry	Coast and Geodetic Survey Office. 726 20th St. N. W.	1881, May 14
Ferrel, William	Coast and Geodetic Survey Office. 471 C St. N. W.	1872, Nov. 16
Fletcher, Robert	Surgeon Genl's Office. 314 Ind. Ave.	1873, Apr. 10
Flint, Albert Stowell	Naval Observatory. 1209 Rhode Island Ave. N. W.	1882, Mar. 25
Flint, James Milton	Smithsonian Inst. Riggs House	1881, Mar. 26
Foote, Elisha (a c)		1871, Mar. 13
Foster, John Gray (b)		1873, Jan. 18
French, Henry Flagg	Treasury Department. 137 East Capitol St.	1882, Mar. 25
Frisby, Edgar	Naval Observatory. 3006 P St. N. W.	1872, Nov. 16
Fristoe, Edward T	Columbian College. College Hill N.W.	1873, Mar. 29
Gale, Leonard Dunnell	1230 Mass. Ave. N. W.	1874, Jan. 17
Gallaudet, Edward Miner	Deaf Mute College, Kendall Green	1875, Feb. 27
Gannett, Henry	Geological Survey. 1881 Harewood Ave., Le Droit Park.	1874, Apr. 11
Gardner, James Terry (c)	State Library, Albany, N. Y	1874, Jan. 17
Garnett, Alexander Young P. (d)	1317 N. Y. Ave. N. W.	1878, Mar. 16
Gihon, Albert Leary	Navy Department. 1736 I St. N. W	1880, Dec. 18

NAME.	P. O. ADDRESS AND RESIDENCE.	DATE OF ADMISSION.
Gilbert, Grove Karl......................	Geological Survey. 'Le Droit Park.....	1873, June 7
Gill, Theodore Nicholas (*a*)..........	Smithsonian Inst. 321-323 4½ St. N.W.	1871, Mar. 13
Godding, William Whiting	Government Asylum for the Insane ...	1879, Mar. 29
Goode, George Brown	National Museum. 1620 Mass. Av. N.W.	1874, Jan. 31
Goodfellow, Edward......................	Coast and Geodetic Survey Office.......	1875, Dec. 18
Goodfellow, Henry (*d*)..................	Bureau of Military Justice, War Dept.	1871, Nov. 4
Gore, James Howard	Columbian College. 1305 Q St. N. W.	1880, Mar. 14
Graves, Edward Oziel (*c*)......	....	1874, Apr. 11
Graves, Walter Hayden (*c*)......	Denver, Colorado.....................	1878, May 25
Greely, Adolphus Washington (*c*).....	....	1880, June 19
Green, Bernard Richardson..........	1738 N St. N. W........................	1879, Feb. 15
Green, Francis Mathews..............	Bureau of Navigation, Navy Dept.......	1875, Nov. 9
Greene, Benjamin Franklin (*a c*).....	West Lebanon, N. H....................	1871. Mar. 13
Greene, Francis Vinton...............	War Department. 1915 G St. N. W......	1875, Apr. 10
Gunnell, Francis Mackall (*c*).........	600 20th St. N. W......................	1879, Feb. 1
Hains, Peter Conover (*c*)	Office Light House Engineer, Charleston, S. C.	1879, Feb. 15
Hall, Asaph (*a*)	Naval Observatory. 2715 N St. N. W.	1871, Mar. 13
Hanscom, Isaiah (*b*)...................	....	1873, Dec. 20
Harkness, William (*a*)...............	Naval Observatory. 1415 G St. N. W.	1871, Mar. 13
Hassler, Ferdinand Augustus (*c*)...	Tustin City, Los Angeles Co., Cal.........	1880, May 8
Hayden, Ferdinand Vandeveer (*ac*)	Geological Survey. 1803 Arch street, Philadelphia, Penna.	1871, Mar. 13
Hazen, Henry Allen.....................	Army Signal Office. 1209 R. I. Av. N.W.	1882, Mar. 25
Hazen, William Babcock..............	Army Signal Office. 1601 K St. N. W.	1881, Feb. —
Henry, Joseph (*a b*)...................	....	1871, Mar. 13
Henshaw, Henry Wetherbee.........	Bureau of Ethnology. 903 M St. N.W.	1874, Apr. 11
Hilgard, Julius Erasmus (*a*).........	Coast and Geodetic Survey Office. 1709 Rhode Island Ave. N. W.	1871, Mar. 13
Hill, George William....	Nautical Almanac Office. 318 Ind. Ave. N. W.	1879, Feb. 1
Holden, Edward Singleton (*c*)........	Madison, Wisconsin	1873, June 21
Holmes, William Henry.	Geological Survey.....................	1879, Mar. 29
Hough, Franklin Benjamin (*c*)......	Agricultural Department...............	1879, Mar. 29
Howell, Edwin Eugene (*c*)	Rochester, N. Y........	1874, Jan. 31
Howgate, Henry W......................	....	1873, Jan. 18
Humphreys, Andrew Atkinson (*a*)..	S. E. Corner 15th and K Sts. N. W....	1871, Mar. 13
Huntington, David Lowe..............	Army Med. Museum. 1709 M St. N.W.	1877, Dec. 21
Jackson, Henry Arundel Lambe (*c*)	War Department.....................	1875, Jan. 30
James, Owen (*c*).......................	Hyde Park, Penna.......	1880, Jan. 3
Jeffers, William Nicolson (*d*)	Navy Department.....................	1877, Feb. 24
Jenkins, Thornton Alexander (*a*)..	2115 Penn. Ave. N. W................	1871, Mar. 13
Johnson, Arnold Burgess..............	Light House Board, Treasury Dept. 501 Maple Ave., Le Droit Park.	1878, Jan. 19
Johnson, Joseph Taber...............	937 New York Ave. N. W.............	1879, Mar. 29
Johnston, William Waring...........	1401 H St. N. W.......................	1873, Jan. 21
Kampf, Ferdinand (*b*)...............	....	1875, Dec. 18
Keith, Reuel (*c*)........	....	1871, Oct. 29
Kidder, Jerome Henry...............	Navy Department. 1601 O St. N. W.	1880, May 8
Kilbourne, Charles Evans...........	Army Signal Office. Lexington House.	1880, June 19
King, Albert Freeman Africanus...	726 13th St. N. W	1875, Jan. 16
King, Clarence (*d*).....................	....	1879, May 10
Knox, John Jay.....................	Treasury Dept. 1127 10th St. N. W....	1874, May 8
Kummell, Charles Hugo..............	Coast and Geodetic Survey Office. 608 Q St. N. W.	1882, Mar. 25
Lane, Jonathan Homer (*a b*)........	....	1871, Mar. 13
Lawyer, Winfield Peter................	Mint Bureau, Treasury Department. 1912 I St. N. W.	1881, Feb. 19
Lee, William	2111 Penn. Ave. N. W...............	1874, Jan. 17
Lincoln, Nathan Smith..............	1514 H St. N. W.......................	1871, May, 27
Lockwood, Henry H. (*d*)............	....	1871, Oct. 29
Loomis, Eben Jenks	Nautical Almanac Office. 1413 College Hill Terrace N. W.	1880, Feb. 14
Lull, Edward Phelps	Navy Department. 1313 M St. N. W....	1875, Dec. 4
Lyford, Stephen Carr (*d*).............	Ordnance Office, War Department......	1873, Jan. 18
Macauley, Henry Clay (*c*)............	....	1880, Jan. 3
McGuire, Frederick Bauders........	1306 F St. N. W. Res., 614 E St. N. W.	1879, Feb. 15
Mack, Oscar A. (*b*)...................	....	1872, Jan. 27
McMurtrie, William...................	Agricultural Dept. 1728 I St. N. W......	1876, Feb. 26

NAME.	P. O. ADDRESS AND RESIDENCE.	DATE OF ADMISSION.
Mallery, Garrick............................	Bureau of Ethnology. P. O, Box 585. Res., 1323 N St. N. W.	1875, Jan. 30
Marvin, Joseph Badger (c)............	....	1878, May 25
Marvine, Archibald Robertson (b).		1874, Jan. 31
Mason, Otis Tufton	Columbian College. 1305 Q St. N. W.	1875, Jan. 30
Meek, Fielding Bradford (a b)......		1871, Mar. 13
Meigs, Montgomery (c)..................	War Department. Rock Island, Ill.	1877, Mar. 24
Meigs, Montgomery Cunning- ham (a)	1239 Vermont Ave. N. W....................	1871, Mar. 13
Menocal, Aniceto Garcia..............	Navy Yard, Washington, D. C	1877, Feb. 24
Mew, William Manuel...................	Army Medical Museum. 942 New York Ave. N. W.	1873, Dec. 20
Milner, James William (b).............		1874, Jan. 31
Morris, Martin Ferdinand (c)........	717 12th St. N. W.	1877, Feb. 24
Mussey, Reuben Delavan	P. O. Box 618. Res., 508 5th St. N. W.	1881, Dec. 3
Myer, Albert J. (a b)		1871, Mar. 13
Myers, William (c)................;......	Office of Commissary General, War Department.	1871, June 23
Newcomb, Simon (a).......................	Navy Department. 1336 11th St. N.W.	1871, Mar. 13
Nichols, Charles Henry (c)............		1872, May 4
Nicholson, Walter Lamb (a)	Topographer of Post Office Dept. 1322 I St. N. W.	1871, Mar. 13
Nordhoff, Charles.....................	New York Herald Bureau. 1027 New York Ave. N. W.	1879, May 10
Osborne, John Walter..	212 Delaware Ave. N. E.......................	1878, Dec. 7
Otis, George Alexander(a b).........		1871, Mar. 13
Packard, Robert Lawrence (e).......	Patent Office. 2022 G St. N. W...........	1875, Feb. 27
Parke, John Grubb (a)...................	Engineer Bureau, War Department. 16 16½ St. N. W.	1871, Mar. 13
Parker, Peter (a)...........	2 La Fayette Square	1871, Mar. 13
Parry, Charles Christopher (c)......	Burlington, Iowa...............................	1871, May 19
Patterson, Carlile Pollock (b)........	....	1871, Nov. 17
Paul, Henry Martyn (c)................	University of Tokio, Japan................	1877, May 19
Peale, Albert Charles (c). ...•........	Schuylkill Haven, Schuylkill Co., Pa.	1874, Apr. 11
Peale, Titian Ramsay (a c)............	....	1871, Mar. 13
Peirce, Benjamin (a b)................		1871, Mar. 13
Peirce, Charles Sanders (c)............	Coast and Geodetic Survey Office. Res., Baltimore, Md.	1873, Mar. 1
Pilling, James Constantine............	Geological Survey. 903 M St. N. W.....	1881, Feb. 19
Poe, Orlando Metcalfe...	Headquarters of the Army. 1507 Rhode Island Ave. N. W.	1873, Oct. 4
Porter, David Dixon (d)................	1710 H St. N. W.	1874, Apr. 11
Powell, John Wesley....................	Geological Survey. 910 M St. N. W.....	1874, Jan. 17
Prentiss, Daniel Webster..............	1224 9th St. N. W..............................	1880, Jan. 3
Pritchett, Henry Smith (c)	Washington University, St. Louis, Mo.	1879, Mar. 29
Rathbone, Henry Reed (c)............		1874, Jan. 17
Ridgway, Robert (c)......................	Smithsonian Inst. 1214 Va. Av. N.W.	1874, Jan. 31
Riley, Charles Valentine...............	Agricultural Dept. 1700 13th St. N.W.	1878, Nov. 9
Riley, John Campbell (b)		1877, May 19
Ritter, William Francis McKnight..	Nautical Almanac Office. 16 Grant Place.	1879, Oct. 21
Rodgers, Christopher Raymond Perry (c)	1723 I St. N. W..................................	1872, Mar. 9
Rodgers, John (b).		1872, Nov. 16
Rogers, Joseph Addison (c)......... ...	Naval Observatory.............................	1872, Mar. 9
Russell, Israel Cook......................	Geological Survey......................•......	1882, Mar. 25
Sands, Benjamin Franklin (a).......	816 15th St. N. W.............................	1871, Mar. 13
Saville, James Hamilton	342 D St. (La. Ave.) N. W. Res., 1315 M St. N. W.	1871, Apr. 29
Sawyer, Frederic Adolphus (e)	....	1873, Oct. 4
Schaeffer, George Christian (a b)....		1871, Mar. 13
Schott, Charles Anthony (a)..........	Coast and Geodetic Survey Office. 212 1st St. S. E.	1871, Mar. 13
Searle, Henry Robinson................	1223 10th St. N. W............................	1877, Dec. 21
Seymour, George Dudley..............	607 7th St. N.W. Res., 1007 9th St. N.W.	1881, Dec. 3
Shellabarger, Samuel...................	Room 23, Corcoran Building. Res., 812 17th St. N. W.	1875, Apr. 10
Sherman, John............................	1317 K St. N. W...............................	1874, Jan. 17
Sherman, William Tecumseh (a d)..	War Department. 817 15th St. N. W...	1871, Mar. 13
Shufeldt, Robert Wilson................	Surg. Genl's Office. 819 17th St. N.W.	1881, Nov. 5

NAME.	P. O. ADDRESS AND RESIDENCE.	DATE OF ADMISSION.
Sicard, Montgomery (c)	Ordnance Bureau, Navy Department. 1404 L St. N. W.	1877, Feb. 24
Sigsbee, Charles Dwight	Hydrographic Office, Navy Dept. 3319 U St., West Washington.	1879, Mar. 1
Skinner, Aaron Nicholas (e)	Naval Observatory. 1726 10th St. N.W.	1875, Feb. 27
Smith, David (c)	Navy Department	1876, Dec. 2
Smith, Edwin	Coast and Geodetic Survey	1880, Oct. 23
Spofford, Ainsworth Rand	Library of Congress. 1621 Mass. Ave. N. W.	1872, Jan. 27
Stearns, John (c)		1874, Mar. 28
Stone, Ormond (c)	Leander McCormick Observatory, University of Virginia.	1874, Mar. 28
Story, John Patten	Army Signal Office. 921 17th St. N.W.	1880, June 19
Taylor, Frederick William	Smithsonian Institution. 1120 Vermont Ave. N. W.	1881, Feb. 19
Taylor, George (e)	804 E St. N. W. Res., 1120 Vermont Ave. N. W.	1873, Mar. 1
Taylor, William Bower (a)	Smithsonian Inst. 457 C St. N. W	1871, Mar. 13
Thompson, Almon Harris (c)	Ivanpah, Greenwood Co., Kansas	1875, Apr. 10
Tilden, William Calvin (c)	Army Medical Museum	1871, Apr. 29
Todd, David Peck (c)	Amherst, Mass	1878, Nov. 23
Toner, Joseph Meredith	615 Louisiana Ave	1873, June 7
Twining, William J. (b)		1878, Nov. 23
Upton, Jacob Kendrick (d)	Cooke & Co., cor. 15th St. and Penn. Ave. 1721 De Sales St.	1878, Feb. 2
Upton, William Wirt	2d Comptroller's Office, Treasury Dept. 810 12th St. N. W.	1882, Mar. 25
Upton, Winslow	Army Signal Office. 1441 Chapin St. N. W.	1880, Dec. 4
Vasey, George	Agricultural Dept. 1437 S St. N. W	1875, June 5
Waldo, Frank	Army Signal Office. 1427 Chapin St. N. W.	1881, Dec. 3
Walker, Francis Amasa (c)	Mass. Inst. of Technology, Boston, Mass.	1872, Jan. 27
Ward, Lester Frank	Geological Survey. 1464 R. I. Av. N.W.	1876, Nov. 18
Warren, Charles (e)	Bureau of Education. 1208 N St. N. W.	1874, May 8
Webster, Albert Lowry	Geological Survey. P. O. Box 591	1882, Mar. 25
Welling, James Clarke	Columbian College	1872, Nov. 16
Wheeler, George M. (c)	Engineer Bureau, War Department	1873, June 7
Wheeler, Junius B (a c)	West Point, New York	1871, Mar. 13
White, Charles Abiathar	Geological Survey. Le Droit Park	1876, Dec. 16
White, Zebulon Lewis (c)	Providence, Rhode Island	1880, June 19
Wilson, Allen D.	Geological Survey.	1874, Apr. 11
Wilson, James Ormond	Franklin School Building. 1439 Mass. Ave. N. W.	1873, Mar. 1
Winlock, William Crawford	Naval Observatory. 1903 F St. N. W.	1880, Dec. 4
Wolcott, Christopher Columbus (d)	War Department	1875, Feb. 27
Wood, Joseph (c)	Asst. Engineer B. & P. R. R.	1875, Jan. 16
Wood, William Maxwell (c)	Navy Department	1871, Dec. 2
Woodward, Joseph Janvier (a)	Army Med. Museum. 620 F St. N.W.	1871, Mar. 13
Woodworth, John Maynard (b)		1874, Jan. 31
Yarnall, Mordecai (b)		1871, Apr. 29
Yarrow, Harry Crécy	814 17th St. N. W	1874, Jan. 31
Zumbrock, Anton	Coast and Geodetic Survey Office. 306 C St. N. W.	1875, Jan. 30

Number of *founders* 44
    "   members *deceased* 28
    "   "   *absent* 52
    "   "   *resigned*.............................. 12
    "   "   *dropped*.............................. 5
    "   "   *active*................................. 149

Total number enrolled............................. 246

BULLETIN

OF THE

PHILOSOPHICAL SOCIETY OF WASHINGTON.

203D MEETING.   OCTOBER 8, 1881.

The Society, in accordance with the notice of adjournment at its last June meeting, resumed its sessions.

The President (Mr. J. J. WOODWARD) in the Chair.

Thirty-eight members present.

Mr. G. K. GILBERT read a communication on

THE QUATERNARY CLIMATE OF THE GREAT BASIN.

The matters contained in this communication were a summary of certain chapters which will appear from the pen of Mr. Gilbert in the Second Annual Report of the Director of the United States Geological Survey now in press. The observations of which the communication was a resume were made in his capacity of Geologist in charge of the Exploration of the Utah Division.

Remarks were made on Mr. Gilbert's communication by Mr. THOMAS ANTISELL.

Mr. E. B. ELLIOTT also made a communication on

ACCRUED INTEREST ON GOVERNMENT SECUTITIES.

Mr. W. B. TAYLOR exhibited to the Society a photographic print from a single negative including about 140 degrees of panorama. The ordinary camera does not usually comprise more than about 60 degrees, and requires as a necessary condition of good definition perfect stability of the lens and the plate. In the present case, an inspection of the two houses presented in the rural view, (especially of the longer one near the middle of the picture,) with the curved road winding between them to the right, shows that a revolving camera was employed; the long sensitive plate having evidently been simultaneously moved transversely in the reverse direction to that of the objective. This perfect co-ordination of the revolving and sliding movements could be obtained by a mechanical gearing; and the extended landscape be thus successively impressed upon advancing portions of the plate—probably through a vertical slit in a diaphragm immediately in front of the plate. That the corelation of movement has been very perfect is evidenced by the admirable precision of every detail in the photograph. It will be observed that the three men standing in different parts of the field of view are one and the same individual, who has had time to pass behind the instrument, and to twice take a new position in advance of the moving camera. By bending the long card into a concave arc somewhat more than the third of a cylinder, and placing the eye at the axis of curvature, it will be seen that the various slight distortions of perspective (particularly in the houses) are completely corrected.

Mr. J. M. TONER exhibited, *apropos* to the approaching centennial of the surrender of Cornwallis at Yorktown, certain well preserved specimens of coins and medals of national historic interest, viz:

(1.) Bronze copy of medal given to Washington on the evacuation of Boston.

(2.) A bronze copy of a medal of Lafayette.

(3.) A bronze copy of a medal of Columbus.

(4.) A very fine half dollar of 1785.

(5.) A very fine Washington cent of 1791.

————————

204TH MEETING.   OCTOBER 22, 1881.

The President in the Chair.

Forty members present.

Mr. A. B. JOHNSON presented the following communication on

RECENT INVESTIGATIONS BY THE LIGHT-HOUSE BOARD ON THE ANOMALIES OF SOUND FROM FOG SIGNALS.

Among our erroneous popular notions is one which occasionally brings practical men, even ship-masters, to grief. It is the idea that sound is always heard in all directions from its source according to its intensity or force, and according to the distance of the hearer from it. Instances of this fallacy have accumulated, and they are emphasized by shipwrecks caused by the insistance of mariners on the infallibility of their ears, who have accepted unquestioned the guidance of sound signals during fog as they have that of light-houses during clear weather. The fact is, audition is subject to aberrations, and under circumstances where little expected. We have learned by sad experience that implicit reliance on sound signals may, as it has, lead to danger if not to death.

The wreck of the steamer Rhode Island, on Bonnet Point in Narragansett Bay, which happened on November 6, 1880, when a million dollars in property was lost, was caused, it was said, by the failure of the fog-signal on Beaver Tail Point to sound at that time. Thereupon the Light-House Board, which has charge of the sixty and more fog-signals on our coasts, made an investigation which showed that the fog-signal was in full operation when the wreck took place; but it also brought out the fact, that while there was no lack in the volume of the sound emitted by the signal, there was often a decided lack in the audition of that sound, so much so that it would not be heard at the intensity expected, nor at the place expected; indeed it would be heard faintly where it ought to be heard loudly, and loudly where it ought to be heard faintly; that it could not be heard at all at some points, and then further away it could be heard better than near by; that it could be heard and lost and heard and lost again, all within reasonable ear shot, and all this while the signal was in full blast and sounding continuously.

The following table, A, will give the results obtained by the officer of the navy who investigated these phenomena, and reported to the Light-House Board:

TABLE A.

Observations on Beaver Tail Fog-Signal, Rhode Island, made on November 16, 1880, from a sail-boat, Thermometer at beginning 58°, ending 67° ; Wind moderate from the West ; Weather clear and cold, with a bright sun. Time, beginning 11.15 A. M. .

Number of Observation.	Distance from Beaver Tail Fog-Signal in statute miles.	Intensity of sound in scale of 10.	REMARKS.
1	½	10	
2	⅞	2	
3	1 1/16	1	
4	1¼	10	
5	1⅜	1	
6	1½	0	
7	1⅝	0	
8	1⅞	1	Close to Bonnet Point changed course and ran almost due south.
9	1⅛	1	1½ miles from last station.
10	1	0	¼ mile from last station.
11	⅞	1	" " "
12	⅝	4	" " "
13	½	10	" " "
14	⅜	10	About opposite Beaver Tail, ½ mile from last station, and in the axis of trumpet.
15	½	10	About ½ mile from last station, and running for Newport, heading nearly northeast.
16	1	10	About ½ mile from last station.
17	1¼	5	" ½ " "
18	1½	2	" ¼ " "
19	1⅞	2	" ¼ " "
20	2⅛	1	" ½ " "
21	2½	0	" ¼ " "
22	3½	0	" ½ " "
23	3⅞	2	" ½ " "
24	4	10	About ¼ mile from last station, just off Ft. Adams.
25	4¼	10	Under the lee of Fort Adams.
26	4½	2	
27	4⅝	2	
28	4¾	2	
29	5	2	Newport.

Last summer, I had an opportunity while on a light-house steamer, to experience something of the variations in the audition of the Beaver Tail fog-signal. When the steamer left the light-

Table A. November 16 th 1880.

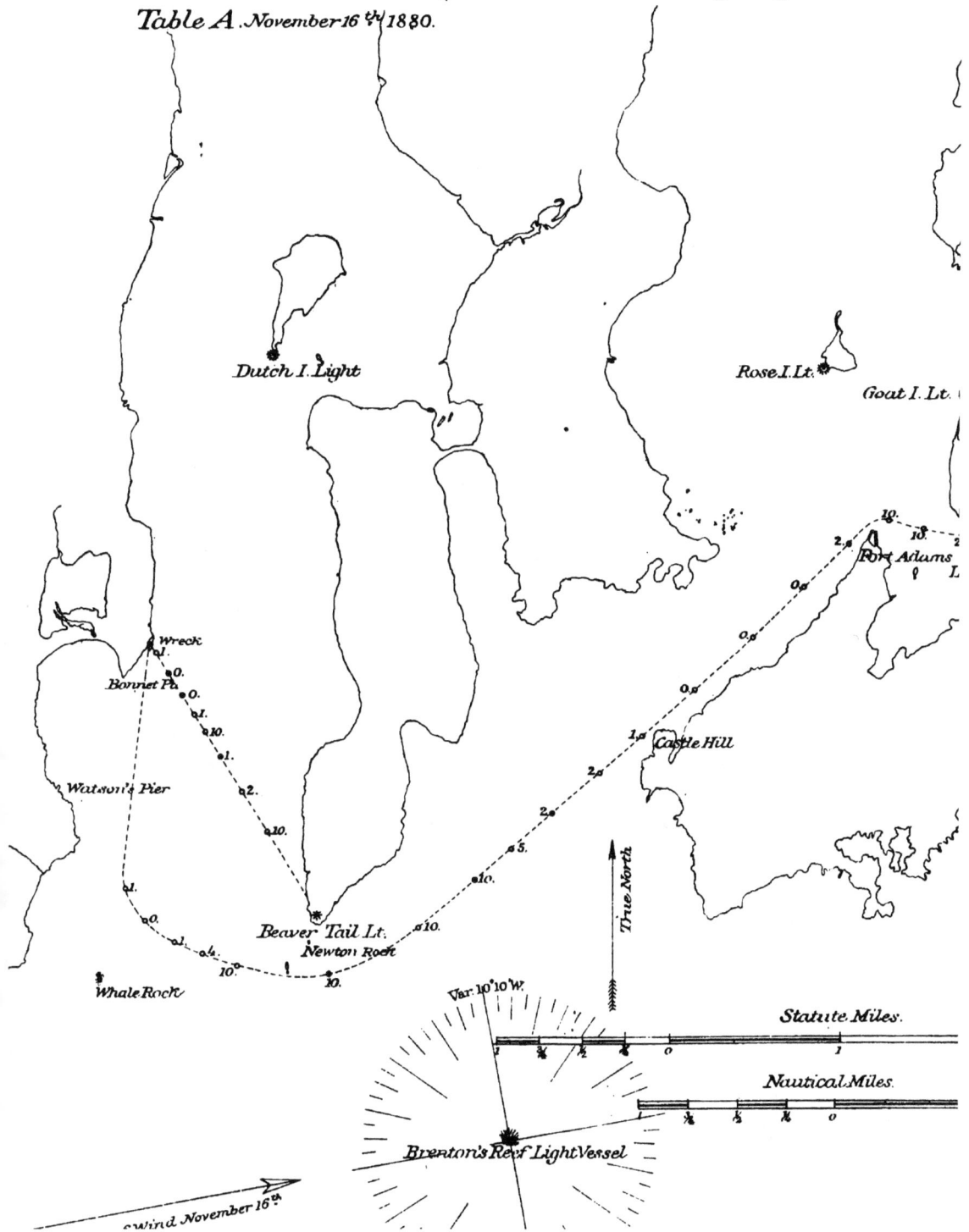

Dutch I. Light

Rose I. Lt.

Goat I. Lt.

10.
2.
10.
2
Fort Adams
L.
0.

0.

Wreck
1.
0.
Bonnet Pt.
0.
1.
10.
1.
0.

Castle Hill
1.

Watson's Pier
2.
2.
10.
2.
5.
1.
10.
0.
10.
True North
Beaver Tail Lt.
10.
Newton Rock
1.
10.
10.

Whale Rock

Var. 10°10'W.

Statute Miles.
2   ¾   ½   ¼   0   1

Nautical Miles.
¾   ½   ¼   0

Brenton's Reef Light Vessel

Wind November 16 th

house landing, the fog-signal was to sound for a given time, and to commence when the steamer had reached a given point, half a mile distant. When that point was reached, we could see by the steam-puffs coming from the 'scape pipe, that the signal was being blown; but we could not hear its sound; nor did we, as we continued on our course, running away from the light station for the next five minutes. When near to Whale Rock, less than a mile and a half distant from the signal, the steamer was stopped, silence was ordered fore and aft, and we all listened intently. The expert naval officers thought they heard a trace of the fog-signal, but my untrained ears failed to differentiate it from the moan of the whistling buoy close to us. Yet the blasts of the ten-inch steam whistle, for which we were listening, can often be heard at a distance of ten miles.

Soon after, I had another opportunity to further observe the operations of this signal. We left Narragansett Pier, R. I., on Aug. 6, 1881, at 4 P. M., in a dense fog, with a strong breeze from the W. S. W., and a heavy chop sea. We wished to ascertain how far the Beaver Tail fog-signal could be heard dead to windward and in the heaviest of fogs. At Whale Rock, one and one-third miles from it, we did not hear a trace of it. Then the steamer was headed directly for Beaver Tail Point, and we ran slowly for it by compass, until the pilot stopped the steamer, declaring we were almost aboard of the signal itself. Every one strained his ears to hear the signal but without success; and we had begun to doubt of our position when, the fog lifting slightly, we saw the breakers in altogether too close proximity for comfort. We passed the point as closely as was safe; and, when abreast of it and at right angles with the direction of the wind, the sound of the fog-signal broke on us suddenly and with its full power. We then ran down the wind to Newport, and carried the sound with us all the way. The fog continuing during the next day, the signal kept up its sound, and we heard it distinctly and continuously at our wharf, though five miles distant.

On the night of May 12, 1881, about midnight, the Galatea, a propeller of over 1500 tons burden, with a full load of passengers and freight, bound through Long Island Sound from Providence to New York, grounded in a dead calm and a dense fog on Little Gull Island, about one-eighth of a mile from and behind the fog-signal, and got off two days later without damage to herself or loss of life or freight. It was as usual alleged that the fog-signal, a steam siren, at Little Gull Light, was not in operation at the time of the accident, and the Light-House Board, also, as usual, immediately ordered an investigation. This was made by the Assistant Inspector of the Light-House District, a naval officer, who reported that after taking the sworn evidence of the light-keepers at Little Gull and the other light-stations within hearing distance, of other Government officers who were, for the time being, so located that they might have had knowledge of the facts, and of the officers of vessels that were within ear shot, including those of the Galatea, he reached the conclusion that the fog-signal was sounding at the time of the accident; and that, although the fog-signal was heard at Mystic, fifteen miles distant in another direction, and although it was heard on a steam tug a mile beyond the Galatea; that it was heard faintly, if at all, on that vessel; and if heard at all, was so heard as to be misleading, though the Galatea was but one-eighth of a mile from the source of the sound.

This report is in itself full of interest. It appears that this officer spent several days steaming around Little Gull, while the fog-signal was in full blast, in various kinds of weather, and that he found the aberrations in audition here were as numerous and even more eccentric than those before mentioned as experienced at Beaver Tail. The results of his observations are given in Tables B and C; and in each case the condition of the atmosphere as to humidity, pressure, temperature and motion are shown, as is also the then tidal condition.

TABLE B.

Fog Signal Tests at Little Gull Island, Long Island Sound, July 11, 1881. Time 10 A. M. Wind, N.N.E., force 2. Barometer, 29.77; Thermometer, 61. Weather at commencement, dark, overcast with squalls of Scotch mist from N.N.E. It began to clear at 11:30 A.M.

Number of Observation.	Time of Observation.	Distance from Little Gull Island fog signal in stat. miles.	Intensity of sound in scale of ten.	REMARKS.
	h. m.			
I	10 10	1⅝	I	
2	10 15	2⅜	½	A faint murmur is put at ½ of 1, in scale of 10.
3	10 18	2½	o	
4		3⅜	o	

Number of Observation.	Time of Observation.	Distance from Little Gull Island fog signal in stat. miles.	Intensity of sound in scale of ten.	REMARKS.
	h. m.			
5	10 25	3⅝	0	
6		3½	0	
7		·3½	½	About ½ mile from last station.
8	10 50	3½	1	
9		3⅝	0	
10		3⅝	1	About ½ mile from last station.
11		3¾	2	About ½ mile from last station.
12	11 09	3½	2	Changed course and ran a little S. of W.
13		3¾	3	
14	11 15	2⅞	3	
15	11 25	2½	4	
16		2¾	5	
17	11 35	2½	7	
18		2⅛	7	
19		1½	8	
20	11 55	½	9	
21		½	10	
22	12 03	⅜	10	About ½ mile from last station.
23	12 07	⅜	7	
24		1⅞	2	
25	12 14	1⅞	1	
26	12 19	2¼	1½	
27	12 23	2¾	½	Changed course.
28	12 40	2¾	½	Faint murmur.
29	12 52	3½	0	Changed course.
30	1 01	2	½	
31	1 06	1⅝	1-2	
32	1 12	1⅝	5	
33	1 18	¾	10	
34		⅝	10	Almost west of fog-signal.
35		1¼	10	
36	1 35	1½	8	Changed course.
37		1⅝	8	
38	1 42	⅞	10	Stood N. E.; sound gradually increasing.
39	1 52	½	3	
40	1 55	⅞	2	Changed course.
41		¾	2	
42	2 01	⅜	2	
43	2 02	⅛	10	
44		⅜	10	
45		¾	8	
46		1	7	
47		1¾	5	
48	4 29	2	2	
49		2¾	1	
50	4 38	3⅜	0	Lost the sound.
51		3¾	0	
52	4 45	4¼	0	Bartletts Reef light-ship; wheels stopped and no sound.

TABLE C.

Observations at Little Gull Island, Long Island Sound, July 15, 1881, commencing at 6.30 A. M. Thermometer, 59° Fahr. Barometer, 29.80. Wind, W.N.W., force 3, hauling to the westward and increasing gradually.

Number of Observation.	Time of Observation.	Distance from Little Gull Island fog-signal in stat. miles.	Intensity of sound in a scale of ten.	REMARKS.
	h. m.			
1	6 32	1¾	10	
2	6 57	2¼	10	Changed course, running S. by W. ½ W.
3		2¼	8	About ½ mile from last station.
4		2⅜	7	
5		3¼	4	
6	7 17	3¾	3	Changed course, running E.
7		3⅝	2	About ½ mile from last station.
8		3¾	1	" " "
9		3½	5	" " "
10	7 28	3⅜	7	Changed course, running N. by W. ½ W.
11		2½	8	
12		2½	5.	About ½ mile from last station.
13		2	5	Changed course, running W.
14	7 50	2¾	5	
15		2⅞	3	
16		3⅛	2	
17	8 00	3¾	0	Sound lost.

On August 3d, I had an opportunity to hear this fog-signal myself, and to note its audibility. The wind was from the south and very light; the air was damp, smoky, hazy, and, as the sailors say, hung low; the barometer stood at ⁻29.90; the tide was about flood. Our steamer was run for six miles in the axis of the siren's trumpet, which was sounded for our benefit at its full force. Note was made every third minute in a scale of ten of the intensity of the sound, and it was found that the audition decreased normally with the distance for the first two miles; at 2¼ miles it had fallen off one-half; at 3 miles it had fallen to one-tenth its power; at 3¼ miles away we could hear but a faint murmur, and when 4 miles distant, we had lost it completely; and yet there seemed to be no reason why we should not have heard it clearly at three times that distance.

The next morning was calm, but heavy with white fog; yet we heard the Little Gull siren distinctly though it was 10¼ miles off, as we lay at our dock in New London. The steamer ran out of the harbor, but was compelled to anchor so thick was the fog ; yet we heard Little Gull though 7½ miles off, at a force of 6 in the scale of ten, and the sound was so clear cut and distinct that we could differentiate it from the siren at the New London light, which was much nearer to us.   The steamer worked round to inspect the neighboring lights, and we heard the Little Gull siren when at North Dumpling light station, 7 miles off, at a force of 6 ; at Morgan's Point Light, 10 miles off, at a force of 5, and we continued to hear it at an intensity of from 5 to 6 as we worked around among the other lights, within a compass of 10 miles, till the fog broke and the siren ceased.

Opportunity soon occurred for making more critical experiments. On a fine day we ran out to Little Gull, had the siren started under full steam, and then, following out a pre-arranged program, ran round Little Gull Island in such way, as to describe a rectangle of about 8 by 10 miles, its longest side running nearly north and south.   No fixed rate of speed was maintained, but the steamer slowed, backed, or stopped, as was necessary.   The atmosphere was what the sailors call lumpy, and Prof. Tyndall calls non-homogeneous.   Prof. Henry, when writing of a like condition, said : *" As the heat of the sun increases during the first part of the day, the temperature of the land rises above that of the sea, and this excess of the temperature *produces upward currents of air,* disturbing the general flow of wind, both at the surface of the sea and at an elevation above."   Observations were made and noted in a scale of ten, of the force or intensity of the signal's sound as it reached us at the end of each minute.   The following Table D shows a sufficient number of the results for our purposes, taken from the tabulated schedule of our notes.   The table also shows the condition of the atmosphere during our observations.

---

*L. H. Board's Rep. for 1875, page 116.

TABLE D.

Observations at Little Gull Island, Long Island Sound, August 9, 1881, commencing at 10 A. M. Thermometer—Dry Bulb, 73°.09, Wet Bulb, 73° Fahr.   Barometer, 29.77   Wind, S. W., force, 3.   Cir. Strat. Clouds about the horizon.

Number of Observation.	Time of Observation.	Distance from Little Gull Island in statute miles.	Intensity of sound in scale of ten.	Number of Observation.	Time of Observation.	Distance from Little Gull Island in statute miles.	Intensity of sound in scale of ten.
	h. m.				h. m.		
1	10 30	0¼	10	16	12 04	2⅝	9
2	10 32	0⅓	10	17	12 08	2¼	9
3	10 34	0½	10	18	12 13	2⅛	5
4	10 36	1	10	19	12 20	2⅛	3
5	10 37	1¼	0	20	12 28	3¼	1
6	10 48	2	0	21	12 35	3½	0½
7	10 57	3	0	22	12 41	3⅜	0
8	11 02	3	0	23	12 45	3	1
9	11 08	3 1/16	1	24	12 57	2½	0
10	11 15	3½	3	25	12 58	2⅜	0
11	11 23	4⅛	4	26	1 02	1½	1
12	11 38		8	27	1 20	1¾	0½
13	11 42	2¾	9	28	1 24	1⅝	0½
14	11 54	3	9	29	1 30	0¾	0
15	11 57	3¼	9	30	1 32	0¼	10

At 4 P. M. two of us went in a row boat to Little Gull from the steamer which lay to her anchor half a mile off, and verified the fact that the fog-signal had been in full operation during the time of our observations by the report of the steamer's mate, who had been left there for that purpose. It then occurred to us to investigate still more closely what appeared to be a space—a circle of silence—in which we had, during the experiments of the morning, failed to hear the signal. After having had the siren put in full operation again, we pulled toward the nearer end of Great Gull Island, the siren sounding meantime with earsplitting force. When about 600 yards away we suddenly lost the sound as completely as if the signal had stopped. Pulling toward the steamer, not more than 200 yards, we reached a position at right angles with the axis of the siren's trumpet when we suddenly heard the sound again at its full force. Thus, in pulling 500 yards, we passed from complete audition of the signal to absolute inaudition; and then we passed back again to complete audition by pulling 200 yards in

another direction. All this took place within half an hour in open water, always in full view of the signal station, and without any visible obstacle being interposed or removed.

While on the island we learned that one of the light-house keepers, who had been on leave, had just returned from Sag Harbor, twenty miles away to the southeast. He had failed to hear the signal at all, until opposite the eastern end of Great Gull Island, and until he was within half a mile of the siren which was in full operation.

On the next morning our steamer anchored about a mile north of Little Gull; the wind was light, the air was clear, and the day was warm and beautiful. As it had been preceded by a warm night the atmosphere was homogeneous, and it was expected that we should have a day of normal audition and barren of curious phenomena. After the siren had commenced its noise we ran down to a point within half a mile of the light-house, and then steamed for Plum Island, running a little south of east for six miles, when we returned as nearly as might be on our own track. The results were curious. We lost half the force of the sound when within a quarter of a mile of the siren; a moment later we had lost four-fifths of it. Running another half mile we were off the middle of Great Gull Island, and the sound had increased to a force of four; in five minutes more it had dropped to three; from that on, until we reached the end of our six mile run, it gradually weakened, and it had dropped to a force of two when we turned and ran back to our anchorage. It is particularly curious that the sound had the same intensity at three-sixteenths of a mile from its source, and at six whole miles from that point, while it varied from two to ten in a scale of ten between those points. The results of the trip are more fully and exactly given in Table E.

Thinking that possibly this peculiarity might have been induced by those differences of temperature in the strata of the atmosphere suggested by Dr. Tyndall as probable cause for such phenomena, effort was made to ascertain something of these differences by sending a thermometer to the upper air. In the course of the afternoon we made a kite some six feet high, attached to it a self-registering thermometer, and after a number of trials succeeded in getting it up about five hundred feet, and in hauling it safely in again after it had been up over an hour. The thermometer had a wet bulb, and beside was protected from the direct rays of the sun; but it registered only half a degree more of heat at its highest point than it had done in the pilot-house. The course the kite took showed no difference between the air currents alow and aloft.

TABLE E.

Observations at Little Gull Island, Long Island Sound, August 10, 1881, commencing at 10:30 A. M. Dry Bulb Thermometer, 76°, Wet Bulb, 75°. Barometer, 29.40. Wind, W. by N., force 3, and steady throughout. Day clear and beautiful.

Number of Observation.	Time of Observation.	Distance from Little Gull Island in a direct line in statute miles.	Intensity of sound in a scale of ten.	Number of Observation.	Time of Observation.	Distance from Little Gull Island in a direct line in statute miles.	Intensity of sound in a scale of ten.
	h. m.				h. m.		
1	10 36	$1\frac{1}{16}$	10	7	10 59	$2\frac{1}{16}$	2 to 3
2	10 40	$0\frac{3}{4}$	10	8	11 07	$2\frac{1}{2}$	2 to 3
3	10 44	$0\frac{1}{4}$	5	9	11 29	$2\frac{5}{8}$	2 to 3
4	10 45	$0\frac{3}{16}$	2	10	11 45	$5\frac{1}{16}$	2 to 3
5	10 49	$0\frac{1}{4}$	4	11	11 5?		
6	10 53	$1\frac{1}{4}$	3	12	12 02	6	2

The Light House Board has known from the first that aberrations in audibility might occur near any fog-signal. When the fog-trumpet was set up at Beaver Tail Point in 1856, the Naval Secretary of the Board, then Lieutenant, now Rear Admiral Jenkins, U. S. N., in company with Mr. Daboll, its inventor, found, in returning to Newport, that .they lost the sound of the signal between Beaver Tail and Fort Adams, and recovered it again between the Fort and Newport, as did later observers, and that this failure to hear it did not result from any failure of the signal to operate.

The Board's publications show that Prof. Henry, its scientific adviser, had the subject for many years continuously under advisement, and that between 1865 and 1878, many experiments were made, and various reports on them were submitted to the Board, as to the use and value of its several kinds of fog-signals. In 1870 the Board directed General Duane, of the U. S. Engineers, then and still in its service, to make a series of experiments to ascertain the comparative value of its different signals. In his report the General said, speaking of the steam fog-signals on the coast of Maine :

* " There are six steam fog-whistles on the coast of Maine; there have been frequently heard at a distance of twenty miles, and as frequently cannot be heard at the distance of two miles, and this with no perceptible difference in the state of the atmosphere.

" The signal is often heard at a great distance in one direction, while in another it will be scarcely audible at the distance of a mile. This is not the effect of wind, as the signal is frequently heard much farther against the wind than with it; for example, the whistle on Cape Elizabeth can always be distinctly heard in Portland, a distance of nine miles, during a heavy northeast snow-storm the wind blowing a gale directly from Portland toward the whistle."

*   *   *   *   *   *   *   *   *   *

" The most perplexing difficulty, however, arises from the fact that the signal often appears to be surrounded by a belt, varying in radius from one to one and a half miles, from which the sound appears to be entirely absent. Thus, in moving directly from a station, the sound is audible for the distance of a mile, is then lost for about the same distance, after which it is again distinctly heard for a long time. This action is common to all ear-signals, and has been at times observed at all the stations, at one of which the signal is situated on a bare rock twenty miles from the main land, with no surrounding objects to affect the sound."

Prof. Henry, in considering the results of Gen. Duane's experiments, and his own, some of which were made in company with Sir Fred'k Arrow and Capt. Webb, H. B. M. Navy, both of the British Light-House Establishment, who were sent here to study and report on our fog-signal system, formulated these abnormal phenomena. He said they consisted of:

" 1. The audibility of a sound at a distance and its inaudibility nearer the source of sound.

" 2. The inaudibility of a sound at a given distance in one direction, while a lesser sound is heard at the same distance in another direction.

" 3. The audibility at one time at a distance of several miles, while at another the sound cannot be heard at more than a fifth of the same distance.

" 4. While the sound is generally heard further with the wind than against it, in some instances the reverse is the case.

" 5. The sudden loss of a sound in passing from one locality to another in the same vicinity, the distance from the source of sound being the same." †

These experiments were not confined to our own shores. Dr. Tyndall, the well known English physicist, who stands in the same relation to the British Light-House Establishment that Prof. Henry did to our own, writes thus:

---

*Annual Rep't L. H. Board 1874, pp. 99–100.
† L. H. B. Annual Rep. 1875, page 106.

" With a view to the protection of life and property at sea, in the years 1873 and 1874, this subject received an exhaustive examination, observational and experimental.   The investigation was conducted at the expense of the Government, and under the auspices of the Elder Brethren of the Trinity House [the governing body of the British Light-House Establishment.]

" The most conflicting results were at first obtained.   On the 19th of May, 1873, the sound range was 3⅓ miles; on the 20th it was 5½ miles; on the 2d of June 6 miles; on the 3d more than 9 miles; on the 10th 9 miles; on the 25th 6 miles; on the 26th 9¼ miles; on the 1st of July 12¾ miles; on the 2d 4 miles, while on the 3d, with a clear, calm atmosphere and smooth sea, it was less than 3 miles." *

The officer who made the reports, as to the fog-signals at Beaver Tail and Little Gull, after the accidents to the steamers Rhode Island and Galatea heretofore mentioned, was the Assistant Inspector of the Third Light-House District, Lieut. Comd'r F. E. Chadwick, U. S. N.; and it was he who had charge of the Light-House steamer while the foregoing observations were being made, after Capt. George Brown, U. S. N., the Inspector—to whom I am indebted for many courtesies on this trip—was called elsewhere by other official duties. Mr. Chadwick brought to this work an unbiased mind, trained in the severest schools of scientific investigation.   His object in all his experiments was simply to ascertain the exact truth for practical official purposes.   He had not proposed, even to himself, to make any generalizations from his observations.   But he kindly answered certain of my questions as to the opinions which had forced themselves upon him, and his answers are here set down for the consideration of those who use these fog-signals overmuch as a guide for their ships.

" It seems to me" he said " that navigators should understand that when attempting to pick up a fog-signal attention must be given to the direction of the wind, and that if they are to windward, (in a moderate breeze,) the chances are very largely against hearing it, unless close to; that there is nearly always a sector of about 120° to windward of the signal in which it either cannot be heard at all, or in which it is but faintly heard.   Thus, with the wind E. S. E., so long as they are bearing from the signal between N. E. and South, there is a large chance that the signal will not be audible until it is very close.

" As they bring the signal to bear at right angles with the wind, the sound will almost certainly in the case of light wind increase, and it will soon assume its normal volume—being heard almost without fail in the leeward semicircle.

" Fog, to my mind, and so far as my experience goes, is not a factor of any consequence whatever in the question of sound.   Signals may be heard at great dis-

---

*Sound, by Tyndall, 3d Edition English, page 324.

tances through the densest fogs, which may be totally inaudible in the same directions and at the same distances in the clearest atmosphere.   It is not meant by this last statement that the fog may assist the sound; as at another time the signal may be absolutely inaudible in a fog of like density, where it had before been clearly heard.   That fog has no great effect can easily be understood when it is known, (as it certainly is known by observers,) that even snow does not deaden sound—there being no condition of the atmosphere so favorable for the far reaching of sound signals as is that of a heavy N. E. snow storm, due supposably to the homogeneity produced by the falling snow.

" It seems to be well established by numerous observations that on our own northern Atlantic coasts the best possible circumstances for hearing a fog-signal are in a northeast snow storm, and, so far as these observations have extended, they seem to point to the extraordinary conclusion that they are best heard with the observer to windward of the signal; and that in light winds the signal is best heard down the wind, or at right angles with the wind.

" The worst conditions for hearing sound seem to be found in the atmosphere of a clear, frosty morning on which a warm sun has risen and has been shining for two or three hours.

" The curve of audibility in a light or moderate breeze, in general, is similar to that plotted by Prof. Henry, as in the accompanying diagram.

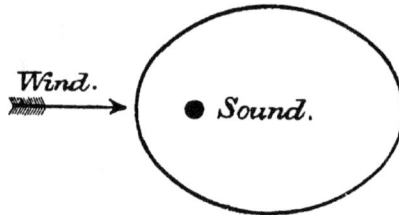

" I think it is established that there are two great causes for these phenomena, non homogeneity of the atmosphere, and the movement of the wind; how this latter acts no one can say.   The theory of retardation of the lower strata of the atmosphere near the earth's surface, as advanced by Prof. Stokes, of England,* seems good for moderate winds, but it hardly holds in cases where the siren is heard from eighteen to twenty miles to windward during N. E. gales."

While the mariner may usually expect to hear the sound of the average fog-signal normally as to force and place, he should be prepared for occasional aberrations in audition.   It is impossible at this point in the investigations which are still in progress, to say when, where or how the phenomena will occur.   But certain suggestions present themselves even now as worthy of consideration.

It seems that the mariner should, in order to pick up the sound of the fog-signal most quickly when approaching it from the wind-

*See Henry on Sound, p. 533; or, Sm. Rept., 1878, p. 533; or, L.-H. B. Rept. for 1875, p. 120. See Henry on Sound, p. 512, and Taylor in Am. Jour. Sci., 3d series, XI, p. 100; also, Rept. Brit. Assoc., XXIV, 2d part, p. 27.

ward, go aloft; and that, when approaching it from the leeward, the nearer he can get to the surface of the water the sooner he will hear the sound.

It also appears that there are some things the mariner should not do.

He should place no negative dependence on the fog-signal; that is, he should not assume that he is out of hearing distance because he fails to hear its sound.

He should not assume that, because he hears a fog-signal faintly, he is at a great distance from it.

Neither should he assume that he is near to it because he hears the sound plainly.

He should not assume that he has reached a given point on his course because he hears the fog-signal at the same intensity that he did when formerly at that point.

Neither should he assume that he has not reached this point because he fails to hear the fog-signal as loudly as before, or because he does not hear it at all.

He should not assume that the fog-signal has ceased sounding because he fails to hear it even when within easy earshot.

He should not assume that the aberrations of audibility which pertain to any one fog-signal pertain to any other fog-signal.

He should not expect to hear a fog-signal as well when the upper and lower currents of air run in different directions; that is when his upper sails fill and his lower sails flap; nor when his lower sails fill and his upper sails flap.

He should not expect to hear the fog-signal so well when between him and it is a swiftly flowing stream, especially when the tide and wind run in opposite directions.

He should not expect to hear it well during a time of electric disturbance.

He should not expect to hear a fog-signal well when the sound must reach him over land, as over a point or an island.

And, when there is a bluff behind the fog-signal, he should be prepared for irregular intervals in audition, such as might be produced could the sound ricochet from the trumpet, as a ball would from a cannon ; that is, he might hear it at 2, 4, 6, 8 and 10 miles from the signal, and lose it at 1, 3, 5, 7, 9 and 11 miles distance, or at any other combination of distances, regular or irregular.

These deductions, some made, as previously mentioned, by several of the first physicists of the age, and some drawn from the original investigations here noted, are submitted for consideration rather than given as directions. They are assumed as good working hypotheses for use in further investigation. While it is claimed that they are correct as to the localities in which they were made, it seems proper to say that they have not been disproved by the practical mariners who have given them some personal consideration, and who have tried to carry them into general application. Hence these suggestions have been set down in the hope that others with greater knowledge and larger leisure may give the subject fuller attention, and work out further results.

If the law of these aberrations in audibility can be evolved and some method discovered for their correction, as the variations of the compass are corrected, then sound may be depended upon as a more definite and accurate aid to navigation. Until then, the mariner will do well when he does not get the expected sound of a fog-signal, to assume 'that he may not hear a warning that is faithfully given, and then to heave his lead, and resort to the other means used by the careful navigator to make sure of his position.

Mr. CLEVELAND ABBE remarked that it seemed to him if these anomalies were due to the refraction of sound in a vertical plane, then a few feet of increase in the altitude of the observer or of the signal itself, would make a great difference in the result. To this .Mr. JOHNSON replied that the observations made on board the vessels were attended with the same results as to degree of audibility, whether the observer were stationed upon the mast, deck, or near the water line of the vessel.

Mr. WILLIAM B. TAYLOR said that the interesting observations presented by Mr. Johnson were in the main entirely corroborative of the results announced by our late President, Prof. Henry ; and the anomalies noted furnished striking confirmation of the explanations and generalizations reached by him, while they as strikingly discredited as incongruous the rival hypothesis of hygroscopic flocculence in the atmosphere as a notable occasion of acoustic disturbance. When we consider the wide areas over which fog-signals are designed to be conveyed—through which spaces the atmosphere can rarely be uniform, either in its temperature or its movements—we can readily understand that from these two prominent conditions of sound-refraction, acoustic rays are commonly propagated in quite sensibly curved or often serpentine directions; and that while these inequalities will sometimes favor audibility at given points, they will as often impair or defeat it. Moreover, these deformations of sound waves are not confined to vertical planes, since it has been shown that *lateral* refractions may exist, giving false impressions of direction as well as of distance.

As we have no means of either controlling or accurately determining these simultaneous differences of wind and temperature, we are forced to admit that the practical difficulties attending these anomalies of sound propagation are insoluble and incurable. But we must not hence abandon sound-signalling as either hopeless or inefficient, since it is the best—or rather the only—method at our disposal of giving warning and guidance to the befogged mariner.

Two partial alleviations of the recognized defects are suggested. The first is to place the siren or the steam whistle at considerable elevations, say on the top of skeleton towers, perhaps higher than those ordinarily employed as light-towers; at which points they could readily be operated from the ground. This would, in many cases, counteract the tendency to local acoustic shadows or bands of silence, though in other cases it would be quite ineffectual. The second expedient is, (if not too expensive,) to greatly multiply the number of such signals at available points about dangerous coasts or inlets, with proper distinctions to clearly specialize their indications, in order that the mariner failing to catch the sound from one direction, might have the probability of picking up the sound from a different azimuth. As these sound instruments may be operated at considerable distances from the engine, and even at practically inaccessible positions, on rocks or on buoys, *danger points* especially should be guarded by fog-signals, not necessarily of great power, but capable, at least, of covering the radius of actual insecurity.

Remarks were made by Mr. WILLIAM B. TAYLOR on the relation of fog and snow storms to audibility.

With regard to fog, Mr. TAYLOR said, we are not to conceive the sound vibrations as passing alternately through air and water, (as a ray of light does,) but taking into view the average wave-length of sound (several feet ordinarily) and the enormous number of water particles contained in that space, we must contemplate the whole mass as a homogeneous medium taking up the sound waves in the same manner, whether the air were perfectly dry, or were precipitating excessive moisture in the form of rain. In the absence of sensible wind, the air thus supersaturated with moisture would be practically very homogeneous, and thus generally well adapted to the normal transmission of sound.

A similar remark applies to falling snow, (when not accompanied with strong wind,) with the additional circumstance that, while the precipitation and congelation would tend to warm the upper regions of the air, any melting of the snow as it fell would cool the lower region. This condition of relative warmth above and cold below is favorable to the conveyance of sound to a distance—as first pointed out by Prof. Osborn Reynolds, of Manchester,—by reason of the expanding spherical wave-front being slightly more accelerated above than below, (in accordance with well known principles,) and thus causing the horizontal or slightly rising sheets of sound to be dished downward.

The next communication was by Mr. WILLIAM HARKNESS on the relative accuracy of different methods of determining the solar parallax.

This paper is published in full in the *American Journal of Science* for November, 1881, No. 131, vol. 22, pp. 375–394.

205TH MEETING.   NOVEMBER 5, 1881.

The President in the Chair.

Forty-three members present.

MR. J. C. WELLING presented the following communication on

ANOMALIES OF SOUND SIGNALS.

In the year 1865 Prof. Henry, while making some observations on the intensity of sounds, discovered that a sound moving against the wind, and which was inaudible to the ear of an observer on the deck of a vessel, might sometimes be regained by ascending to the mast-head; that is, sound is sometimes more readily conveyed by the upper current of the air than by the lower.

This fact, with other corroborative facts, did not, he says, reveal its full significance to him until he was able to interpret it by the aid of the hypothesis of Prof. Stokes, (Transactions of the British Scientific Association for 1867, Vol. 24,) according to which there is—when the wind˙blows—a difference of velocities between the upper and the lower strata of the atmosphere, resulting from the retardation of the lower stratum by friction with the ground. This unequal movement of the atmosphere disturbs the spherical form of the sound waves, and tends to make them somewhat of the form of an ellipsoid, the section of which by a vertical diametral plane, parallel to the direction of the wind, is an ellipse, meeting the ground at an obtuse angle on the side towards which the wind is blowing, and at an acute angle on the opposite side. But as sound moves in a direction perpendicular to the front of the sound waves, it follows that sounds moving with a favorable wind tend to be tilted downwards toward the ground; and sounds moving against an opposing wind tend to be tilted upward until, finally, they pass above the head of a listener standing on the ground.

The effect of different elevations on the audibility of the same sound has been brought within the sphere of scientific experiment. In some experiments made by Prof. Reynolds in 1874, on "a flat meadow," by the aid of an electrical bell, placed one foot from the ground, it was found that elevation affected the range of sound against the wind "in a much more marked manner than at right angles." He adds: "Over the grass no sound could be heard with the head on the ground at twenty yards from the bell, and at thirty yards it was lost with the head three feet from the ground, and its full intensity was lost when standing erect at thirty yards. At seventy yards, when standing erect, the sound was lost at long intervals, and was only faintly heard even then; but it became continuous again when the ear was raised nine feet from the ground, and it reached its full intensity at an elevation of twelve feet."*

In some experiments made by Prof. Henry, in 1875, he found that while sound moving at right angles to the wind could not be heard as far as sound moving with the wind, yet it was equally true

---

* London, Ed., and Dub. Ph. Mag. for 1875, Vol. 50.

of sounds moving against the wind and at right angles to the wind, that they could both be better heard on the top of a high tower than on the surface of the ground.*

Baron Humboldt, in observations made on the intensity of sounds at the Falls of the Orinoco, remarked their greater audibility by night than by day, and referred their comparative weakness by day to the effect of atmospheric disturbances arising from ascending currents of rarified air and descending currents of heavier air, which broke up the homogeneity of the atmosphere, and thereby obstructed the transmission of sound. It is a necessary complement of this hypothesis that sound which fails to be transmitted through the atmosphere, because of "the reflections which it endures at the limiting surfaces of the rarer and the denser air," is liable to be returned to the hearer in the shape of aerial echoes rebounding from the acoustic cloud which the primary sound is not able to pierce; and hence the logical place assigned to echoes by Dr. Tyndall, when, adopting and applying the Humboldt hypothesis, he says that "rightly interpreted and followed out, these aerial echoes lead to a solution which penetrates and reconciles the phenomena from beginning to end." "On this point," he says, "I would stake the issue of the whole inquiry. * * * The echoes afford the easiest access to the core of this question." †

The conflicting hypotheses of Humboldt and Stokes, as respectively applied by Tyndall and Henry in interpreting the abnormal phenomena of sound, are here cited as prefatory to some much older observations made under the same head by Dr. W. Derham, in his elaborate paper entitled "Experiments and Observations on the *Motion of Sound*, and other things pertaining thereto," as read before the Royal Society in 1708. This paper, written in Latin, is the report of a systematic inquiry into phenomena pertaining to the velocity and motion of sounds, and treats only incidentally on the intensity of sounds; but, nevertheless, it contains some interesting statements under this latter head.‡

The subject of echoes is the first which engages the writer's attention. He says that echoes produced by sound-reflecting objects situated near a sounding body may sometimes be heard through many

---

* Rep. of Light-House Board, 1875, p. 119.
† "Sound," p. xxiv.
‡ Phil. Trans. of Royal Society, Jan. and Feb., 1708.

miles, as well as the primary sound, or even better than the latter. He observes that echoes produced by the firing of cannon on the Thames river, between Deptford and Cuckold's Point, came to his ears in a multiple form, repeated five or six times, and the terminal crash of the echo was the loudest. This last feature was observed even when the multiple sounds were nine or ten in number. To this he adds: "When I have heard the crashes of heavy artillery, especially in a still and clear atmosphere, I have often observed that a *murmur* high in the air preceded the report. And in thin fog I have often heard the sound of cannon running in the air, high above my head, through many miles, so that this murmur has lasted fifteen seconds. This continuous murmur, in my opinion, comes from particles of vapor suspended in the atmosphere which resist the course of the sound waves, and reverberate them back to the ears of the observer after the manner of undefined echoes.*

Mr. Richard Townley, an intelligent observer, having written to Dr. Derham, in a letter from Rome, that "sounds are rarely heard as far at Rome as in England and in other northern regions, and having cited in support of this statement some observations drawn from the firing of cannon in the castle of St. Angelo, Dr. Derham caused an enquiry on this point to be made in Italy, under the auspices of the British Minister at Florence. The enquiry was conducted by Joseph Averani, a Professor in the University of Pisa. Guns were fir d at Florence, and observers were stationed at different points ir. Leghorn and its vicinity to mark the effect of the reports. The observers stationed in the Light-House and the Marzocco tower, in the lower part of the city, heard no reports, but observers stationed on an old fortress in the upper part of the city, and other observers placed on Monte Rotondo, about five miles from Leghorn in the direction of Mount Nero, (and, therefore, more in the direction of the wind which was blowing across the path of the sound,) were able to hear the reports.

Another series of experiments was made on water, by firing cannon at Leghorn, and stationing observers at Porto Ferrajo in the Island of Elba, a distance of about sixty miles. In this case the reports were better heard in still air than when the wind was either favorable or unfavorable, and were not heard at all points equally well, but only at those which were a little the more elevated.†

---

* Derham, p. 10.   † *Ibid.*, pp. 18, 19, 20.

As to the result of these observations, it was easy for Dr. Derham to conclude that sounds are heard as far in Italy as in England, when the conditions of the atmosphere are the same; and these experiments are here cited only for the light they shed on the comparative antiquity of the observation that elevation has an important bearing on the audibility of sounds.

As to the causes which really affect the intensity of sounds, Dr. Derham seems to have had a very obscure and imperfect notion. His observations under this head are mainly a bundle of contradictions, and the causes of these variations he prudently leaves to be investigated by others, seeing, as he says, "that it equally exceeds the grasp of his mind to discover them, and to assign what may be the proper medium or vehicle of sound." He does not, however, fall into the error of measuring the acoustic transparency of the atmosphere by its optic transparency, for he says that the clearest day he can remember, when wind and everything else seemed to concur in promoting the force and velocity of sound, was a day when he could not hear the firing of cannon at a distance easily penetrated by their reports on former occasions. The effect of clear or foggy air on sound, he says, is very uncertain, but as to *thick fogs* and snow, he affirms that they are certainly powerful dampers of sound, an observation now abundantly proved to be erroneous.

From some observations made by Gen. Duane, at Portland, Maine, in 1871, it appears that the fog-signal at that point is often surrounded by a belt of silence, varying from one to one and a half miles in radius.

From some observations made by Prony, Mathieus, and Arago, at Villejuif, and by Humboldt, Bouvard, and Gay-Lussac, at Montlhéry, in France, the two towns being 11.6 miles from each other, it was noticed that while every report of the cannon fired at Montlhéry was heard with the greatest distinctness, nearly every report from Villejuif failed to reach Montlhéry. The air at the time was calm, with a slight movement of wind from Villejuif toward Montlhéry, or "against the direction in which the sound was best heard." These observations were made in 1822.

In 1872, Prof. Henry observed the same non-reciprocity of sound in approaching the Whitehead fog-signal on the coast of Maine. At a distance of six miles the signal was heard; at a distance of three miles from the shore the sound of the signal was lost, and was not regained until the vessel approached within a quarter of a mile of the station. During all this time of silence the sound of the steamer's whistle was distinctly heard at the Whitehead station; that is, a lesser sound was heard from the steamer to the station, "while a sound of greater volume was unheard in the opposite direction." The wind at the time was blowing in favor of the steamer's whistle, and against the fog-signal.*

In a paper presented to the Royal Society in 1874, Prof. Reynolds showed that the form of the sound-wave is liable to flexure from changes in the temperature of the atmosphere as well as from the unequal motion of wind.†

These abnormal phenomena of sound, considered in connection with the hypothesis of Prof. Stokes, as enlarged and applied by Prof. Henry, may be reduced into the following generalizations which, if accurate in point of logical form, and true in point of the facts to which they are applied, may be stated under the guise of aphorisms, as follows:

1. "Where the condition of the air is nearest that of a calm, the larger will be the curve of audition, and the nearer will the shape of the curve approach to a circle, of which the point of origin of the sound, or the point of perception will be the centre." [This aphorism is stated abstractly from any consideration of temperature refraction which, so far as it exists, will always tend to modify the shape of the curve of audition.]‡

2. Apart from all consideration of temperature refraction, a sound will be heard furthest in the direction of a gentle wind, because the portion of the sound-wave thrown down from above, in this case, is re-enforced by the sound reflected from the surface, and will thus more than compensate for the loss by friction.||

3. Other things being equal, the area of audition will be proportionally diminished in the case of sounds moving against winds more or less strong, because the sonorous waves will be refracted above the ears of the observer. (Stokes, Henry and Reynolds.)

---

* Rep. Light-House Board, 1874, p. 108.

† London, Ed., and Dublin Phil. Mag. for 1875, Vol. 50, p. 52.

‡ Light-House Report for 1875, p. 125.

|| *Ibidem.* Cf., Tyndall's Sound, p. 311. Cf., Reynolds in Lon., Ed., and Dub. Ph. Mag. for 1875, Vol. 50, pp. 63, 68.

4. The area of audition will be diminished in the case of a sound moving with an overstrong favoring wind, because the sound-waves in this case will be so rapidly and strongly thrown down to the ground that the intensity of the sound will suffer more diminution from absorption and friction than can be supplied by the upward reflection of the sound rays conspiring with the gradual downward flexure of the sound-waves, as in the case of a gentle favoring wind.*

5. Sounds moving *against* a gentle wind will, *cæteris paribus*, be heard further than similar sounds moving *with* an overstrong favoring wind, for reasons already implied, because the downward flexure of the sound-waves, being excessive in the latter case, tends to extinguish the conditions of audibility more rapidly than is done by the slight upward refraction in the former case.

6. When sounds moving against the wind are heard further than similar sounds moving with a wind of equal strength, it is because of a dominant upper wind blowing at the time in a direction opposite to that at the surface.†

7. A sound moving against the wind, and so refracted as in the end to be thrown above the head of the observer will, at the point of its elevation, leave an acoustic shadow. But this acoustic shadow, at a still further stage, may be filled in by the lateral spread of the sound-waves, or may be extinguished by the downward flexure of the sound waves, resulting from an upper current of wind moving in an opposite direction to that at the surface, or resulting in a less degree from an upper stratum of still air. Under these circumstances, there will be areas of silence enclosed within areas of audition.‡

8. As sounds may be refracted either by wind, or by changing temperatures, or by both combined, it follows that, under many circumstances, a sound lost at one elevation may be regained at a higher elevation.‖

9. As sounds moving against the wind are liable to become inaudible (by being tilted over the head of the observer) even before

---

* Light-House Report, 1875, p. 125.

† Light-House Report for 1877 : Experiments on Sound, p. 13.

‡ Experiments on Sound, 1877, p. 8.

‖ Henry and Reynolds.   Cf., Delaroche, Ann. de Chim., 1816, Tome I, p. 180.

their intensity has been extinguished, we may find in this fact an explanation of the statement made by Reynolds, that "on all occasions the effect of wind seems to be rather against distance than distinctness." *

10. As sounds may be inaudible at certain distances and elevations without being wholly extinguished, it follows that the comparative inaudibility of sounds at different times cannot always be cited as an evidence of their relative intensities. The comparative inaudibility may be a function of variable refraction rather than of variable intensity. Hence the law of inverse squares, though perfectly true in its theoretical application to the measurement of the intensity of all sounds, cannot always be legitimately used to calculate backwards from the audibility of a sound, as empirically ascertained at a given point and elevation, to its relative intensity as previously heard at the same point and elevation.

11. The hypothesis of Stokes, as applied by Henry, does not exclude the hypothesis of Humboldt, but reduces the latter to a very subordinate and inappreciable place in interpreting the abnormal phenomena of sound.

12. The hypothesis of Stokes, as applied by Henry, does not exclude the reasoning or the experimental proofs by which Prof. Reynolds demonstrates that differences in temperature exert a refracting power in sound, but finds in that refraction an influence which may sometimes accelerate and sometimes retard the refraction produced by wind.†

The next communication was by Mr. C. H. KOYL, Fellow of the Johns Hopkins University, on

THE STORAGE OF ELECTRIC ENERGY.

After discussing the subject from an historical point of view, concluding with a description of the improved form of secondary battery lately invented by M. Faure, the author proceeded to state the

---

* Lon., Ed., and Dub. Ph. Mag. for 1875, Vol. 50, p. 63.

† Rep. Light-House Board 1875, p. 125, cf. Reynolds; Lon., Ed., and Dub. Ph. Mag. for 1875, Vol. 50, p. 71.

results of some investigations carried on independently in this country by Mr. J. A. Maloney and Mr. Franz Burger, of Washington, and afterward by himself in connection with them.

Mr. Maloney and Mr. Burger had been aiming to interpose in the circuit of the electric lamp a reservoir of energy which should perform the same function for the electric lamp that a gasometer did for a gas-burner, viz., prevent its flickering by keeping a constant or nearly constant potential on the main line, even though the current from the source should be irregular.

A long course of experiment convinced them that plates of lead immersed in dilute sulphuric acid form a combination preferable to any other for giving return currents when once these plates have been made part of an electric circuit. They noticed what they believed to be an oxide of lead formed on one plate, and since the thicker the coating of oxide the greater the effect, they began to regard this layer as a sort of sponge which, in some way, held the electricity, and they concluded to increase the holding capacity of the cell by increasing the thickness of the sponge. Oxide of lead was accordingly purchased and painted on, with results which were surprising. The storage of electricity in large quantity was effected. This was of course independent and without any knowledge of Mr. Faure's work in Europe, but the chief merit of their inquiry lies in the rapidity with which they grasped the idea of *mechanically* increasing the sponge-like coating.

While they were testing the capabilities of the battery and were still endeavoring to improve it, the announcement was made of Mr. Faure's similar inventions. Soon after the battery was submitted for experiment to three members of this Society, and subsequently the co-operation of the author was invited for further study of the subject.

On examining the plates during their summer investigations they found reason for believing that the published theory of the action of the cell was but partly correct; for after the plates had been charged the changes of color and, therefore, of chemical constitution, upon which the return current was supposed to depend, were found, in general, not to take place until the return current had been passing for some time. If so, in something else than chemical combination must lie the storage capacity of these cells. The conclusion arrived at from their investigations was that the change of red-lead into peroxide upon one plate and into spongy lead upon the other required only a small part of the oxygen and hydrogen liberated by the primary current and that the remainder was mechanically held in the coatings.

Several minor considerations support this view, and the principal experiments upon which the proof should rest, viz., the liberation of the gas in a vacuum or by slight application of heat in general succeed. Some anomalies, however, are presented which require further study, but which the author hopes soon to reconcile with the theory of mechanical storing.

A discussion followed, in which several members participated.

206TH MEETING.   NOVEMBER 17, 1881.

The President in the chair.

Thirty-eight members present.

The communication for the evening was by Mr. G. K. GILBERT

ON BAROMETRIC HYPSOMETRY.

This communication was reserved by the author, and his views and investigations in connection with this subject will be found in a paper contributed by him to the Second Annual Report of the Director of the United States Geological Survey.

A brief discussion ensued, and one or two points were questioned

---

207TH MEETING.   DECEMBER 3, 1881.

The President in the chair.

Seventy-six members and visitors present.

Under the rules this meeting, being the next preceding the annual meeting, was set apart for the delivery of the address of the retiring President of the Society. Calling Vice-President Hilgard to the chair, the President of the Society, Mr. J. J. WOODWARD, then read the following address:

MODERN PHILOSOPHICAL CONCEPTIONS OF LIFE.

I address you this evening in accordance with the fifth of the new Standing Rules for the government of the Philosophical Society of Washington, adopted in January last, which directs that the stated meeting next preceding the annual meeting for the election of officers shall be set apart for the delivery of the President's Annual Address. By the rules adopted at the first organization of the society the President's address was directed to be delivered on the evening of the annual meeting after the election of officers had taken place. It was found, however, that the elections always occupied the whole meeting, so that the address was necessarily postponed until after the term of office for which the President was elected had expired. During the presidency of the illustrious Professor Henry, who by common consent was re-elected annually, the inconvenience of this arrangement was not felt. But I understood the general sense of the Society last year to be that an annual change of President is desirable, and that this standing rule was adopted in view of that feeling, in order to give the retiring President a convenient opportunity for the delivery of his address before his term of office expires.

For my own part I was last year, and am now, thoroughly convinced of the desirability of electing a new President annually in a society like ours. I think on the one hand that it is a measure well calculated to increase the interest taken in the society by its members, and on the other hand that the preparation of a formal annual address would be too great a tax upon the time of a President re-elected from year to year. I think, too, that there is much propriety in a suggestion which I heard expressed in many quarters last year, that our President should be selected alternately, from what may be called for convenience, the Physical and Biological sides of the society, so that having been myself elected as in some sort a representative of the Biological side, it is my hope that you will at the next meeting elect as my successor a representative of the Physical side. With this brief explanation I will proceed at once to the consideration of the subject I have selected for the present occasion.

I propose to invite your attention this evening to some thoughts on the *Modern Philosophical Conceptions of Life*. The theme is so large that it would be idle to attempt its systematic treatment in the course of a single evening; nor do I pretend to be in possession of any satisfactory solution of this ancient question, of which I might offer you an abstract or outline, pending the fuller presentation of my results elsewhere. Yet I have ventured to hope that a discussion of some of the considerations involved, and a brief statement of certain views that I have been led to entertain, would not be without interest, and perhaps might prove of actual service, especially to those of you who are engaged in biological pursuits.

Undoubtedly the conception of life most popular at the present time is that which assumes all the phenomena of living beings to be the necessary results of the chemical and physical forces of the universe, and claims, or intimates, that wherever this has not yet been proven to be the case the evidence will hereafter be forthcoming. This doctrine, which may conveniently be designated the chemico-physical hypothesis of life, has readily found its way from the speculative writings of philosophers to the rostrums of some of our teachers of chemistry and physics who boldly declare, in their class-lectures and public addresses, that the forces at work in the inorganic world are fully adequate to explain all the phenomena of living beings, and prophesy that the time is soon coming "when the last vestige of the vital principle as an independent entity shall disappear from the terminology of science." [1]

Now, most of these gentlemen are not embarrassed by any very definite or detailed knowledge of the physiological and pathological phenomena which a tenable theory of life must be competent to explain, while they do know, or at least ought to know, a great deal of chemistry and physics; the confidence with which they maintain their creed is therefore readily understood. Much more surprising is it to find the same doctrine embraced by numerous zoologists, physiologists, nay, even pathologists, among them men who cannot for a moment be supposed to be unacquainted with the phenomena to be explained, and of whose abilities and reasoning powers it is impossible for me to think or speak otherwise than respectfully. Yet I cannot but believe that they have adopted the chemico-physical hypothesis, not so much because they are really satisfied with it as a scientific explanation of all the phenomena, as because they are unduly biased in its favor by the utterances of the great philosopher who has done, as I think we will all agree, such good service to biological science by elaborating and popularizing the doctrine of evolution.

It is only natural that such a bias should exist. The discussion of the nature of life—in the case of man at least—has always, and not unreasonably, been conjoined with the discussion of the nature of the soul, and the philosophers who have won highest repute in the latter discussion, have always been willing enough to offer solutions of the life-problem, and have never had any difficulty in finding followers even among those whose special lines of investigation might be supposed to impose upon them the duty of independent inquiry into the meaning of life.

Just as it was in the old time, with regard to this matter, so it is now. When Galen undertakes to discuss the complex phenomena of the Psyche, as manifested by the human species, he openly and continually confesses the extent to which he relies upon the authority of Plato; and when the dicta of the master are such as to require a special effort of faith on the part of the disciple, he honestly exclaims "Plato indeed appears to be persuaded of this, as for me, whether it be so or not, I am unable to dispute the question with him."[2]

In like manner, did they venture to be as frank as Galen was, most of the modern biologists who have adopted the chemico-physical theory of life would, I presume, confess "as to this matter our opinions are derived from Mr. Herbert Spencer's Principles of Biology—what are we that we should venture to dispute as to questions like these with him."

Nevertheless in striking contrast to this chemico-physical hypothesis of life, which is to be regarded as the fashionable faith of the hour, there still survives in many quarters, and especially among physicians, a disposition to regard indiscriminately almost all the phenomena of living beings as peculiar manifestations of a vital principle. So strong, indeed, is the faith of some of these modern vitalists, that they seem to shut their eyes to the evidence already in our possession as to the actual participation of known chemical and physical forces in the operations going on within living bodies, and appear almost to resent the willing aid that chemistry and physics afford to the physiological investigator of the present day.

Nay, further than this, in the inevitable reaction that is beginning to make itself felt against the avowed revival of the materialism of Epicurus and Lucretius—for we all know now that the chemico-physical hypothesis of life is not a new induction of modern science, but an ancient Greek speculation reappearing in modern petti-coats—that other Greek speculation of the threefold Psyche, the doctrine taught by Plato and Aristotle, and which Galen accepted on their authority, the doctrine of a vegetable, an animal, and a rational soul, a human trinity coexisting in every human being, is once more rehabilitated and finding followers—likely, indeed, as I think, to obtain more followers than perhaps any of you yet suppose. And these followers are by no means confined to metaphysicians or churchmen, they can be found also already among the biologists. It is an English biologist of good repute, and of no mean abilities, who takes occasion, in a technical biological work published this very year, to express his belief that the Greek conception of the threefold Psyche "appears to be justified by the light of the science of our own day." [3]

For myself I must confess at once that I am quite unable to join either of these opposing camps as a partizan. I cannot accept the more strictly vitalistic views, because I am compelled continually to recognize the operation of purely chemical and physical forces in living beings. On the other hand, there are whole groups of phenomena characteristic of living beings, and peculiar to them, for which the chemico-physical hypothesis offers no intelligible explanation.

From this point of view the various processes and functions of living beings may indeed be divided into two classes, of which the first may be regarded with more or less certainty as the special re-sults, under special conditions, of the very same forces that operate in the inorganic world ; while the second, to which alone I would apply the term vital, are not merely in every respect peculiar to living beings, and hitherto utterly inexplicable by the laws of chemistry and physics, but are so different in character from the phenomena of the inorganic world that it does not seem rational to attempt to explain them by these laws.

Let me refer briefly to the processes and functions belonging to the first class. Here I place all those more strictly chemical processes by which, within the very substance of vegetable pro-toplasm, inorganic elements are combined into organic matter,

as well as those which produce all the various subsequent transformations, whether in plants or animals, of the organic matter
thus prepared.   This general conception includes of course, in the
case of the higher animals, all the chemical phases of the processes
of digestion, assimilation and tissue-metamorphosis or metabolism,
including secretion and excretion; in the case of the lower animals
and plants, so much of these several functions as belongs to each
species.

Now please to understand that when I say I recognize all the
chemical phases of these processes to be the results of the ordinary
chemical laws, I do not entertain any mental reservation with regard
to the unrestricted application of these laws.   I cannot for a moment agree with those physiologists who have imagined the vital
principle to thwart, or interfere with, or counteract these laws in
any way.   I know, indeed, that we are far from being as thoroughly
acquainted, as we may by and by hope to be, with the chemical
phenomena of living beings; that many of the questions are very
difficult, so that as yet, with all our labor, we have obtained but
partial or even contradictory results; but I find in this only a reason
for further investigation—no logical difficulty of a radical kind.
In a general way I recognize that the matter of which living beings
are composed is built up of elementary substances belonging to the
inorganic world, and that it consists of atoms possessed of the very
same properties, and obedient to the very same laws as like atoms
in inorganic bodies.   Yet I confess I find in all this no reason for
denying the existence of a vital principle; only I do not figure this
principle in my mind as a hostile power interfering in any way with
the chemical tendencies of the atoms present; I liken its operations
rather to those of the chemist in his laboratory who obtains the
results he needs only on the condition of most rigid obedience to
chemical laws.

Intimately associated with some of the chemical processes just
enumerated are those chemical processes of respiration, in which
the chemical affinities of the oxygen of the atmosphere are directly
or indirectly the means of promoting tissue metamorphosis, as well
as of reducing at once to simpler forms some portion of the various
complex substances derived from the food.   These chemical processes are undoubtedly the chief original sources of the heat and
mechanical power manifested by animals.   Of course they receive
heat also from without by conduction and radiation; but this is a

small matter to the heat generated within them; of course, too, mechanical power is continually transformed into heat within the body of animals, but this neither increases nor diminishes the total amount of energy liberated.

I yield my hearty assent to that modern scientific induction [4] which sees in the potential energy of the complex chemical compounds supplied to animals by their food, the essential source of all the actual energy of the body, whether manifested in the form of heat or work. In a general way the reduction of these complex chemical compounds by oxidation into the much simpler ones, urea, carbon dioxide, and water, is the means by which potential is converted into actual energy. In the case of plants, too, the source of any little heat that may be developed under special conditions, and of such sluggish motions as actually occur, is doubtless to be found in the reduction to simpler combinations by oxidation of a part of the organic matter already formed. The chief function of the vegetable world, however, is to build up, by means of the solar energy, those complex and unstable organic compounds that supply the animal world with food. Nevertheless, while I yield my hearty assent to this generalization, and freely admit that it is more than a mere deduction from the general doctrine of the conservation of energy—that in fact it affords the most satisfactory explanation yet suggested for a large number of observed phenomena—it is my duty to caution you against the erroneous supposition that any one has ever yet succeeded in affording a rigorous demonstration of the truth of the generalization by an adequate series of actual experiments.

Various attempts have, indeed, been made of late years to determine experimentally both for animals and for man, the potential energy contained in the food of a given period, and the actual energy liberated during the same time in the form of heat and work. I think, however, that all practical physiologists who have looked into the question will agree with me that the numerical results hitherto obtained must be received with the utmost caution. [5] Difficulties exist on both sides of the problem. It is comparatively easy, no doubt, to obtain a close approximation to the quantity and composition of the food; but to represent numerically what becomes of it in the body, to deduct correctly what passes through unchanged, and ascertain with reasonable accuracy the amount of carbon dioxide, water, and urea, into which the rest is transformed;

these are questions which have taxed the utmost resources of investigators, and as to which our knowledge is yet in its infancy.

On the other hand, the direct measurement of the resulting heat and work has hitherto proved still less satisfactory. It would seem to be a very simple thing to place an animal in a calorimeter, and measure the heat-units evolved in a given time, as Lavoisier and Laplace attempted to do in the latter part of the last century, and we have been told that "Lavoisier's guinea-pig placed in the calorimeter gave as accurate a return for the energy it had absorbed in its food as any thermic engine would have done."[6] But this assertion is not supported by the results of actual experiment. We know now that many precautions, unknown to Lavoisier, must be taken to secure any approach to accuracy in calorimetric experiments with animals, and just as the method is being brought to something like perfection by arranging for the respiratory process and its influence on the results, and by other necessary modifications of the primitive rude attempts,[7] doubts are beginning to arise as to whether after all the conditions in which the animal is placed in the calorimeter are not so far abnormal as seriously to vitiate the results;[8] so that in fact the most approved numerical expressions of the heat-production of the body to be found in the books are based rather upon calculation of the amount that ought to be produced by the oxidation of an estimated quantity of food than upon actual calorimetric observations.

Nor do we find it any easier when we attempt the actual measurement of the amount of work produced by an animal from a given amount of food. Indeed, in attempting to formulate an equation between the potential energy of the food and the actual amount of heat and work in any given case, we are met with the special difficulty that the animal does not evolve less heat because it is doing work than it does when it is at rest; on the contrary, it actually evolves more heat, consuming for the purpose more food than usual—or if this is not forthcoming, consuming a part of its own reserve of adipose tissue—so that from this source fresh complications of the problem arise.

The labor and ingenuity with which all these difficulties have been encountered is certainly worthy of the highest praise, and I willingly admit the probably approximate truth of the figures generally in use, say $2\frac{1}{4}$ to $2\frac{3}{4}$ million gramme-degrees as the daily average heat-production of an adult man, and 150,000 to 200,000 metre-killogrammes as his capacity for daily mechanical work.[9] Nevertheless these figures are after all only probable approxima-tions, and there still exists, with regard to these questions, a large and inviting field for the application of chemical and physical methods to physiological research.

All the mechanical work done by living beings is effected by means of certain contractions of their soft tissues. The movements of the amœba, so often described of late years, may be taken as the type of the simplest form of these contractions. Similar move-ments occur, with more or less activity, in the protoplasm of all young cells, and in the higher animals are strikingly illustrated by the movements of the white corpuscles of the blood and the wan-dering cells of the connective tissue. In the lowest animal forms these simple amœboid movements of the protoplasm are the only movements, but in the higher forms, besides these, certain special contractile tissues make their appearance, by which the chief part of the mechanical work done is effected; these are the striated and unstriated muscular fibres.

On account of the extreme minuteness of the little protoplasmic bodies in which the amœboid movements are manifested, the inves-tigation of the mechanical means by which these movements are effected has not as yet been attempted, although a great mass of details have been accumulated by actual observation with regard to the phenomena themselves and the conditions under which they occur. Very little more has been done with regard to the con-tractions of the unstriated muscular fibres. The striated muscles, however, have been made the subject of a host of researches, and I suppose the conclusions to which we may ultimately be led by these can be regarded, with but little reservation, as applicable to the function of the unstriated muscles, and also to the simpler amœboid protoplasmic contractions.

Yet, notwithstanding the vast amount of experimental labor and speculative ingenuity that has been lavished, since the time of Hal-ler, upon the question of the contraction of the striated muscle, it must be confessed in the honest language of Hermann,[10] that the problem still mocks our best endeavors. For myself, I am un-willing to believe that the phenomena of muscular contraction, or indeed, of any of the varieties of protoplasmic contraction by which animals effect mechanical work, will not by and by be fully and satis-factorily explained on chemico-physical principles. I cannot for a moment give my adherence to the dogmatism of those modern vitalists who insist that the contractions of a muscle, or of an amœba, are essentially vital phenomena; for this would be to claim that life can create force. But it would be folly to shut our eyes to the circumstance that no chemico-physical explanation of muscular contraction yet offered has been so convincingly supported by facts as to command the universal assent of competent physiologists.

Of the various hypotheses devised to explain muscular contraction, those which regard the phenomena as in some way resulting from electrical disturbances have long enjoyed great popularity. Such of these hypotheses as still survive are based upon the electrical manifestations actually observed in living muscles. It has been pretty generally accepted in accordance with the observations of Du Bois-Reymond, whose brilliant series of experiments in animal electricity [11] is deservedly renowned, that even quiescent living muscles are in a state of electrical tension. If, for example, a muscle composed of parallel longitudinal fibres, be exposed with suitable precautions, and divided near each extremity by a transverse incision, the surface of the muscle will be found to be positive to the cut ends, and if one of a pair of non-polarizable electrodes, connected with a suitable galvanometer, is placed in contact with the surface of the muscle and the other in contact with one of the cut ends, the existence of a current is made manifest. The conditions are, moreover, such that while the maximum effect is produced when the equator of the surface is connected with the centre of one of the cut ends; more or less current will also be manifested whenever any two points of the surface are thus connected with the galvanometer, provided they are not equidistant from the equator. In such cases the point most distant from the equator is always negative. The electro-motive force of this natural current of the quiescent muscle varies greatly, but has been found by Du Bois-Reymond to amount sometimes to as much as .08 Daniell in one of the thigh muscles of the frog.[12] In muscles of different form, or cut differently from what has just been described, the currents are somewhat differently arranged, but the example just given must suffice for my present purpose.

In accordance with the observations of the same investigator, it is claimed that during a muscular contraction the electrical tension diminishes, the normal muscle-current experiences a negative variation, and this occurs in such a way, that as the wave of actual contraction moves along the muscle, which it does, according to the observations of Bernstein and Hermann,[13] with a velocity of about 3 metres per second, it is preceded by a wave of negative variation. This negative variation is indeed so trifling, if the muscle contracts but once, that it is difficult to observe it; but when the contractions succeed each other with great rapidity, as in artificially produced tetanus, it may become sufficient to neutralize completely the deflection of the galvanometer due to the current of the quiescent muscle.

But the belief that the electrical currents, shown to exist in the quiescent muscles in these experiments, exist also in uninjured animals has not remained unchallenged. Since 1867 it has been attacked especially by Hermann,[14] who has endeavored to show that these currents are produced only under the special conditions of the experiments, and that there are in reality no natural muscle-currents at all. It was well known that the currents observed in the experiments varied greatly under different circumstances, and it seemed a significant fact that they should be most intense when the muscle was removed from the body and had both ends cut off. If the muscle was removed with its tendinous extremities still attached, the current was usually found to be very feeble, or entirely absent, until the ends were well washed in salt and water, or dipped in acid. Du Bois-Reymond had explained this by supposing the natural ends of the muscle to be protected by what he called a parelectronomic layer of positive elements that must be removed before the natural current could be made manifest. On the other hand, Hermann has endeavored to show that the parts injured by the knife, or acted on by the salt or acid, enter at once into the well-known condition of rigor mortis, and only become negative to the still living portions of the muscle in consequence of this change. That electrical disturbances actually occur in contracting muscles he admits, but endeavors to show that they are due simply to the fact that the changes preceding contraction make the affected part of the muscle negative to every part less modified or wholly unaltered. Hence, if an uninjured muscle be caused, under proper precautions, to contract simultaneously in all its parts, it will be found that the contraction is wholly unaccompanied by any muscle-current.[15]

Observations that appear to support these views of Hermann have been brought forward by Englemann.[16] On the other hand

Du Bois-Reymond has defended his views with vigor, and sharply criticised, of course, the labors and logic of his assailant.[17] I need not at present express any opinion as to the merits of this voluminous controversy. It is enough for my purpose to indicate the questions at issue as sufficiently important and uncertain to be well worthy of independent experimental criticism.

Suppose, however, this criticism should result in showing that Hermann is wholly in the wrong, and that the muscle-currents observed by Du Bois-Reymond really exist in healthy muscles. How, then, shall these currents explain the phenomena of muscular contraction? I presume that no physiologist of the present day is misled by the superficial comparison, which Mayer and Amici were led by their microscopical studies of the muscles of insects to make between the striated muscular fibre and a Voltaic pile.[18] But the molecular theory by which Du Bois-Reymond has endeavored to explain his natural muscle-currents and their negative variation would appear to open up an inexhaustible mine of speculative possibilities for those who are inclined to speculate.

Yet the old experiment of Schwann[19] has always been a stumbling-block in the way of any theory that would explain muscular contraction by the action of a force which must increase inversely as the square of the distance between the molecules, for the force of the contraction, as it actually occurs, diminishes as the muscle shortens ; and hence we find so good a physiologist as Radcliffe[20] reviving, in a modified form, the old hypothesis of Matteucci,[21] in accordance with which the electrical tension of the fibre, in the state of rest, causes a mutual repulsion of the molecules, and so elongates the muscle, while the contraction is merely the effect of the elasticity of the tissue, which asserts itself so soon as the repulsive force is diminished by the negative variation that precedes contraction.

In consequence of these and other difficulties many physiologists are beginning to regard the electrical phenomena as subordinate accidents of the chemical processes that go on in muscle, and endeavor to explain muscular contraction as resulting directly from these chemical processes themselves. Arthur Gamgee[22] has adopted as most probable the chemical hypothesis of Hermann.[23] This assumes the contraction to result from the decomposition of a complex nitrogenous compound supposed to be contained in the muscular tissue, and named inogen. During contraction inogen breaks down into carbon dioxide, lactic acid, (Fleischmilchsäure,) and gelatinous myosin. The rearrangement of molecules necessary to produce the latter body determines the contraction. Subsequently the gelatinous myosin combines with the necessary materials furnished by the blood, and becomes inogen again. This decomposition and recomposition goes on also while the muscle is at rest, but, as then the gelatinous myosin is reconverted into inogen as rapidly as it is formed, no contraction results.

Du Bois-Reymond declares all this to be merely unsupported hypothesis.[24] Gamgee himself admits that it is, after all, not very clear why the gelatinous myosin should contract. Michael Foster,[25] who wholly rejects this particular chemical hypothesis, nevertheless seems quite sure that the true explanation will be found to be a chemical one. He insists that muscular contraction is essentially a translocation of molecules, and declares that whatever the exact way in which this translocation is effected may be, it is fundamentally the result of a chemical change, or, as he describes it, "an explosive decomposition of certain parts of the muscle-substance."

The purpose I have in view does not require, fortunately, that I should attempt to decide whether these more purely chemical theories of muscular contraction, or the more purely electrical theories, are best entitled to confidence. My object has been effected, if I have impressed you with the fact that wide differences of opinion still exist as to the nature of the process, and that further investigation is indispensable for the settlement of existing controversies.

The subject just briefly discussed brings us naturally to the consideration of the nature of the action of the motor nerves, by which, in all animals possessed of a muscular and nervous system, the contraction of the muscles is regulated and determined.

The hypothesis which identifies the nervous currents with electricity was propounded in the posthumous work of Hausen[26] in 1743, and, notwithstanding all the difficulties and objections it has encountered, still survives in a modified form in many contemporaneous minds. Those who hold to this view appeal in its support to the electrical phenomena actually observed in nerves in accordance with the investigations of Du Bois-Reymond. These observations have long been widely accepted as conclusive proof that natural currents exist in the quiescent nerve of the same general character as those attributed to the quiescent muscle, which I outlined a few minutes ago. The electro-motive force of this current was found by Du Bois-Reymond[27] to be equal to .022 Daniell in the sciatic nerve of the frog. When a nervous impulse passes along the nerve the natural current is diminished; it experiences a negative variation, which, according to Bernstein,[28] when the impulse results from a very potent stimulation, may more than neutralize the natural current. The same physiologist has shown that this negative variation moves along the nerves of the frog at the rate of 28 metres per second; that is, at the same rate as the nervous impulse itself, as determined without reference to the electrical phenomena.

As in the case of the muscle-currents, these phenomena have been differently interpreted by Hermann,[29] who denies the existence of any natural nerve-current in uninjured nerves, and ascribes those observed in the experiments to the circumstance that the parts of the nerve dead or dying, in consequence of the section, become negative to the living nerve. The negative variation produced by the stimulation of a nerve he explains by assuming that the stimulated part of the nerve becomes, in consequence of the changes resulting from the stimulation, negative to the unstimulated parts. I will not attempt to enter to-night into the merits of the controversy still in progress with regard to this question; nor will I pause to discuss the exceedingly curious and interesting phenomena of electrotonus,[30] concerning which, I will only say that the question has even been raised by Radcliffe as to how far these phenomena are peculiar to nerves, and how far they may be regarded as mere phenomena of the electrical currents employed, which would be equally manifested under similar circumstances if a wet string or other bad conductor should be substituted for the nerve.[31]

However these disputes may be ultimately decided; whatever the actual facts with regard to the electrical manifestations in nerves at rest or in action, may ultimately prove to be, there is a group of easily repeated elementary experiments which seem to show pretty distinctly that whatever the nervous impulse may be, it is not merely an electrical current.

It was known already when Haller wrote[32] that a string tied tightly around a nerve, although it in no wise interferes with the passage of electrical currents, puts a speedy end to the transmission of nervous impulses. With this old experimental difficulty uncontradicted, it seems strange that anyone should declare at the present time that "the main objections raised to the electrical character of nerve energy is based upon its slow propagation."[33] In fact this latter objection is altogether a subordinate difficulty which may perhaps be entirely explained away; the main experimental objection does not relate to the velocity, but to the conditions of the propagation of the nervous impulse. If, instead of tying a string around it, the nerve be merely pinched or bruised well with a pair of forceps so as to destroy its delicate organic texture; if it be compressed tightly by a tiny metallic clamp; if it be divided by a sharp knife, and the cut ends brought nicely into contact, or brought in contact with the extremities of a piece of copper wire, it will still conduct electrical currents as well as ever, but can no longer transmit the nervous impulse. So, too, there are certain poisons, such as the woorara, which completely destroy the capacity of the nerve for transmitting nervous impulses, without in the least diminishing its conductivity for electricity.[34]

In view of these and other practical difficulties, the best instructed modern physiologists no longer attempt to identify the nervous impulse with the electrical phenomena by which it is accompanied. Du Bois-Reymond himself has suggested that the nervous agent "in all probability is some internal motion, perhaps even some chemical change, of the substance itself contained in the nerve-tubes, spreading along the tubes."[35] Herbert Spencer came to the conclusion that "nervous stimulations and discharges consist of waves of molecular change"[36] flowing through the nerve-fibres; and I suppose that most physiologists at the present time think of the nervous current in some such way as this. Even those who attach most importance to the electrical phenomena will, I take it, agree with Michael Foster, that these "are in reality tokens of molecular changes in the tissue much more complex than those necessary for the propagation of a mere electrical current."[37]

We do not, however, as yet possess any sufficient foundation of facts on which to build a reasonable hypothesis as to the nature of the molecular disturbances that accompany a nervous impulse. The labors of the physiological chemists have taught us nothing with regard to the changes that go on, except that the axis-cylinder which, in the inactive living nerve is alkaline, becomes acid after long continued activity, or after death.[38] We can measure the velocity with which the impulse travels; we can study the conditions under which it arises; we can believe, as I certainly do, that it will ultimately receive a chemico-physical explanation, but its real nature we do not yet know.

So far as we can ascertain, the phenomena of the conduction of nervous impulses by the sensitive nerves are so similar to those of the conduction of motor impulses, that any explanation ultimately adopted for the one will probably apply to the other also. When, however, we ascend to the study of the nervous centres, by which sensitive and motor nerves are connected together, and attempt the interpretation of the complex functions of nerve-cell, ganglion, spinal cord, and brain, we find that none of the hypotheses hitherto brought forward to explain the observed phenomena repose on any defensible chemico-physical basis.

I cannot, of course, undertake to give to-night even the most meagre outline of the wondrous mechanism which physiological experiments show must exist. That reflex actions, co-ordinated muscular movements, and all the complex phenomena of this class, do depend upon a wonderfully complex mechanism, and occur in strict accordance with the ordinary chemical and physical laws, I do not for a moment doubt, and I cordially invite the co-operation of the chemists and physicists to aid the physiologists in the explanation of this mechanism, for we stand only upon the threshold as yet.

If now we turn from the more general discussion of muscular contraction and nervous action, to the consideration of the several functions carried on in animals, by means of special arrangements of the muscular and nervous systems, we continually encounter the preponderating influence of purely physical laws. The introduction of air into the lungs of breathing animals, and its expulsion thence, is effected in a purely mechanical way, while the exchange of the carbon dioxide of the blood with the oxygen of the inspired air occurs in strict obedience to the laws of the diffusion of gases.

The ordinary laws of hydraulics govern the circulation of the blood and lymph, and all the complex visible motions of the body are executed in accordance with the ordinary laws of mechanics; nor is it at all necessary for me to insist upon the purely physical nature of the operations of the organs of the special senses, conspicuously the eye and the ear. For example, so far as concerns the means by which images of external objects are formed sharply upon the retina, the eye is as purely a physical instrument as the telescope or the microscope. But I need not dwell upon this group of phenomena, because the importance of the role of the ordinary physical laws in this domain is conceded, I suppose, by the extremest of the vitalists of the present day.

We see, therefore, that, with regard to a large part of the phenomena of living beings, there are grounds for affirming either that they have already been satisfactorily explained by a reference to established chemical and physical laws, or at least that they are of such a character that it is reasonable to hope they may be thus explained at some future time. Is it possible, then, to return, as some have done of late years, to the old speculation of Des Cartes, and look upon living beings as mere machines? To do so, it will not suffice to image to yourselves ordinary machines in which fuel yields force. To satisfy the chemico-physical hypothesis of life you must suppose machines that build themselves, repair themselves, and direct, from time to time, new applications of their energy in accordance with changes in the environment; nay, more—machines that accouple themselves together, breeding little machines of the same kind that grow by and by to resemble their parents, and all this self-directed, without any engineer. But even Des Cartes required an engineer—the soul—to run his man-machine, and the logic which compelled him to this view applies just as forcibly to all the modern machine conceptions of living beings.

I have already asserted that there are whole groups of phenomena characteristic of living beings, and peculiar to them, which cannot be intelligently explained as the mere resultants of the operation of the chemical and physical forces of the universe. These phenomena I refer—I avow it without hesitation—to the operations of a vital principle, in the existence of which I believe as firmly as I believe in the existence of force, although I do not know its nature any more than I know the nature of force. If, for convenience, at any time, I compare the living body to a machine, I must compare the vital principle to the engineer—it is the director, the manager if you will, but it does not supply the force that does any part of the work. Let us consider, then, in the remainder of this discourse, the phenomena which indicate the guidance of the vital principle.

The first group of phenomena belonging to this second class are those forced upon our attention whenever we attempt to study the question of the origin of life. It has seemed to some of our contemporaries that, in accordance with the doctrine of evolution, as deduced by Mr. Herbert Spencer from the great truth of the persistence of force, life ought always to arise spontaneously out of inorganic matter whenever the necessary materials and other conditions of life are brought together. Indeed, if there be nothing more or other in life than force, I confess I do not understand how this conclusion can be logically escaped; and yet, when we come to interrogate nature, we find that, in point of fact, things do not happen so.

The sun may stream all the enormous energy of his rays upon the slime of the Nile, but he generates no monsters; nay, not even a bacterium, except in the presence and under the direction of pre-existing life. Our biological knowledge has so far advanced that it is easy for us to get together mixtures of matter, for the most part derived from pre-existing living beings, which are peculiarly well fitted to supply the materials needed for the building up of a variety of low forms of life, and the extent of our present knowledge of the conditions favorable to the development of these low forms of life is shown by the rapidity with which they do develop from a few individuals to countless millions, if only a few individuals are introduced as parents into our flasks and brood-ovens. The species to which the countless progeny belongs, depends always upon the species of the parents we introduced by design or accident, and if parents of several species are introduced we may imitate on a tiny scale the great struggle for existence, and witness the survival of the fittest. Never, however, has the spontaneous generation, out of inorganic matter, of a single living form been yet observed.

Speculative considerations have, indeed, from time to time led certain enthusiasts to desire earnestly that it might be observed; and when we consider on the one hand the influence of pre-existing bias, and on the other the intricacy of some of the experimental processes in question, it is by no means necessary to charge dishonesty upon those who, from time to time, have actually fancied that their desires have been realized to the extent of the spontaneous generation of bacteria at least. When we consider the immense development of the trade in canned food, which could not exist for a single summer's day, if these experimenters were not mistaken, it will be seen how little need there was for renewed scientific experiment to refute their conclusions; but it is a noteworthy fact that among those who have contributed most by exact research to recent scientific demonstrations of the truth, that life never arises except from pre-existing life, are to be found some of the most earnest and eloquent advocates not merely of the doctrines of evolution, but of its supposed corollary, the chemico-physical hypothesis of life.

I sympathize heartily with those who, recognizing that the supposition of the spontaneous origin of life on our globe is flatly contradicted by the facts of science, have endeavored to escape the difficulty by imagining the earliest parent living forms to have been brought to our earth on the surface of meteoric stones or other cosmical bodies. This hypothesis, put forward originally on purely theoretical grounds, has recently acquired a certain degree of support from the published observations of Hahn and Weinland,[39] who believe they have recognized the remains of humble coralline forms in thin sections of meteoric stones collected in Hungary. Yet these observations, if indeed they should prove to be correct, would rather afford indications of the existence of life in other worlds than ours, than show that living forms could survive the high temperature to which such cosmical masses must be exposed during their transit through our atmosphere; and even should we find reasons for ultimately adopting this hypothesis, we should not have solved the problem of the origin of life, but only removed it entirely beyond the domain of further scientific investigation.

If, however, we reject this view, and still mean to support the chemico-physical hypothesis of life, we shall have to resort to a still more improbable supposition. We shall have to suppose that although in the present order of things life can only arise out of pre-existing life, the order of things was at some past time so far different that life could then arise out of inorganic matter; a supposition which implies an instability in the course of nature that is contradicted by all the teachings of science.

I willingly admit that, in view of our present scientific notions of the cosmogony, it is impossible to believe that life always existed upon this planet. I willingly admit that life on the earth must have had a beginning in time. But we do not know how it began. Let us honestly confess our ignorance. I declare to you I think the old Hebrew belief, that life began by a creative act of the Universal Mind, has quite as good claims to be regarded a scientific hypothesis as the speculation that inorganic matter ever became living by virtue of its own forces merely.

If we turn now to the consideration of the processes of growth, we shall find additional reasons for believing in the existence of a vital principle. Let us consider first, in the most general way, the conditions under which those strictly chemical processes occur, to which I have already alluded, and by which the inorganic atoms are combined into organic matter. I repeat it, I do not for a moment question that the actual force by which these processes are compelled exists in the solar rays, and that it is, after all, the solar energy thus stored up in the vegetable protoplasm and its products that supplies, by its subsequent liberation, all the force manifested by living beings. Yet, let me beg you to observe that in all the myriads of years during which the solar energy has streamed upon the earth, that energy has never, on any occasion that we know of, determined the combination of inorganic atoms into organic matter, except within the substance of already living protoplasm. The water and carbon dioxide and ammonia in the atmosphere and in the soil, come into contact with each other, within the substance of porous inorganic clods on the surface of the soil, much as they do in the substance of protoplasm, and the equal sun warms both alike; but in the clod they remain water, carbon dioxide, and ammonia; in the protoplasm, provided only that it is living protoplasm, they combine into starch or oil, or even into protoplasm itself. The essential condition, then, of this storing up of the solar energy for the subsequent use of living beings is the presence of life, and in these fundamental operations the mighty force of the sun acts, in the fullest sense of the words, the part of the servant of life.

The view thus suggested, that we have here to do with something more than the mere operation of the inorganic forces, is still further strengthened when we come to consider more in detail the phenomena of the growth of living beings, whether plants or animals. The better we become acquainted with these phenomena the more fully we become convinced that we have to do with processes for which the inorganic world affords no parallel.

Linnæus, indeed, declared, "lapides crescunt," using the very same phrase which he applied also to plants and animals.[40] But it is impossible to maintain this assertion without adopting the most superficial view of the growth of living beings, and defining the process to consist merely in increase of size. That this should have appeared reasonable, in the time of Linnæus, need excite no surprise; but it seems strange to find so astute a thinker as Mr. Herbert Spencer repeating the old fallacy in the first chapter of his Inductions of Biology, and declaring: "Crystals grow, and often far more rapidly than living bodies."[41] Then, after instancing the formation of geological strata by the deposit of detritus from water, as well as the formation of crystals in solutions, as examples of growth in the inorganic world, he asks: "Is not the growth of an organism a substantially similar process?" and adds: "Around a plant there exist certain elements that are like the elements which form its substance, and its increase in size is effected by continually integrating these surrounding-like elements with itself; nor does the animal fundamentally differ in this respect from the plant or the crystal."

Now, as opposed to this, I must express my belief that the more we know of the actual details of the process of growth in plants and animals the more clearly it will be seen that this process does differ so fundamentally from that by which a crystal is formed and increases in size, or from any increase in size of inorganic bodies, that the same scientific term cannot, with any propriety, be applied to both, however long popular usage may have given to both a common name. When inorganic bodies increase in size the additional atoms are deposited on their external surfaces; or, if a fluid, after penetrating the interstices of some porous body, deposits there any material held in solution, the mass, indeed, is increased thereby, but not the size. When, however, vegetable protoplasm grows, it does not merely integrate with itself certain elements around it like the elements which form its substance; the needed elements exist in compounds quite unlike itself, and it combines them together into protoplasm in all parts of its mass, so that it grows by a process of intussusception wholly unlike anything that occurs in the inorganic world. In the case of animal protoplasm, the mode of growth by intussusception is the same, but the capability of combining together. mere inorganic elements into its own substance is lost; and, besides these, a certain amount of pre-existing vegetable or animal protoplasm must be present in the food, or growth will not go on.

In both cases, when the growth has proceeded to a certain extent—within certain definite limits—a new characteristic phenomenon occurs in a growing mass of vegetable or animal protoplasm; it multiplies by division, its whole mass participating in the act, in accordance with one or other of a few definite methods. This process is repeated again and again. The progeny may separate, without modification, as independent forms, or, as in the case of the more complex organisms, they may cohere together, and the process culminates by groups of them undergoing certain definite and peculiar transformations, after which further multiplication becomes rare or ceases altogether, and the growth of the complex organism is thus limited.

I cannot, of course, attempt this evening to describe all the known details of the process of growth which I have thus hastily sketched; to give you a really satisfactory account of them would require a series of lectures. But I do not hesitate to say that the more fully you know these details the more unscientific you will think the attempt to class them as in any way similar to the circumstance that inorganic crystalline compounds seem "each to have a size that is not usually exceeded without a tendency arising to form new crystals, rather than to increase the old." It is, at the best, a waste of words to attempt to explain complex phenomena by comparing them to simpler ones which are fundamentally unlike them.

I have but now referred to a process by which, in the growth of the more complex living beings, the small primitive protoplasmic mass, out of which each individual arises, subdivides and produces a numerous brood of protoplasmic masses, at first closely resembling the parent mass, but after a time differing from it more and more, and finally undergoing transformations into definite and peculiar forms. This process, which does not take place in any disorderly manner, but in a very characteristic and definite way in each individual form, is designated by the term development. In point of fact, so far as it consists in the mere growth and multiplication of the individual elements that compose the organism, and the increase in size of the organism itself on account of these processes, it is properly designated by the term growth. In so far, however, as the individual elements are differentiated, and the wonderful architecture of the living being, with its organs and systems, is completed thereby, it is properly designated by the term development.

Nothing like the process of development as thus defined exists in the inorganic world, and in all the attempts at such a comparison that it has been my fortune to meet, the most fundamental facts of the development of living beings have been persistently ignored. Among these fundamental facts I invite your attention especially to the circumstance that there is something in the miscroscopic mass of protoplasm, out of which, even in the case of the highest and most complex living beings, each individual arises, that goes even further in determining the direction in which the individual shall develop than the pabulum, or environment, or all the mighty chemical and physical forces that are brought into play as the process goes on. In a word, the individual developes after the pattern of its parent, or not even all the solar energy can compel it to develop it at all.

We are thus brought face to face with the facts of sexual generation, and especially of heredity, with all their wide bearings on the great biological questions of natural selection and the origin of species. Into the details of these large questions the limits of the hour will not permit me to enter. Could I take time to do so, I am satisfied that at every step I should be able to collect for you additional evidence of the existence of a vital principle. Still I regret this the less because most of you, I think, are so familiar with the modern literature of these subjects, and especially with the admirable writings of Mr. Darwin, that I feel sure, if I can succeed in giving you a clear outline of my views, much that I should say, had I time, will suggest itself to your own minds. In a general way, however, when we study, in the history of life upon this globe, the double phenomena of long continued persistence of type, and of slow variation continually occurring, we will find that almost all biologists, whatever their theory of life, explain these phenomena on the one hand by heredity, on the other by the sensibility of the organism to the influence of the environment.

Both heredity and the influence of the environment may be very conveniently studied in those simplest organisms in which each individual consists of a single minute mass of naked protoplasm, as in certain rhizopods, for example, the amœba. These tiny creatures produce a progeny which preserves the parental type as closely as is done by the offspring of the higher animals. Their sensibility to the influence of the environment is manifested in several ways. They grow, that is they appropriate materials from the environment, in the way I have already specified; they manifest automatic movements, that is, on encountering food, obstacles, or other disturbing external circumstances, movements result the direction and energy of which are in no wise determined by the character or force of the external influences, or as they may be conveniently termed the stimuli by which these movements are provoked; and finally, simultaneously with the process of growth, a certain metamorphosis, or metabolism, of the protoplasm is continually going on resulting in the formation of excrementitious substances which are continually being excreted.

The processes of growth and metabolism exhibit different degrees of intensity in accordance with variations of the environment, and whatever physical theory of the mode in which the protoplasmic motions are produced we may adopt, the mechanical force manifested can only be supposed to proceed from the decomposition of a part of the protoplasm itself into simpler compounds, that is, from a particular kind of metabolism. Hence you will I think, be quite prepared to hear me speak of all the circumstances in the environment that so act upon living protoplasm as to increase its growth or metabolism, as stimuli, and of the property of living protoplasm by which all its responses to stimuli are guided, as irritability, instead of limiting these terms to the phenomena of automatic movement only, as was formerly done. This irritability of living protoplasm determines the direction in which its internal forces shall be manifested. Speaking of it as I do, perhaps you would wish me to call it sensibility rather than irritability, and I do not know that I should object very strenuously to any one who wished to do this. But however you may name it, it is this vital property of all living protoplasm that produces the sensibility to changes in the environment which has been the main factor in the gradual evolution, during the ages, of the highest and most complex from the simplest and lowest living forms.

Against this view it has been urged with much ingenuity that protoplasm is the material substratum of life, and life merely a property of protoplasm; that is, if the words have any meaning at all, that life is the resultant only of the forces inherent in the inorganic atoms of which the protoplasm is built up. Now, in the first place, no one has ever yet been able to show, by any conceivable synthesis, how the forces known to belong to the several kinds of inorganic atoms of which protoplasm is composed, could by their combination, produce the characteristic phenomena of living protoplasm, namely, the phenomena of irritability, as I have just described them. But, in the second place, this speculation appears to be pretty flatly contradicted by the circumstance that, although protoplasm can only be formed within the substance of previously existing living protoplasm, it can continue to exist, it does continue to exist as protoplasm after it has ceased to live. Not merely can it persist for a time without chemical change as dead protoplasm, it can subsequently serve as food and be reconverted into living protoplasm once more. Bear in mind, however, that this change can only be effected within the substance of the living protoplasm of the animal. that assimilates this food. It is not effected by the chemistry of digestion, that merely makes peptone of the protoplasm; merely makes it soluble enough to pass into the substance of the protoplasmic masses that are to appropriate it. These considerations, then, would seem to show that the material, protoplasm, cannot be rightly believed to be of itself the cause and essence of life.

If I should pause here, it seems to me that I should have brought forward adequate reasons for believing in the existence of a vital principle. But I cannot pause here. Beyond and above all this there is another great group of phenomena peculiar to living beings— a group of phenomena concerning which, in my own individuality, I have knowledge at least as positive as any I possess of the existence of force, and which I am led, by a logic quite as convincing as that by which any general proposition with regard to the external world is proven, to believe exists in like kind and degree in the case of my fellow-man. I refer to the phenomena of the perceiving, emotional, willful, reasoning human mind. Into the argument that makes it highly probable that a similar but less and less perfect mind exists in the animal world, and identifies with mind the sensibility of the lowest animal forms, and even that of vegetable protoplasm, I will not attempt to enter to-night. Mr. Herbert Spencer himself has presented this view with so much ingenuity, that, without committing myself to an approval of all his details, I must content myself by referring you to his writings for one of the best discussions of this matter. It will be sufficient for my present purpose to close this discourse by the presentation of a few considerations in relation to mind as it exists in man.

For myself I know mind only as a manifestation of life, if indeed it is not the essence of life. But the old doctrine of Epicurus, handed down to us in the poem of Lucretius, that in some way or fashion mind is produced by the clashing together of the atoms, has been boldly revived of late years, and transmuted into a form more plausible to modern thought, although just as unsupported by any actual knowledge of facts.

No one has done this more boldly or more cleverly than Mr. Herbert Spencer has done in his First Principles, and of course you are all familiar with the ingenious argument, in favor of this view, which runs through that masterly work. It would be, from many points of view, profitable, but it would be a very laborious task to attempt the critical discussion of his argument. It must suffice, for my present purpose, to point out that two of the fundamental assumptions upon which that argument is based are wholly undemonstrated. The first assumption is, that mind is itself a force;[42] the second, that mind cannot be conscious of itself, but only of the external world.[43]

If I could bring myself to believe that mind is, in any proper sense of the word, a force, and that such popular metaphorical expressions as mental force or mental energy accurately described the phenomena, I should certainly expect to find at least some shadow of proof for Mr. Herbert Spencer's assertion, that mental operations fall within the great generalization of the correlation and equivalence of the forces. On the contrary, however, you will find, on reading his lucid periods, that his whole argument relates to those physical conditions in the organs of sense and in the muscular and nervous systems, which are the antecedents of perception—which are, in fact, the things really perceived—and in no sense constitute the perceiving mind. Between strictly mental phenomena and the physical forces no one has as yet even attempted to establish a numerical equivalent; nay, more, the correlation of thought with the physical forces is not only undemonstrated, it is utterly unthinkable. You can conceive several different ways, it matters not whether true or false, in which the motions we know as heat might be converted into those we know as light, and so on with the other physical forces; but you cannot represent mentally any intelligible scheme by which any of the physical forces can be converted into the simplest or most elementary thought.

As to the question of self-consciousness, it seems as if the great philosopher were reasoning in a circle. He first assumes that the fundamental condition of all consciousness is the antithesis between subject and object,—which is true only with regard to consciousness of perception, the form of consciousness by which we become acquainted with the non ego,—and then he concludes that there can be no consciousness of the ego because it cannot fulfil these conditions. That is, in a word, he denies consciousness of the ego, because it is not consciousness of the non ego. Really it appears to me that, as against such a philosophy as this it is not amiss to appeal to "the unsophisticated sense of mankind," of which Mr. Mansel speaks.[44] But there is fortunately a better philosophy than this; a philosophy which recognizes the validity of the mind's self-consciousness as at least fully equal to the validity of its consciousness of the conditions of the body by which it obtains a knowledge of the external world. By this self-consciousness I know, with a certainty which no doubt can ever disturb, that I have a mind; and by rightly applying my reasoning powers to the data of my self-consciousness, I can learn much that will be useful to me with regard to my mental processes and the methods of employing them. But here I have to stop. I can learn nothing, whether by consciousness or by reasoning, with regard to the real nature of my conscious mind, and however much it may long for immortality, neither philosophy nor science afford any foundation of proof upon which it might build its hopes.

I have already said that I know mind only as a manifestation of life. Its operations are intimately connected with the chemical and physical phenomena of living beings, and it exercises over them a certain directing influence, the nature of which we do not understand. The obedience of our voluntary muscular actions to the mandates of the guiding will is a familiar illustration of this directing influence. On the other hand, all the knowledge of the external world on which the mind exerts its reasoning power reaches it through the organs of sense and the nervous system. Indeed, our studies of the phenomena of sensation compel us to conclude that what our mind really perceives, when it takes cognizance of the external world, is merely the ever-changing panorama of our own cerebral states. It should be anticipated, therefore, that disturbed or morbid conditions of the brain would lead to irregular or disorderly mental operations; and the circumstance that this really happens, affords no better proof of the materiality of thought than is afforded by the circumstances of our ordinary normal thought.

So, too, since the cerebral changes, which the mind perceives, are themselves of a purely chemico-physical nature, it should be anticipated that, like the metabolic processes in other tissues, they would be accompanied by an increased excretion of characteristic waste-products, by evolution of heat and by afflux of blood. Experimental investigation has been directed to each of these points, and some important observations have no doubt been made; but much of the testimony is conflicting, and our knowledge is still so incomplete that further inquiry in each direction is greatly to be desired.

This is particularly the case with regard to the chemical questions connected with the metabolism of the brain. In the first place our knowledge of the chemical composition of brain-substance is still in its infancy. The view that its characteristic ingredient is the phosphorized nitrogenous body described in 1865 by Liebreich under the name of protagon has been strongly controverted by Diaconow, Hoppe-Seyler, and Thudicum, while recently it has been reaffirmed by Gamgee, and Blankenhorn.[45] But even should this view turn out to be well founded, we have yet everything to learn with regard to the transformations protagon undergoes during functional activity, and the nature of the resulting waste products.

Long before Liebreich announced the existence of protagon, however, the attention of the physiological chemists had been directed to the prominence of phosphorous as an element in the composition of the cerebral substance, and it had been suggested that a part of the phosphoric acid excreted in the urine might be derived from the metabolism of the brain. As early as 1846 Bence Jones[46] had observed an excess of phosphatic salts in the urine during certain brain diseases, notably acute inflammations, and an observation published in 1853 by Mosler[47] appeared to indicate that a similar excess followed intellectual activity.

Byasson [1868] in his essay on the relation between cerebral activity and the composition of the urine,[48] reports a number of urinary analyses which support the view that the excretion of alkaline phosphates by the kidneys is habitually increased during mental work. This opinion has also received a certain degree of support from the more recent papers of Zuelzer[49] and Struebling;[50] nevertheless it is impossible to study the detailed observations upon which it is based without feeling how meagre and unsatisfactory the evidence relied upon really is. It is at best only sufficient to indicate the importance of further inquiry, and to suggest the necessity of avoiding certain obvious errors of method which complicate and obscure the results of the investigations hitherto made.

The opinion that mental effort is accompanied by an increase in the temperature of the brain was first propounded by Lombard in 1867. Using a delicate thermo-electric apparatus of his own contrivance, he observed during mental effort a rise of the surface temperature of the head, which sometimes amounted to as much as one-twentieth of a degree centigrade.[51]   Subsequent and more elaborate investigations confirmed him in this conclusion, which has also been supported by observations made with thermo-piles by Schiff and Bert, as well as by the use of surface thermometers in the hands of Broca and L. C. Gray of Brooklyn.[52]   Gray claimed to have observed a maximum rise of as much as two and a half degrees Fahrenheit.   These physicians and some others have also investigated the relative temperature of the two sides of the head, of different regions on each side, the variations produced in certain regions by voluntary muscular movements, and those resulting from localized brain diseases.[53]

To attempt any discussion of these interesting studies, and their conflicting results, would lead me altogether beyond my prescribed limits.   It is enough for my present purpose to point out that the recent investigations of François Frank [54] would seem to indicate that the variations of temperature actually observed are chiefly due to changes in the cerebral circulation.   Plunging suitable sounds, connected with a thermo-electric apparatus, into the brains of animals to different depths, Frank found that the deeper parts of the brain are always warmer than its superficial layers.   The superficial layers are continually cooled by radiation, and their temperature is a degree, or more than a degree centigrade, lower than that of the deeper parts.   Even these, however, are .1° to .2° centigrade cooler than the blood in the thoracic aorta, and it will therefore readily be understood that a relaxation in the muscular coats of the cerebral vessels, permitting the more rapid circulation of a larger quantity of blood, would be promptly followed by an increase in the temperature of the superficial parts of the brain.   None of the observers I have cited have reported a surface temperature of the head during mental effort that is too high to be accounted for in this way ; and if, as I willingly concede is probable, there is really an increased heat-production in the brain itself, it is wholly masked by the more considerable change due to afflux of blood.

Now a consideration of the phenomena of blushing, and certain well known sensations in the head, might lead us to expect that emotional and mental conditions would prove to be attended by increased activity in the circulation of the blood in the brain ; yet many difficulties have hitherto been encountered in the attempt to demonstrate experimentally that this is true. Mosso of Turin supposed that he had succeeded in doing this with his plethysmograph.[55] The instrument is essentially a cylinder of water, into which the arm is introduced and so fastened in place by a caoutchouc membrane that the slightest increase or diminution in the volume of the arm will cause the rise or fall of the water, through a tube connected at one end with the interior of the cylinder and at the other with a suitable recording apparatus. The pen or pencil of this apparatus inscribes a curve that rises or falls with the fluid in the tube. Among the curious observations made with this instrument, Mosso reports that the mental operations and emotions of the persons he experimented on were accompanied by a fall of the curve, which he regarded as proof that more blood goes to the brain and less to the arm during emotion, or mental action, than at other times. But the following year these observations were repeated with great care, and with an improved plethysmograph by Basch, of Vienna,[56] who failed to verify them. Most of the phlegmatic Germans on whom he experimented did sums in their heads, and otherwise exerted their minds, without producing the slightest modification of the curve, and none of them appear to have been as emotional as Dr. Pagliani, of whom Mosso relates that, his arm being in the plethysmograph, when the revered Prof. Ludwig entered the room the curve fell as if he had received an electric shock. Basch has cautiously investigated the causes of the varying quantity of blood in the arm in these experiments, and has clearly shown how many general and local conditions concur in producing the result. Especially has he emphasized the effect of variations in the abdominal circulation, which appear to exercise a much more considerable influence upon the size of the arm than any changes that occur in the brain.

In subsequent works Mosso has stated that during mental effort, such, for example, as is required to multiply small numbers in the head, the radial pulse, as recorded by the sphygmograph, is shown to become somewhat more frequent, and the recording lever does not rise so high as at other times.[57] Thanhoffer, who has pointed out that in these observations the influence of respiration on the pulse was neglected, concluded, nevertheless, from his own sphygmographic observations, that after due allowance is made for this complicating influence, it must be conceded that cerebral activity does exercise a certain effect upon the pulse, and in the direction stated.[58] Eugène Gley, in a recently published essay, claims to have obtained similar results, and states that at the same time the sphygmographic trace of the carotid artery shows a higher upstroke of the recording lever, and other indications of dilatation of the vessel.[59] While these observations are not sufficiently numerous, or free from objections, to be accepted without question as proof that an increased supply of blood to the brain invariably accompanies mental effort, they are certainly sufficient to encourage further labor in this interesting field.

But if the arguments in favor of the purely material nature of our mental operations that have been based upon the imperfect results of the three lines of investigation I have just referred to must be rejected as utterly fallacious, what shall we say of the logic that attempts to draw a similar conclusion from the results of those inquiries into the phenomena of personal equation which aim at determining the time that must be allowed for the mental operation involved?[60] Do we, then, indeed need the beautiful experiments of Hirsch and Donders[61] to prove that thought occupies time? Whence, indeed, do we derive our primitive conceptions of time save from our consciousness of the succession of thought? And how could even the shortest time be occupied by even an infinite number of thoughts if each thought did not occupy at least some time, however brief?

I have thus, gentlemen, attempted to show that we are logically compelled to invoke the existence of a vital principle in order to account for certain important groups of phenomena occurring in living beings which cannot possibly be explained by the chemical and physical forces of the universe. These phenomena form a series, at one end of which we find the mere irritability or sensibility of the humblest mass of living protoplasm ; at the other the reasoning faculty of the human mind. From the one extreme of this series to the other I recognize the manifestations of the vital principle. I willingly confess that I know nothing of the ultimate nature of this principle, except that it must be very different from the chemical and physical forces whose operations I have learned to recognize in the organic as well as in the inorganic world ; nevertheless I am compelled by my study of the phenomena to conclude that it exists. I know that Mr. Huxley, only last summer, declared in the International Medical Congress at London, that the doctrine of a vital principle is the "asylum ignorantiæ of physiologists;"[62]

but this ancient sarcasm has now been applied to so many things that it has long since lost whatever sting it may once have possessed, when it was fresh and new. And I also know that one of the chief characteristics of true science is the sharpness with which it enables us to discriminate between that which we have proven and really know and that which we have not proven and do not know. Better far is it, and a thousand times more in accord with the simple honesty of science, to acknowledge frankly the truth that phenomena occur in living beings which the inorganic forces do not explain, than to mistake our wishes for discoveries, to convert conjectures into dogmas, or, worst of all, to transform an undemonstrated hypothesis into a superstitious, aggressive, and intolerant creed.

Nor will the soundness of the conclusions, at which the present generation shall arrive as to this matter, be without its practical effect upon methods of biological research, and the consequent future progress of biological science. It is not a mere metaphysical subtlety, but a subject of practical importance that I have asked you to consider to-night. For if the chemico-physical hypothesis of life be true, the only road of progress in biology lies through the chemical and physical laboratories. Now, I have already this evening more than once indicated how highly I esteem the class of biological work that has already been done in these laboratories, and I have endeavored to show how large is the unexplored biological field that can be explored only in this manner. But in addition to all that we can ever hope to do in this direction—and I insist upon its importance—I insist also upon the importance of other lines of work: I insist upon the importance of the systematic study of the phenomena of growth and development, of generation and heredity, of sensibility and mind. All that can thus be learned we need to know, and not merely for its own sake. This knowledge is indispensable to the right interpretation of the succession of life upon the globe in the past, and the successful direction of the interference of the human will with the future succession of life upon the globe in accordance with human necessities. We shall make slow progress in this direction if we confine our efforts to the application of chemistry and physics to those phenomena of living beings that can be thus explained. The other phenomena, not thus explicable, must also be studied in detail, arranged into orderly groups, and made the basis of such inductions as our knowledge of them may warrant. It is only by pursuing this method that we can hope ultimately to acquire, with regard to the phenomena of living beings, that power to predict, which is the criterion of true science, and that power to control, which we so sorely need.

·

———————

NOTES.

———————

[1] GEORGE F. BARKER—*Some Modern Aspects of the Life Question.* Address as President of the Amer. Ass. for the Advancement of Science. Boston meeting, August, 1880. Proceedings, Vol. XXIX, Part I, p. 23.

[2] GALEN—*Quod animi mores corporis temperamenta sequantur*, Cap. 3. [Kühn's Edit., T. IV, p. 772.]

[3] ST. GEORGE MIVART—The Cat. London, 1881, p. 387.

[4] First taught by J. R. MAYER—*Die organische Bewegung in ihrem Zusammenhange mit dem Stoffwechsel: Ein Beitrag zur Naturkunde.* Heilbronn, 1845.

[5] See, for example, M. FOSTER—*Text Book of Physiology*, 2d Edit., London, 1878, p. 355.

[6] BARKER—*op. cit., supra.*

[7] See H. SENATOR—*Unters. über die Wärmebildung und den Stoffwechsel*, Archiv. für Anat. Phys. und wiss. Med., 1872, S. 1.

[8] FOSTER—p. 368, *op. cit., supra.*

[9] L. LANDOIS—*Lehrb. der Phys. des Menschen*, Vienna, 1879; S. 402.

[10] L. HERMANN—*Handb. der Phys.*, Bd. I, Th. 1, S. 242.

[11] EMIL DU BOIS-REYMOND—*Unters. über thierische Elektricität*, Berlin, 1848–60, and *Gesammelte Abhandl. zur allgemeinen Muskel-und Nervenphysik*, Leipsic, 1875–77.

[12] DU BOIS-REYMOND—*Ges. Abhandl.*, Bd. II, S. 243.

[13] BERNSTEIN—*Unters. über den Erregungsvorgang in Nerven-und Muskelsysteme*, Heidelberg, 1871; also Du Bois-Reymond's Archiv, 1875, S. 526; Hermann in Pflüger's Archiv, Bd. X, 1875, S. 48.

[14] L. Hermann—*Weitere Unters. zur Phys. der Muskeln und Nerven*, Berlin, 1867; also *Handb. der Phys.*, Bd. I, Th. 1, Leipsic, 1879, S. 192 *et seq.*

[15] Hermannn—*Handb. der Phys.*, Bd. I, Th. 1, S. 215.

[16] Engelmann—Pflüger's Archiv, Bd. XV, 1877, S. 116 *et seq.*

[17] Du Bois-Reymond—*Ges. Abhandl.*, Bd. II, S. 319 *et seq.*

[18] Mayer—Müller's Archiv, 1854, S. 214; Amici (1858)—Translation in Virchow's Archiv, Bd. XVI, 1859, S. 414.

[19] Schwann—in *Müller's Handb. der Phys.*, 1837, Bd. II, S. 59.

[20] C. B. Radcliffe—*Dynamics of Nerve and Muscle*, London, 1871.

[21] Matteucci—*Lectures on the Physical Phenomena of Living Beings*, (translated by J. Pereira,) London, 1847, p. 333.

[22] Arthur Gamgee—*A Text Book of the Phys. Chemistry of the Animal Body*, Vol. I, London, 1881, p. 418.

[23] L. Hermann—*Grundriss der Phys. des Menschen*, 5te Aufl., 1874, S. 231.

[24] Du Bois-Reymond—*Ges. Abh.*, Bd. II, S. 320.

[25] Foster—*op. cit.*, p. 79 *et seq.*

[26] C. A. Hausen—*Novi profectus in historia electricitatis*, Leipsic, 1743. I cite from Du Bois-Reymond—*Unters. über thierische Elektricität*, Bd. II, Berlin, 1849, Th. 1, S. 211.

[27] Du Bois-Reymond—*Ges. Abh.*, Bd. II, S. 250.

[28] Bernstein—*op. cit.*, *supra.*

[29] Hermann—*loc. cit.*, note [14], *supra;* also *Handb. der Phys.*, Bd. II, Th. 1, Leipsic, 1879, S. 144 *et seq.*

[30] See especially Du Bois-Reymond—*Unters.*, Bd. II, Th. 1, S. 289, and Pflüger—*Unters. über die Physiologie des Electrotonus*, Berlin, 1859 : An excellent summary of the observations (with the literature) is given by Hermann—*Handb. der Physiologie*, Bd. II, Th. 1, S. 157 *et seq.*

[31] Radcliffe—p. 74 *et seq.*, *op. cit.*, *supra.*

[32] A. von Haller—*Elementa Physiologiæ*, Lib. X, Sect. VIII, § 15, T. IV, Lausanne, 1762, p. 380. He cites as authority the essay of Le Cat, crowned by the Berlin Academy in 1753. [We have in the S. G. O. Library the Berlin edition of 1765, *Traité de l'existence, etc., du fluide des nerfs, etc.*]

[83] BARKER—p. 8, *op. cit., supra.*

[84] CLAUDE BERNARD—*Leçons sur la Phys. et la Path. du système nerveux,* Paris, 1858, T. I, p. 157 and p. 224.

[35] Translation of a lecture given by E. Du Bois-Reymond at the Royal Institution, London, in Appendix No. 1 of H. BENCE JONES' *Croonian Lectures on Matter and Force,* London, 1868, p. 130.

[86] HERBERT SPENCER—*The Principles of Psychology,* Vol. I, New York, 1871, p. 95. Compare also his *Principles of Biology,* Vol. II, New York, 1867, p. 346 *et seq.*

[87] FOSTER—p. 79, *op. cit., supra.*

[88] A. GAMGEE—p. 447, *op. cit., supra.*

[89] O. HAHN—*Die Meteorite und ihre Organismen,* Tubingen, 1881. I cite the Jour. of the Royal Mic. Society, October, 1881, p. 723.

[40] "Lapides crescunt, Vegetabilia crescunt et vivunt, Animalia crescunt, vivunt et sentiunt." This phrase occurs in the first edition of the *Systema Naturæ,* Leyden, 1735. I cite the reprint of FÉE, Paris, 1830, p. 3, as well as the second Stockholm edition, 1740, p. 76. The expression is replaced in the later editions by more guarded language.

[41] HERBERT SPENCER—*The Principles of Biology,* Vol. I, New York, 1866, p. 107.

[42] HERBERT SPENCER—*First Principles,* Amer. Ed., New York, 1864, p. 274.

[43] HERBERT SPENCER—*op. cit.,* p. 65 *et seq.*

[44] As cited by Mr. HERBERT SPENCER, *loc. cit.,* last note.

[45] GAMGEE—p. 425 *et seq., op. cit., supra.*

[46] HENRY BENCE JONES—*On the variations in the alkaline and earthy phosphates in disease,* Phil. Trans. for 1846, p. 449.

[47] MOSLER—*Beitraege zur Kentniss der Urinabsonderung,* etc., Inaug. Diss., cited in Canstatt's Jahresbericht, 1853, Bd. I, S. 134.

[48] H. BYASSON—*Essai sur la relation qui existe à l'état physiologique entre l'activité cérébrale et la composition des urines,* Paris, 1868.

[49] W. ZUELZER—*Ueber das Verhältniss der Phosphorsaüre zum Stickstoff im Urin,* Virchow's Archiv, Bd. 66, 1876, S. 223.

[50] STRUEBLING—*Ueber die Phosphorsaüre im Urin*, Archiv. für exp. Path. und Pharm., Bd. VI, 1876-7, S. 266.

[51] J. S. LOMBARD—*Experiments on the relation of heat to mental work*, The New York Medical Journal, Vol. V, 1867, p. 199.

[52] J. S. LOMBARD—*Experimental researches on the temperature of the head*, Proc. of the Royal Society of London, Vol. 27, 1878, p. 166; IDEM—*The regional temperature of the head*, London, 1879; IDEM—*Experimental researches on the temperature of the head*, London, 1881. MORITZ SCHIFF—*Recherches sur l'échauffement des nerfs et les centres nerveux à la suite des irritations sensorielles et sensibles*, Archives de Physiol. norm. et path., T. III, 1870, p. 5 *et seq.* BERT—*Communication to the Société de Biologie*, read Jan. 18, 1879, in Gazette Hebdomadaire, Jan. 24, 1879, p. 63. BROCA—*Communication to the French Association for the Advancement of the Sciences*, at the Havre meeting of 1877, in Gaz. Hebd., Sept. 7, 1877, p. 577; also Gaz. Méd. de Paris, 1877, p. 457; IDEM in London Med. Record, Jan. 15, 1880. L. C. GRAY—*Cerebral Thermometry*, The New York Med. Jour., Vol. 28, 1878, p. 31; also Chicago Jour. of Nervous and Mental Diseases, Vol. VI, 1879, p. 65.

[53] See, besides the papers cited in the last note, C. K. MILLS in The New York Med. Record, Vol. 14, 1878, p. 477, and Vol. 16, 1879, p. 130; MARAGLIANO and SEPPELLI—*Studies on cerebral thermometry in the insane*, translated by J. Workman, The Alienist and Neurologist, St. Louis, Jan., 1880, p. 44 *et seq.;* R. W. AMIDON—*The effect of willed muscular movements on the temperature of the head*, Archives of Medicine, April, 1880, p. 117.

[54] FRANÇOIS FRANK—*Communication to the Société de Biologie*, May 29, 1880, in Gaz. Hebd., June 11, 1880, p. 392.

[55] ANGELO MOSSO—*Sopra un nuovo metodo per scrivere i movimenti dei vasi sanguini nell'uomo*, Atti della Reale Accademia della Scienza di Torino, T. XI, Nov. 14, 1875. I have not obtained access to the original, but find an abstract in the Archives de Phys. norm. et path., 1876, p. 175. See also BARKER, p. 12, *op. cit., supra.*

[56] BASCH—*Die volumetrische Bestimmung des Blutdrucks am Menschen*, Stricker's Med. Jahrb., 1876, S. 431. See also ROLLET in HERMANN'S *Handb. der Phys.*, Bd. IV, Th. I, Leipsic, 1880, S. 306.

[57] MOSSO—*Die Diagnostic des Pulses in Berzug auf die localen Veränderungen desselben*, Leipsic, 1879; also by the same, *Sulla circolazione del sangue nel cervello dell'uomo*, Rome, 1880.

[58] THANHOFFER—*Der Einfluss der Gehirnthätigkeit auf den Puls*, Pflüger's Archiv., Bd. XIX, 1879, S. 254.

[59] EUGÈNE GLEY—*Essai critique sur les conditions physiologiques de la pensée.*

État du pouls carotidien pendant le travail intellectuel, Archives de Phys. norm. et path., Sept.-Oct., 1881, p. 741.

[60] BARKER—p. 11, *op. cit., supra.*

[61] HIRSCH—*Détermination télégraphique de la difference de longitude entre les observatoires de Genève et de Neuchatel*, Genève et Bale, 1864. DONDERS—in Reichert and Du Bois-Reymond's Archiv., 1868, p. 657.

[62] T. H. HUXLEY—*The connection of the Biological Sciences with Medicine*, The Popular Science Monthly, October, 1881, p. 800.

At the conclusion of the reading the thanks of the Society were voted to the President for his able and instructive address.

208TH MEETING. (11TH ANNUAL MEETING,) DECEMBER 17, 1881.

The President in the chair.

Forty-four members present.

The minutes of the last annual meeting were read and adopted.

The Secretary, Mr. THEODORE GILL, read the list of members who had been elected since the last annual meeting.

The Treasurer read to the Society his report upon the receipts, expenditures, and remaining funds of the Society for the year now about to close. He also read the list of members whose dues had been paid.

The Chair then reported to the Society a resolution of the General Committee, which is as follows:

Resolved, That the President be requested to ask the Society to appoint a committee to audit the Treasurer's report, and to communicate the result of their audit to the Society at its next meeting.

In accordance with this request, and also with that of the Treasurer, it was moved and carried that the Chair appoint a committee of three for the purpose named in the resolution.

The Chair appointed a Committee of Audit, consisting of Messrs. John Jay Knox, G. K. Gilbert, and Robert Fletcher.

Mr. THORNTON A. JENKINS then offered the following resolution:

Resolved, That all persons who have resigned membership in the Society, or failed in their duties as provided for in the rules of the

Society, shall be dropped from the succeeding published list of members.

By a vote of the Society this resolution was referred to the General Committee.

The Society then proceeded to ballot for officers for the ensuing year, and the following officers were elected :

President,	WILLIAM B. TAYLOR.
Vice-Presidents,	J. E. HILGARD. J. C. WELLING.
	J. J. WOODWARD. J. K. BARNES.
Treasurer,	CLEVELAND ABBE.
Secretaries,	THEODORE N. GILL. MARCUS BAKER.

MEMBERS OF THE GENERAL COMMITTEE.

J. S. BILLINGS.	GARRICK MALLERY.
C. E. DUTTON.	SIMON NEWCOMB.
J. R. EASTMAN.	J. W. POWELL.
E. B. ELLIOTT.	C. A. SCHOTT.

WILLIAM HARKNESS.

The rough minutes of the meeting were then read and approved, and the Society adjourned.

209TH MEETING.   JANUARY 14, 1882.

The President, WM. B. TAYLOR, in the chair.

Upon taking the chair President-elect TAYLOR offered a few remarks, and thanked the Society for the honor conferred upon him.

The minutes of the 207th meeting—the 208th being the annual meeting—were then read and approved.

A communication by Mr. BENJ. ALVORD was read, entitled

CURIOUS FALLACY AS TO THE THEORY OF GRAVITATION.

Some years since I noticed in a text book on astronomy, used in one of the most celebrated colleges in the United States, a pretended demonstration that the attraction of gravitation *must* vary inversely as the square of the distances. It was continued in several editions down to about 1850, when that portion was omitted. I always supposed that the author copied it from some old authority; that he was not guilty of inventing it, abused as it was.

In "Hind's Dictionary of Arts and Sciences" (one volume, folio, London, 1769, copy in the Congressional Library) it is found under the article "Attraction."

The first named author announced that "Gravity at different distances from the east *must* vary inversely as the square of the distances." He proceeded substantially as follows:

"The total amount of attraction exerted by the earth upon bodies exterior to it is the same as though that force was all concentrated in the centre. But a force or influence which proceeds in right lines from a point in every direction is diminished as the square of the distance is increased. For, let the centre of the earth be the vertex of a pyramid, cut said pyramid by two parallel bases at different distances from the vertex, making two similar pyramids. *Whatever the nature of gravity, its influence at the distance of each base must be equally diffused over the base. Therefore its intensity or force will be as much less at the greater base, as contrasted with its influence at the nearer and lesser base, as the surface of the latter is to the surface of the former.* But the surfaces of these bases are to each other as the squares of their distances from the vertex. Therefore the force of gravity varies inversely as the square of the distances.—Q. E. D."

Actually he placed Q. E. D. to it as if it was a mathematica, demonstration!

He afterwards said:

"The intensity of light at different distances from the radiant varies inversely as the square of the distances. This proposition is proved in the same manner as that respecting gravity, the reasoning in which applies to *all* emanations from a centre."

Subsequently, when he got to refer to the laws of Kepler, he said:

"They, therefore, became known as *facts* before they were demonstrated mathematically. The glory of this achievement was reserved for Newton, who proved that they were necessary results of the law of universal gravitation."

This sentence would have astonished Newton! It places the cart before the horse. From the empirical laws of Kepler the theory of gravitation was mathematically derived by Newton. Not the reverse. What a confusion of ideas that Kepler's laws could both be demonstrated mathematically and observed as facts? How it belittles the labors of Newton, who should have made his discovery (*de novo* from his own breast) by a geometrical process and not from the observed facts!

But my principal object in referring to this curious fallacy was to give an attempt of my own to show its fallacy by a "*reductio ad absurdum.*"

I can prove by an entirely similar process, with equal plausibility, that the force of gravity must vary inversely *as the cubes of the distances.* Instead of a pyramid take a cone. Let the centre of the earth be the vertex of a cone. Place two spheres or molecules of different sizes,* tangent to the cone, at different distances from the vertex. *Whatever the nature of gravity, its influence at the distance of each sphere must be equally diffused throughout the solid contents or volume of each sphere. Therefore its intensity or force will be as much less at the greater sphere, as contrasted with its influence at the nearer and smaller sphere, as the volume of the latter is to the volume of the former.* But these volumes or solid contents vary as the cubes of their radii, or as the cubes of their distances from the vertex. Therefore the force of gravity varies inversely as the cubes of the distances.

The oracular "Q. E. D." could have been placed to this fallacy with full as much propriety as in the former case, for I have used nearly identical words. Of course they are both pure assumptions. Neither are mathematically true, and the one destroys the other, as they are contradictory. But the first is true as arrived at by severe induction from the observed facts.

If I was a professor of logic, I should give these as specious examples of the danger of false premises, and of the ease with which they could be manufactured.

Indeed, the authors first named would imply that there could in the science of mechanics be no central forces, no empirical laws. Indeed, they would reduce the whole planetary system, the whole cosmos, to a geometrical necessity; and they would lose that interesting exposition in physical astronomy as to the wisdom and beneficence exhibited in the planetary system as it exists.

In the well-known discussion of central forces by Poisson, the equation of the curve when referred to co-ordinate axes is ascer-

---

* The word molecules, being now a favorite word with the physicists, might suit the casuist a little better.

tained, and the change of one constant in the equation causes a change in the nature of the curve. If the law varied *directly as the distance*, the orbits of the planets would be ellipses as now, (but the sun would be at the centre, and not at one foci,) and they would all revolve in the same period about the sun, and on the surface of any planet no attraction towards its centre would exist. This curious result would follow: that any object projected into the air would immediately be carried from the earth, and would perpetually revolve as a satellite, like the moon, around it. All terrestrial objects would be unsettled and float about in the air in the utmost disorder.

If, on the contrary, the law varied inversely *as the cube of the distance*, (according to that precious second fallacy above set forth,) each planet would describe a spiral orbit, (if at first projected towards the sun,) continually winding and winding towards the sun; or, if perchance projected at first *from* it, would move in a spiral curve, causing it to recede farther and farther from the sun; and the eye of Omniscience alone could trace its final wanderings. What a contrast, all these suppositions, to the order, stability, beauty, and beneficence of our planetary system as it exists!

The next communication was by Mr. M. H. DOOLITTLE

ON THE GEOMETRICAL PROBLEM TO DETERMINE A CIRCLE EQUALLY DISTANT FROM FOUR POINTS.

" Describe a circumference equally distant from four given points; the distance from a point to the circumference being measured on a radius or radius produced. In general there are four solutions." (Chauvenet's Geometry, problem 110.)

These four solutions were undoubtedly obtained in accordance with the conception of three given points all either inside or outside of the required circumference. Three other solutions may be obtained from the conception of two given points inside and two outside. Mr. Marcus Baker has suggested that a distance may properly be measured from a given point through the centre of the circle to the opposite side of the circumference. This interpretation increases the number of solutions to fourteen.

This communication gave rise to a brief discussion, participated in by Messrs. HARKNESS, NEWCOMB, and BAKER, the latter pointing out that the problem appears among the exercises of Rouché and Comberousse's Traité de géométrie élémentaire, (2d ed., p. 113, Ex. 124,) a source from which Prof. Chauvenet drew many of his exercises. In Chauvenet's Geometry this problem appears as Exercise 110, page 308, with the statement that there are in general *four* solutions. This statement does not occur in the French work cited, and, therefore, the error appears to be due to Chauvenet himself, a thing somewhat noteworthy, as Chauvenet's works are in general very accurate.

Mr. ALVORD then remarked

ON SOME OF THE PROPERTIES OF STEINER'S "POWER-CIRCLE."

After the consideration of this communication the report of the Auditing Committee, appointed at the 208th meeting, was called for, and, in the absence of the chairman, Mr. Knox, was presented by Mr. Fletcher. The following is the report:

WASHINGTON, *January* 13, 1882.

Mr. President and Gentlemen
 of the Philosophical Society of Washington:

We, your committee, appointed at the annual meeting, December 17th, 1881, to audit the report of the Treasurer for the years 1880 and 1881, have the honor to submit the following report:

We have examined the statement of receipts of dues from members and of interest on bonds, and find the former to be $1,175 and the latter $125, as appears in the Treasurer's statements of accounts for the years 1880 and 1881.

We have examined the vouchers for disbursements for the same period, and find them correct.

We have compared the return checks with the vouchers and with the entries in the bank book, and find them correct.

We have examined the bank book, and found the balance as set forth to be correct, said balance, deducting the amount of two checks not yet returned, being $320.16, with Messrs. Riggs & Co.

The bonds referred to in the statements of assets were exhibited to us by the Treasurer, and consist of $1,000 U. S. 4½s and $500 4 per cent. bonds.

All of which is respectfully submitted.

JNO. JAY KNOX.
ROBERT FLETCHER.
G. K. GILBERT.

The report was adopted, and the committee discharged.

The President, Mr. TAYLOR, then offered a brief communication

ON THE TOTAL LUNAR ECLIPSE OF JUNE 11, 1881.

This was noteworthy for the bright illumination of the moon's disk, which occurred during totality. The features of the moon's surface could be seen almost as distinctly during total eclipse as during full moon. This phenomenon was attributed to the refraction caused by the earth's atmosphere. To an observer stationed upon the moon a bright circle of sunlight would be visible surrounding the earth, and to the light from this source was attributed the illumination of the moon's disk seen during total lunar eclipses.

This communication was discussed by Mr. HARKNESS.

Mr. DALL then presented a brief communication

ON SOME PECULIAR FEATURES OF MOLLUSKS FOUND
AT GREAT DEPTHS.

While considerable difficulty was experienced in separating some of the forms by their shells alone, yet, when their anatomy was examined, some very striking differences were presented. Among the dredgings off the Atlantic coast and in the Gulf of Mexico by the *Blake* were found mollusks claimed to be representatives of two new families having a dentition simulating that of the Docoglossa. One related to the Fissurellidæ and the other referable to the order Rhipidoglossa.

This communication was discussed by Messrs. GILL and ALVORD, after which the Society adjourned.

210TH MEETING.   JANUARY 28, 1882.

President WM. B. TAYLOR in the chair.

Thirty-nine members and visitors present.

Mr. FERREL presented to the Society a communication entitled

ON THE CONDITIONS DETERMINING TEMPERATURE,

but, from lack of time, did not complete its presentation, and asked for a continuance at some future meeting.

Mr. L. F. WARD then read a paper entitled

ON THE ORGANIC COMPOUNDS IN THEIR RELATIONS TO LIFE.

This paper was briefly discussed by Messrs. ANTISELL and ELLIOTT, after which the Society adjourned.

211TH MEETING. FEBRUARY 11, 1882.

President WM. B. TAYLOR in the chair.

Mr. GILBERT presented to the Society a communication

ON ERRORS OF BAROMETRIC OBSERVATIONS PRODUCED BY WIND.

This communication will be published in full in the Report of the Geological Survey.

This communication was discussed by Messrs. BAKER, MASON, and ANTISELL, after which the Society adjourned.

212TH MEETING. FEBRUARY 25, 1882.

President WM. B. TAYLOR in the chair.

Thirty members and visitors present.

Mr. FERREL presented to the Society the concluding portion of a communication offered to the Society at its 210th meeting, January 28th,

ON THE CONDITIONS DETERMINING TEMPERATURE.

The usual formula for the rate of cooling of a heated body in vacuo, first given by Pouillet as determined from the experiments of Dulong and Petit, is of the form:

$$\delta h = Bf(\mu^\tau - \mu^{\tau'})$$

In which

$B =$ the units of heat radiated by a unit of lamp-black surface in a unit of time;

$f =$ the radiating power of the body, lamp-black being unity;

$\tau =$ the temperature of the cooling body;

$\tau' =$ the temperature of the enclosure;

$\mu =$ a constant, of which the value is 1.0077;

$\delta h =$ the heat lost in a unit of time for each unit of surface.

The first part of the second member, $Bf\mu^\tau$, expresses the amount of heat radiated by the body, and the second, $Bf\mu^{\tau'}$, the amount of heat received from the enclosure; the radiating and absorbing powers being usually assumed to be the same, f is common to both.

In applying this formula to bodies in space, protected from the rays of the sun, τ' would represent the temperature of space, by which is meant the temperature at which a body would stand by the heat received from the stars. In applying it to bodies on the earth's surface it may be regarded as the temperature of an imaginary enclosure, from which as much heat would be received as from all surrounding objects, the earth's surface, and the atmosphere, &c., not including the sun, and hence it represents the shade temperature.

If we now suppose the body to be exposed to the direct rays of the sun, the amount of heat thus received must be added to that received from space, or from terrestrial surroundings, that is, to $Bf\mu^{\tau'}$, and the preceding formula then becomes

$$(1) \qquad \delta h = -K\rho f + Bf(\mu^\tau - \mu^{\tau'})$$

In which

$K =$ the units of heat received from the sun on a unit of surface;

$\rho =$ the ratio between the surface receiving rays, projected on a plane perpendicular to the rays, and the whole radiating surface.

As the body receives the rays from one direction and upon one side only, and radiates from all sides, the average amount of heat, $K\rho f$, received over the whole surface and absorbed, must be compared with the amount lost by radiation, and hence the factor f must come in, since only the heat absorbed affects temperature, the absorbing and radiating power here, as usual, being assumed to be the same.

In the case of a spherical body, as the bulb of a thermometer, the value of ρ becomes $\frac{1}{4}$, since the projected receiving surface of the sphere is one-fourth of the whole radiating surface of the sphere. In the case of a long cylinder, in which the radiation from the ends could be neglected in comparison with the whole, the value of ρ becomes $\frac{1}{\pi}$, if the side of the cylinder is exposed perpendicularly to the sun's rays. In the case of a thin disk, with its surface perpendicular to the sun's rays, neglecting the radiation from the edge, the value of ρ would be $\frac{1}{2}$. In the case of such a disk, in which the radiation is from one side only, which would be approximately so in the case of such a disk with the opposite side of polished silver, the value of ρ would be unity.

The amount of heat, K, received from the sun through the atmosphere at the earth's surface is usually expressed by

(2) $$K = Ap^\varepsilon$$

In which

$A =$ the heat received from the sun on a unit of surface at the top of the atmosphere;

$\varepsilon =$ the secant of the zenith distance of the sun;

$p =$ a constant for all zenith distances, but differing in different states of the atmosphere, but always less than unity.

In the case of a static equilibrium of temperature, which was the only case considered, δh vanishes, and the preceding equations, (1) and (2), give

(3) $$\rho Ap^\varepsilon = B(\mu^\tau - \mu^{\tau'})$$

This equation expresses the condition which determines the static temperature, τ, of a body, and it is seen that this depends upon the solar constant A; the form of the body, upon which the value of τ depends; upon the value of p, or the state of the atmosphere; upon the zenith distance, which determines ε; upon the radiating constant, B; and upon the shade temperature, τ'.

Putting for the unit of heat the amount required to raise the temperature of a cubic centimetre or gram of water one degree centigrade, and the square centimetre, second, and degree centigrade, for the units of surface, time, and temperature, respectively, the value of B was determined by the author, from the experiments of Mr. J. P. Nichol on the rate of cooling of a blackened copper ball in vacuum, surrounded by an enclosure of blackened surface, (Proc. Royal Soc. Edin., 1869–70, p. 207,) to be .01808. This value was considered more reliable than that of Pouillet from the experiments of Dulong and Petit, since the latter were made on the rate of cooling of mercury in a glass bulb, and the results had to be reduced to those which would have been obtained with a blackened surface; and the value of the radiating power, f, for glass, which was used in this reduction, Pouillet states, was somewhat hypothetical, and so it left some doubt with regard to the true value of the constant. Pouillet's value of B for the minute-unit was 1.146, and this reduced to the second-unit is .01910. The value $\mu = 1.0077$ required no change to satisfy the results of Mr. Nichol's experiments.

The value of A, deduced from the experiments of Pouillet and Herschel with the actinometer, is .03046 for the mean distance of the sun, both sets of experiments, when reduced to the sun's mean distance, giving very nearly the same value. At the time of the earth's perihelion this is about one-thirtieth greater, and at aphelion as much less.

Pouillet's value of p for clear weather is about 0.75, but others make it considerably less. It can hardly be regarded as a constant, but only as a sort of average of values for clear weather, which may differ very much at different times. According to Tyndal, who maintains that the absorption power of the atmosphere in clear weather depends almost entirely upon the amount of aqueous vapor in it, the value of this constant, even in clear weather, must depend very much upon the hygrometric state of the atmosphere.

With the preceding numerical values of the constants of A and B, the preceding equation gives

$$(4) \qquad\qquad \mu^\tau - \tau' = \frac{1.685\, \rho p^\varepsilon}{\mu^{\tau'}} + 1$$

for determining the value of $\tau - \tau'$, for any zenith distance of the sun, of which the secant is ε, where the value of p and the shade temperature τ' are known. But since the value of B was determined for a vacuum, this formula is only applicable where the radiating body is in a vacuum, and cannot be applied in cases where the body receives or loses heat by conduction or convection.

The first term of the second number of the preceding equation depends upon K, the heat received from the sun, and, therefore, vanishes where the body is in the shade, and we then have $\tau - \tau' = 0$. Hence the temperature of all bodies having the same surroundings must cool down to the same temperature, τ'. This is a necessary consequence of the equality of the absorbing and radiating powers of bodies.

The author had been able to find but few observations of the value of $\tau - \tau'$ to compare with the theoretical value given by the preceding formula. Hooker states that from a multitude of desultory observations made on the Himalaya Mountains at an elevation of 7,400 feet, he concluded that the average effect of the sun's rays on a black-bulb thermometer was 125.7° or 67° (37.2° C.) above the temperature of the air. The shade temperature was, therefore, 14.8° C. With this value of τ', and the value $\rho = \frac{1}{4}$ for the spherical bulb, we get $\tau - \tau' = 41.6°$ at the top of the atmosphere where $p = 1$. The value of p for that altitude, and also the value of ε for the observations, are not accurately known. At the elevation of 7,400 feet, Pouillet's value of $p = .75$ would have to be considerably increased, but the effect of the exponent ε would perhaps bring the value of p^ε equal to about .75. With this value of p^ε the formula gives $\tau - \tau' = 32.4°$, five degrees too small for the observed value.

Again, at the height of 13,100 feet, he found in January, at 9 a. m., the temperature of the black bulb 98° with a difference of 68.2°, and at 10 a. m., 114° with a difference of 81.4°. From the average of these we get $\tau' = -0.4°$ C. and $\tau - \tau' = 41.6°$ C. The preceding formula gives $\tau - \tau' = 45.7°$ C. at the top of the atmosphere where $p = 1$. At the elevation of 13,100 feet the value of p^ε should not be very much less than unity—perhaps about as much less as would reduce the theoretical value 45.7° down to the observed value 41.6°.

It should be remarked here that the theory requires that the two thermometers should have exactly the same surroundings. If the one thermometer is in a vacuum surrounded by a glass bulb and the other outside, this condition is not perfectly fulfilled, and the indication of the thermometer outside in the shade might vary a little from one in the shade within the bulb, unless this bulb is so situated as to have the same temperature as the external shade thermometer.

If, in place of a black-bulb thermometer, we had a thin disk with a blackened side exposed perpendicularly to the sun's rays, and the opposite side of polished silver of which the radiating power is extremely small, we should have in this case the value of $\rho = 1$ very nearly, and with this value of ρ the formula would give, in the first of the examples above, for the top of the atmosphere, $\tau - \tau' = 106.6°$ C., which, added to the shade temperature, 14.8°, would give $\tau = 121.4°$ C. This enormously high temperature is not inconsistent with observation, for water has been made to boil from the effect of the direct rays of the sun at the earth's surface, where the theoretical condition of our formula, that no heat shall be lost by conduction, was not perfectly fulfilled.

A portion of the earth's surface, where the soil is dry and sandy, having little conductivity for heat and exposed to the vertical rays of the sun, would be a case similar to that of an isolated disk radiating sensibly from one side only, and the temperature of such a surface, so exposed, should stand at a very high temperature, but of course not nearly up to the theoretical temperature, since much heat would be conveyed away by the conduction and convection of the air, and also some conducted down into the earth. The temperature of sandy soils is often observed to be as high as 150° F. and upwards, and the preceding theory explains these very high temperatures and the great differences of temperature of different bodies under the same circumstances.

From equations (2) and (3), with the given values of A and B, we get

(5) $$K = .07232 \, \mu^{\tau'}(\mu^{\tau} - \tau' - 1)$$

This is an actinometric formula, giving the amount of heat received from the sun, in absolute heat units, from the observation of the sunshine and shade temperatures. So far as the author's reading extends no such formula has ever been given, but $\tau - \tau'$ has been regarded as a measure of the sun's relative intensity under different circumstances. The formula not only gives the absolute instead of the relative amount of heat received, but it shows that $\tau - \tau'$ is not proportional to K, and consequently not a correct measure of the relative intensities of the sun's rays. With an observed value $\tau - \tau' = 35°$ and $\tau' = 30°$ the formula gives $K = .02806$; but with the same value of $\tau - \tau'$, and with the value of $\tau' = 0°$, it gives $K = .02229$. Hence the value of K is not proportional to $\tau - \tau'$, and differs considerably when the value of $\tau - \tau'$, under different circumstances, is the same. Both these values of K are less than the value of $A = .03046$, as they should be by equation (2). The greater the altitude the more nearly should the value of p approximate to that of unity, and the more nearly should the value of K approximate to that of A.

If the value of p, according to Tyndal, as has been stated, depends upon the hygrometric state of the atmosphere, then the value of K, as given by the preceding formula, for any observed values· of τ and τ', must give the diathermancy, and consequently the hygrometric state of the atmosphere in clear weather, not only for the point of observation, but generally throughout the whole extent of the atmosphere through which the rays pass, for the greater the value of K the greater the diathermananey of the air, and hence the less the amount of aqueous vapor in it.

This was briefly discussed by Messrs. HARKNESS, H. FARQUHAR, and TAYLOR.

Mr. ANTISELL then began the presentation of a communication

ON THE BUILDING UP OF ORGANIC MATTER,

which was unfinished when the hour of adjournment arrived, and its completion went over to the next meeting.

———————

213TH MEETING.   MARCH 11, 1882.

President WM. B. TAYLOR in the chair.

Thirty-seven members and visitors present.

Mr. ANTISELL then presented to the Society the remainder of his communication

ON THE BUILDING UP OF ORGANIC MATTER,

the presentation of which was begun at the last meeting.

A brief discussion of this paper—the session having been prolonged for this purpose—followed, and was taken part in by Messrs. GILL and WARD, who took exceptions to some of the conclusions arrived at in the communication.

———————

214TH MEETING.   MARCH 25, 1882.

President WM. B. TAYLOR in the chair.

Thirty-six members and visitors present.

The President announced to the Society the death, at 3 p. m. this day, of pneumonia, after an illness of two days, of Mrs. Joseph Henry, widow of the first president of the Society.

Mr. A. B. JOHNSON then presented to the Society a communication

ON SOME PECULIAR RAVAGES OF TEREDO NAVALIS.

This communication was discussed by Messrs. ANTISELL, DALL, GILL, HARKNESS, and WHITE.

Mr. ANTISELL called attention to the fact that the existence of the Teredo, as well as that of other destructive mollusks brought to our harbors by shipping, along our entire coast is well known, and that, in view of this fact, it is a matter of surprise that provision was not made for guarding against this danger. To this it was answered by Mr. Johnson that the wharf was a temporary one, being only needed for three months, and that, although the presence and destructive powers of the Teredo were recognized by the Board, it did not appear that in any previous case the destructive action of the Teredo was so rapid as to render special precaution necessary in this case. Upon a question from Mr. Harkness it was asserted by Mr. Johnson that a pile, examined on September 15 by divers, and found sound—chips cut by divers from the pile under water were found unbored by the Teredo—broke down on September 19, thus indicating a destruction of a pile in four days.

The accuracy of the observation of September 15, that the chips were unbored, was questioned by Mr. Dall, who asserted that the Teredo in its youngest stage attacks the wood, and that the hole made is at first very minute, and is gradually enlarged and deepened as the mollusk grows. So that a pile which appears sound on the surface may, in fact, already be seriously injured by Teredo borings. In San Francisco Bay the work of destruction of piles by the Teredo, and their renewal goes on continually, and it is estimated that a complete renewal of all the piles in the bay occurs every seven years. The mollusk works and breeds the year round in waters above a temperature of 60° F. It attacks the hard woods, as lignum vitæ, quite as readily as softer woods, but the destruction in such case is less rapid. Such woods, however, as palmetto, consisting of bundles of tough fibres interspersed with soft or spongy material, are only slightly, if at all, injured.

Mr. GILL called attention to the fact that the Dutch Commissioners, appointed in consequence of the great ravages of the Teredo on the coast of Holland in about 1859, found creosote the best preventive. They further found that the activity of the Teredo was, to a certain extent, dependent upon meteorological conditions since the years 1720, 1755, 1782, 1820, and 1850, were seasons of great drought, and consequent increase of salinity of the sea-water along the coast, and in those years the destruction caused by the Teredo was unusually great.

Respecting the geological age of the Teredo, Mr. WHITE exhibited to the Society fossilized wood from the cretaceous formation showing Teredo borings.

Mr. BILLINGS then presented to the Society a communication

ON THE VENTILATION OF THE HOUSE OF REPRESENTATIVES,

which was unfinished when the hour of adjournment arrived, and went over to the next meeting.

Adjourned.

215TH MEETING. APRIL 8, 1882.

President WM. B. TAYLOR in the Chair.

Forty-eight members and visitors present.

Mr. BILLINGS then continued the presentation of the communication begun at the last meeting

ON THE VENTILATION OF THE HOUSE OF REPRESENTATIVES,

of which the following is an abstract:

The difficulties to be overcome, and the means used for this purpose were explained, and plans and sections of the Hall of the House of Representatives at the Capitol, in Washington, were shown. The amount of fresh air required is about one foot per second per person, if an approach to perfect ventilation is desired. The imperfect form of ventilation by dilution requires from forty to fifty feet per minute. When a hall is occupied only one or two hours, the cubic space is important, but in long sessions it is the supply rather than the space that must be looked to.

To produce the requisite movement of the large amount of air used, special force must be supplied. This may be propulsion—the plenum method, or by aspiration—the vacuum method, or a combination of the two. The effect of wind and rain on aspirating systems was alluded to. In the majority of such halls the plenum system, by means of a fan, is used. The difficulty in introducing this large amount of air into a hall depends partly on the necessity for avoiding unpleasant currents, and partly on the cost of heating and supplying power. The question of cost, however, in such halls as are referred to, is usually a minor consideration, but if the tastes of individuals as to temperature are to be consulted— that is, if each man is to have his air at the temperature which suits himself—the cost becomes a serious matter.

The effects of various positions of fresh air inlets were pointed out, and stated to depend largely upon the tendency of air to adhere to surfaces over which it passes, as shown by the investigations of Savart and others. The difference between the upward and downward system were pointed out.

The various modes of heating were described, more especially with reference to their effect upon the air, and the influence of moisture was discussed. Probably the importance of moistening the air is less than has been supposed, and the methods employed for this purpose have been beneficial only indirectly.

The system of heating and ventilation of the Hall of the House was then described, and compared with that of the English Houses of Parliament, the Chamber of Deputies at Versailles, and the Grand Opera House at Vienna, and Frankfort on Main.

The great importance of skilled superintendence was pointed out, and the necessity for continuous records was insisted on.

Remarks upon this communication were made by Messrs. ANTISELL, ELLIOTT, MUSSEY, and POWELL.

Mr. HILGARD then presented a communication

ON SIEMENS' DEEP SEA THERMOMETER AND CARRÉ'S ICE MACHINE.

Remarks on this communication were made by Messrs. ANTISELL, DALL, DUTTON, and E. J. FARQUHAR, after which the Society adjourned.

———————

216TH MEETING.   APRIL 22, 1882.

President WM. B. TAYLOR in the chair.

Thirty-six members and visitors present.

The Secretary read a list of names of persons who had been

elected to, and had accepted membership in, the Philosophical Society, viz: Ezra Westcott Clark, Henry Flagg French, Henry Allen Hazen, Charles Hugo Kummel, Israel Cook Russell, William Wirt Upton, Albert Lowry Webster.

Mr. Ferrel then presented to the Society a communication

ON SOLAR RADIATION AT SHERMAN, WYOMING.

The next communication was by Mr. C. A. White

ON ARTESIAN WELLS ON THE GREAT PLAINS.

This communication has been essentially reproduced with the title, "Artesian Wells upon the Great Plains," (subscribed C. A. White,) in the American Review for August, 1882, No. 135, pp. 187–196.

Mr. Antisell called attention to previous attempts on the part of the Government to obtain water on the great plains by boring artesian wells. During the surveys and explorations of the 39th parallel, for the purpose of ascertaining the feasibility of building a railroad to the Pacific Ocean, special attention was given to the matter of obtaining water by means of artesian wells, and at that time he reached the same conclusion essentially as that now presented by Mr. White. Mr Antisell's published report upon this subject may be found in volume 7 of the Pacific Railroad Reports published in 1854.

Mr. Mussey called attention to boring now in progress along the line of the Southern Pacific Railroad in New Mexico; boring being in progress at the expense of the railroad company for the purpose of supplying water for locomotive purposes.

Mr. Gilbert considered the argument conclusive as to the failure of artesian wells on the great plains to be of any practical value for irrigating purposes, but for some other uses, such as stock raising, farm uses, etc. Some wells in favorable localities had proved a success, and others would also undoubtedly prove successful. Geological prophecy is generally, however, to be made with great caution, and to be received with caution equally great, a proposition which was supported by citing several cases in the experience of himself and others.

On the close of this discussion Mr. ELLIOTT presented a communication

ON THE CREDIT OF THE UNITED STATES, PAST, PRESENT AND PROSPECTIVE.

This communication will be published in another form.

Remarks upon this paper were made by Messrs. GILL and W. B. TAYLOR, after which the Society adjourned.

217TH MEETING.   MAY 6, 1882.

President WM. B. TAYLOR in the chair.

Twenty-eight members and visitors.

The President announced to the Society the death of two of its members, Mr. WILLIAM J. TWINING, Major U. S. Engineers and Commissioner of the District of Columbia, and Mr. JOHN RODGERS, Senior Rear Admiral U. S. Navy and Superintendent U. S. Naval Observatory. He further announced to the Society that the proposition for a federation of the Anthropological, Biological, and Philosophical Societies had been discussed by the General Committee, but that thus far no action had been taken.

The first communication was by Mr. ELLIOTT COUES,

ON THE POSSIBILITIES OF PROTOPLASM.

The following is an abstract of this communication, which has been published at greater length under the title—"Biogen : a Speculation on the Origin and Nature of Life. Abridged from a paper on the 'Possibilities of Protoplasm,' read before the Philosophical Society of Washington, May 6th, 1882. By Dr. ELLIOTT COUES. Washington : Judd & Detweiler, printers and publishers. 1882." (8vo., pp. 27.)

Referring to previous papers on the subject of Life, by Mr. WOODWARD and Mr. WARD, the speaker opposed any purely chemico-physical theory, and adhered to the doctrine of the actual existence of a "vital principle." Granting that all substances, including protoplasm, have been evolved from nebulous matter; that evolution to the protoplasmic state is necessary for any manifestation of life, and even that life necessarily appears in matter thus elaborated, it does not follow that the result of the processes by which matter is fitted to receive life is the *cause* of the vitality manifested. For all that is known to the contrary protoplasm and vitality are simply concomitant; or if there is any causal relation between them, vital force is the cause of the peculiar properties of protoplasm, not the result of those properties. There really exists a potency or principle called "vital," in virtue of which the chemical substance called protoplasm manifests vitality, that is to say, *is alive*, and in the absence of which no protoplasmic or other molecular aggregation of matter can be alive. The chemico-physical theory simply restates abiogenesis or "spontaneous generation," of which we know nothing scientifically. The grave doubt that "life is a property of protoplasm" will persistently intrude until some one shows what is the chemico-physical difference between living and dead protoplasm; none being known.

Noting that chemistry and physics had combined to manufacture an egg which would do everything to be expected of an egg, except to hatch, the speaker summed his charge thus: The atheistic physicist, denying mind in nature, declares that matter alone exists. Matter in motion is all there is; the cosmos being matter in motion in virtue of material forces alone. This is simply to invent a kind of perpetual motion machine, and leave out even the inventor; for such a machine invented itself and set itself going. Then the materialistic chemist takes this self-started machine and declares it has laid an egg that will hatch. On any such theory a God is not only superfluous but impossible. Yet the result of the alleged self-evolution of self-created matter through chemical elements to organic compounds has been the creation of a protoplasmic soul so constituted that it must believe in a God; and if matter be that God, matter contradicts itself, for the constitution of the human soul requires that its God must be other than its protoplasmic self; while if matter be not that God, there must be some other.

The speaker argued for the existence of the soul as something apart from and unlike matter, defining "soul" as that quantity of spirit which any living body may or does possess. No idea can attach to the term "spirit" from which all conceptions of matter are not absolutely excluded. Spirit is immaterial, self-conscious force; life consists in the animation of matter by spirit.

The substance of mind and the substance of matter were noted as equally hypothetical. To the former was given the name

Biogen, or "soul-stuff," and it was defined as spirit in combination with the minimum of matter necessary to its manifestation. The analogy between biogen and luminiferous æther, or the hypothetical substance of light, was discussed. The drift of the speaker's speculation on the vital principle as an ens realissimum was toward a restatement, in scientific terms, of the old *anima mundi* theory. Modern materialistic and atheistic notions about life were denounced as every one of them disguises of the monstrously absurd statement that a self-created atom of matter could lay an egg that would hatch.

The whole matter being beyond the scrutiny of the physical senses is remote from the scope of exact science; but it is irrational and unscientific to deny it, as is virtually done when science excludes it from any share in life-phenomena, by presuming to explain life upon purely material considerations. No chemico-physical theory of life is tenable that does not satisfactorily explain the chemico-physical difference between, for example, a live amœba and a dead one; an explanation which has never yet been, and probably cannot be, given.

A general discussion of the points involved in this paper followed. Mr. POWELL pointed out what he regarded as a fundamental and fatal error in the reasoning, viz., that the axiom that the whole equals the sum of all its parts, had been assumed throughout to be true *qualitatively* as well as quantitively. Furthermore, he maintained that logical consistency required that those who believe in force should believe also in the vital principle, and *vice versa.* As for himself, however, there was neither force nor vital principle, but only matter in motion. Three relations are always to be borne in mind, viz., quantity, quality, and succession, whereas the physicist falls into error by considering only the quantitive relation.

So much of the support of the views of Mr. Coues as might be derived from the common consensus of mankind was criticised by Mr. Gill as unsound, since the common consensus of mankind has often been found at fault; the supposed flatness of the earth, the motion of the sun around the earth, etc., are examples where this criterion fails. Paraphrasing an eminent philosopher's dictum, he thought there was a tendency of biologists ignorant of philosophy and philosophers ignorant of biology to make a distinction between organic and inorganic matter, and call in a "vital force." He likened living and dead protoplasm to an electric battery in action and at rest, and maintained that life is a property of matter, and that it cannot be conceived of separated from matter.

Mr. HARKNESS avowed his belief in force, and hence in vital force, and further in a little religion, and was, therefore, moved to make inquiry concerning the chemical difference between living and dead matter.

Mr. WARD pointed out that very diverse views were held upon this subject by two classes of thinkers who do not come into intellectual contact. Furthermore, while not asserting that a belief in vital force was a superstition, attention was drawn to the fact that infantile races attribute all phenomena to supernatural agencies, and that, with increasing knowledge, there is a decrease in the number of these appeals to supernatural agencies.

The corner stone of modern science, said Mr. DOOLITTLE, is *measure*. We must have a biometer. What electrical science would be without ohms, astronomy without graduated circles, chemistry without the balance, such is biology without a *measure*. Is there more life in two mice than in one mouse? In a horse than in a mouse? Until we can answer these questions substantial progress in biology is not to be expected.

The term automatic, as used here, he considered a confession of biologic ignorance. Automatic motion, as used in the discussion, seemed to mean simply motion which cannot be relegated to any known law.

After some further desultory discussion the Society adjourned.

218TH MEETING. MAY 20, 1882.

President WM. B. TAYLOR in the chair.

Thirty-two members and visitors present.

A series of resolutions concerning the death of Admiral JOHN RODGERS, a member of this Society, which resolutions had been adopted by the General Committee, were read by the Secretary; after which Prof. CHARLES W. SHIELDS, of Princeton College, read to the Society a communication

ON THE PHILOSOPHICAL ORDER OF THE SCIENCES.

This communication has been published by Scribner's Sons in a volume entitled " The Order of the Sciences. An Essay on the Philosophical Classification and Organization of Human Knowledge." By Charles W. Shields, Professor in Princeton College. 103 pp., 12mo. New York, Charles Scribner's Sons, 1882.

This communication was discussed by Messrs. WARD, POWELL, ANTISELL, TAYLOR, ALVORD, and BAKER.

219TH MEETING.   JUNE 3, 1882.

President WM. B. TAYLOR in the chair.

Twenty-two members and visitors present.

The first communication offered was by Mr. ALVORD

ON THE COMPASS PLANT.

This communication has been published with the title " On the Compass Plant," by Benjamin Alvord, in the American Naturalist for August, 1882, No. 16, pp. 625–635.

Remarks were made on the exhibition of polarity in other vegetable types by Messrs. HENRY FARQUHAR and THEODORE GILL.

Mr. E. B. ELLIOTT next presented to the Society a communication

ON SOME FORMULÆ RELATING TO GOVERNMENT SECURITIES.

Mr. C. H. KUMMELL then presented a communication

ON COMPOSITION OF ERROR FROM SINGLE CAUSES OF ERROR.

This was unfinished when the hour of adjournment arrived, and its completion went over to the next meeting.

Adjourned.

220TH MEETING.   JUNE 17, 1882.

President WM. B. TAYLOR in the chair.

Twenty-three members and visitors present.

Mr. C. H. KUMMELL continued his communication

ON COMPOSITION OF ERROR FROM SINGLE CAUSES OF ERROR.

which was begun at the last meeting.

This paper is expected to appear in full in the Astronomische Nachrichten.

Remarks upon this paper were made by Messrs. E. B. ELLIOTT and W. B. TAYLOR.

Mr. MARCUS BAKER then presented the following communication

ON A GEOMETRICAL QUESTION RELATING TO SPHERES.

On January 17, 1882, Mr. Doolittle called the attention of the Society to the geometrical problem *To determine a circle equally distant from four given points in a plane,* and showed that the statement in Chauvenet's Geometry, (p. 308, Ex. 110,) that this problem admits of *four* solutions is erroneous, there being in general *fourteen* solutions. The extension of this problem to spheres and five points in space is nearly as simple as for the case of circles and four points in a plane.

Let it be proposed to solve the following :

PROBLEM.—*To determine a sphere equally distant from five given points.*

The distance to a sphere, considered here, is to be measured along a diameter, produced if necessary, and hence for any position we have two distances, one a maximum, the other a minimum.

Solution.—Case I. Through any four of five given points, a, b, c, d, e, as, for example, b, c, d, e, describe a sphere; the fifth point, a, will in general fall within or without this sphere, of which call the radius R and centre C; also, let $\propto$ be the distance from the centre of this sphere to the point a. Then two spheres described with centre C and radii $\frac{1}{2}(R \pm \propto)$ fulfil the condition of being equidistant from the five points.

Every distinct group of four of the five given points in like manner gives two solutions; hence of this kind there are in all *ten* solutions.

Case II. Through any three of the five given points, a, b, c, d, e, as a, b, c, pass the circumference of a circle; from the centre of the circle erect a perpendicular. This perpendicular is the locus of all points equidistant from points a, b, c. Join the points d and e by a line; bisect this line by a plane perpendicular thereto. This plane is the locus of all points equidistant from d and e. The intersection of these two loci is the centre of two spheres equidistant from the five points.

Every distinct group of three of the five given points in like manner gives two solutions; hence of this kind there are in all *twenty* solutions.

Therefore, in general there are *thirty* spheres equally distant from five given points.

The next communication was by Mr. H. A. HAZEN

ON THE RETARDATION OF STORM CENTRES AT ELEVATED STA-
TIONS, AND HIGH WIND AS A PROBABLE CAUSE.

In the absence of Mr. Hazen the following abstract was read by the Secretary, Mr. Baker:

In his tenth paper, published in the January, 1879, number of the American Journal of Science, Prof. Elias Loomis advanced certain evidence, based on barometric observations, to show that apparently the progress of a storm centre was much more rapid at the surface of the earth than at elevations above it. It is the purpose of this article to put forth certain facts which, it is hoped, will tend to elucidate the subject.

Not long since, before this Society, Prof. G. K. Gilbert showed that a high wind had a tendency to depress the barometer column, as determined from his discussion of certain observations made by the Signal Service at the summit and along the side of Mount Washington, New Hampshire. If now a wind can produce such a depression, it would seem as if the wind accompanying a storm and continuing its force at a high station some time after the passage of the storm centre at the base, might cause the apparent retardation.

It is very desirable that special experiments be made, under natural conditions, directly testing the influence of high winds on the barometer column.*

It seems possible to indirectly ascertain such influence from a barometric computation of the height of a mountain by means of observations taken during different wind velocities. Table I gives such a computation of the height of Mount Washington from observations at the base and summit in May, 1872 and 1873.

---

* Direct experiments have been made, using a blower for the air current, and an air-tight receiver for the barometer, at short distances, a condition of things, however, which can never occur in nature.

TABLE I.

Mean amount to be added to the true difference of elevation between the summit and base of Mount Washington in order to give the computed difference, arranged according to the force of the wind.

	WIND FORCE IN MILES PER HOUR.													
	0 to 10.		11 to 20.		21 to 30.		31 to 40.		41 to 50.		51 to 60.		Above 61.	
	Cases.	Am't.	C.	A.	C.	A.	C.	A.	C.	A.	C.	A.	C.	A.
May, 1872	77	—27.1	25	—18.6	30	—3.1	43	+13.8	65	+10.5	32	+33.9	50	+51.4
May, 1873	104	—43.5	134	—22.0	183	+4.1	135	+15.6	99	+34.9	61	+52.4	27	+80.1

In the above table, for May, 1872, all winds under 10 and above 40 are included, and in May, 1873, all the cases, except a few which were omitted because of serious errors in the observations.

The table shows this remarkable peculiarity that, though with winds above sixty-one miles per hour, the mean computed difference in height is too great by sixty-six feet; with winds under ten miles per hour the mean difference is too small by thirty-five feet. We conclude, then, that some other cause must produce the results, or must act in conjunction with the wind. Taking the wind above sixty-one miles per hour I have found ten cases in which the height was too small by about fifteen feet, also a great number of cases in which, though the wind continued strong from the same direction, yet the computed height continually became less, showing that the wind does not produce a direct effect upon the indications of the barometer. On projecting the curves of pressure we find that there is a uniformity in the occurrence of small and large differences of elevation with the maxima and minima of pressure, the least being found when the pressure is high, and the greatest when it is low.

Grouping a second time, then, with respect to the maxima and minima of pressure, we have Table II.

TABLE II.

Mean amounts to be added to the true difference of height between the summit and base of Mount Washington to obtain the computed difference.

DATE.	LOCALITY.	MAXIMA OF PRESSURE.		MINIMA OF PRESSURE.	
		Cases.	Amount.	Cases.	Amount.
May, 1872	Mt. W. and base	81	— 32.5	70	+ 57.4
May, 1873	Mt. W. and base	102	— 61.6	137	+ 67.3
Jan., Feb., Mar., Oct., Nov., Dec., 1880.	Mt. W. and mean of B. and P.	119	— 29.1	120	+ 127.0

As the first two horizontal rows of figures apply only to observations for the month of May, and as it would be very desirable to have results for the colder months when the fluctuations are much increased, I have added a third set of figures for the summit of Mount Washington, compared with the mean of Burlington and Portland as the base, and computed the difference of elevation from observations taken at 7 a. m., 3 p. m., and 11 p. m., Washington time, during January, February, March, October, November, and December, 1880.

It is evident from Table II that during the prevalence of relatively high pressure, elevations computed barometrically will, in general, be too small, and, on the other hand, when the pressure is low, the computed heights will be too great. This also explains the coincidence of too great computed heights with high winds, for the reason that the highest winds always occur with relatively low pressure; on the contrary, when the wind is light, the pressure is generally high.

May not this retardation be due to the effect of varying temperature? When a "low" has passed a station at sea level the temperature frequently falls steadily, thus contracting the atmosphere and causing its withdrawal from the upper regions, and a still further fall in pressure there. This process will continue until the fall caused by the low temperature is counterbalanced by the rise due to the advancing "high." The following is given as an illustration :

Observations of air-pressure and temperature at Denver and Pike's Peak, Colorado, in November, 1880.

Day.	Hour. Wash. Time.	Temp. Pike's Peak.	Mean Temp. Pike's Peak and Denver.	PRESSURE.	
				Pike's Peak.	Denver.
		°	°	″	″
14	7 a. m. ____	— 5	6	17.75	24.69
	3 p. m. ____	+ 2	20	17.75	24.64
	11 p. m. ____	6	19	17.82	24.59
15	7 a. m. ____	10	22	17.83	24.50
	3 p. m. ____	14	34	17.71	**24.28**
	11 p. m. ____	11	16	17.57	24.48
16	7 a. m. ____	1	6	17.28	24.41
	3 p. m. ____	— 6	1	17.18	24.44
	11 p. m. ____	— 14	— 6	17.22	24.58
17	7 a. m. ____	— 31	— 20	**17.13**	24.54
	3 p. m. ____	— 19	— 10	17.25	24.49
	11 p. m. ____	— 16	— 12	17.42	24.42
18	7 a. m. ____	— 9	— 6	17.48	24.33
	3 p. m. ____	— 4	7	17.41	24.23
	11 p. m. ____	— 5	6	17.32	24.08

From these observations we see that, although the air-pressure was at a minimum at Denver, November 15, 3 p. m., yet, owing to the extraordinary cold, the pressure continued to fall at Pike's Peak, (which is 8,840 feet above Denver,) and did not reach its lowest point until forty hours afterward, or November 17, 7 a. m. Extending the same reasoning to the diurnal range of air-pressure we shall find a satisfactory solution of the retardation. From hourly observations at the summit and base of Mount Washington I find that while the morning maximum occurs at 8 : 30 a. m. at the base, it does not occur till noon at the summit, during this part of the day the temperature is rising rapidly; and hence we may suppose that it produces the continued rise in air-pressure at the summit overbalancing the diurnal range; in like manner the afternoon minimum occurs at 6 p. m. at the summit, or two hours later than at the base, as the temperature begins falling at 2 p. m. This may account for the difference at the two stations. On comparing

the night maximum and morning minimum I find little or no retardation ; this is what we might expect from the fact that at this
time there is little or no change in temperature.

The President, Mr. TAYLOR, called the attention of the Society
to the remarkable halo witnessed by many people in Washington
last Thursday, June 15, saying that in some respects it was remarkable, and presented some theoretical difficulties.   While it had
been seen by a number of those present, none had made any scientific observations of it or taken any measurements.   A number of
other halos were mentioned which, like this, occurred between 10
and 11 a. m., and it was thought worth while to consider whether
halos appeared oftener at those hours than at others, and if so,
why.

221ST MEETING.   OCTOBER 7, 1882.

The President in the chair.

Forty-one members present.

The consideration of the minutes of the last meeting was postponed.

The PRESIDENT welcomed the members to a renewal of the meetings of the Society after the summer vacation.

He also announced that vacancies had been created in the Committee by the resignation of Dr. J. J. Woodward, a Vice-President
of the Society, on account of prolonged illness, and of Mr. Marcus
Baker, one of the Secretaries, by reason of assignment to duty in
California.   The General Committee had elected Mr. E. B. Elliott
a vice-president in place of Dr. Woodward, and Dr. J. S. Billings
a secretary in place of Mr. Baker.   The vacancies resulting therefrom in the membership of the Committee had been supplied by
the election of Dr. D. L. Huntington, U. S. A., and Prof. C. V.
Riley.

Mr. A. S. CHRISTIE made a communication

ON A SYSTEM OF STANDARD TIME.

A prime meridian (say Greenwich) time would, in general, give
the hours of the local natural day dissymmetrical with respect to

the zenith of the clock face and the zero point of the hour numbers. Turning the dial plate until the prime meridian hour of local mean noon comes to the zenith, eliminates the first mentioned element of dissymmetry, and is a partial adaptation of prime meridian time to local convenience.   The second element of dissymmetry is inherent in the nature of numbers, and cannot be eliminated whilst they are retained ; for symmetry demands that the zero point shall be either *everywhere* or *nowhere*, neither of which conditions can be satisfied by the symbols now in use.   Rejecting them, therefore, and adopting a series of hour symbols having no absolute numerical, but only an ordinal, significance, is another and final step in the adaptation of prime meridian time (such only as to the hour-zero) to general use.

A consideration of what symbols to adopt will immediately suggest, that an abandonment of the artificial, and a return to the simplicity of nature, constitutes the real and complete solution of the problem.   That problem may now be stated : To avoid the discordance of local time on different meridians (a discordance which cannot be removed) by the adoption of the same standard time on all meridians, so that the hour and fraction of the hour shall be the same at the same instant everywhere ; which standard time shall be marred by no dissymmetry with respect to the globe, alien in no land, essentially local everywhere, cosmopolitan and impartial as the sun himself.

The mere statement of the problem is almost sufficient.   The system of time must consist in simply telling *where the sun is* with respect to our terrestrial meridians—the answer in every case must be the same in all quarters of the globe.   To limit the geographical knowledge necessary, insure uniformity, and afford hour-zeros, twenty-four equi-distant meridians should be agreed upon as such hour zeros, and named from some country through which, or city near which, they pass.   Regard now the dial plate of the clock as the earth, the north pole at center, and meridians, twenty-four of which are actually drawn, radiating to the circumference.   (Mr. Henry Farquhar suggests that the dial plate be an actual planisphere.)   Bring the local meridian to the zenith and let the hour-hand, revolving once each day, point to the mean sun.   The time read from such a chronometer will be the natural, or sun time, proposed in this paper.   Space here forbids details with respect to the theory itself, or mention of the objections urged against its practicability; but it may be said in conclusion, in answer to an objection raised by Prof. Coffin, that the longitude of any place is given at once by the clock face at meridian transit of the mean sun, without any subtraction whatever.

Mr. Henry Farquhar urged some objections to the device of reckoning time by meridians an hour apart, as not being sufficiently local to avoid a longitude correction in tables of sunrise and other astronomical events, nor sufficiently universal to escape confusion at points nearly 30 minutes from the standard meridians. He thought the need of a universal standard time, already greatly increased by railway and telegraph communication, would become still more strongly felt in the future. Inconvenience resulting from the occurrence of the 24th hour during daylight at any place, could be obviated by numbering hours beyond 24 and retaining the same day. It would not be suitable to reckon time everywhere from Greenwich midnight, since that would involve a change of day at local 10 A. M. in Sydney, (nearly noon in New Zealand) or, if the hours after 10 A. M. were counted as 25, 26, etc. of the previous day, a discrepancy in date between Australia and Europe. Hours might be reckoned from midnight at 6h. east of Greenwich, noon at 6h. west; though 5¼h. west, a meridian passing near Cumberland, Maryland, would be preferable. The longitude of a place would be the time of mean noon at that place, and count from the last-named meridian westward, from 6h. to 30h., and not from 0h. to 24h. The longitude of Washington, then, would be 23h. 53.2m., that of San Francisco, 26h. 54.6m., Honolulu, 29h. 16.4m., Auckland, 7h. 5.7m., Calcutta, 12h. 51.7m., and Greenwich, 18h. 45.0m. The 6h. meridian would pass through Bering Straits and be the line adopted for the change of date.

East of British India the day would be understood to change at 24h., which hour would arrive at some time less than 6h. after midnight. For the rest of the world, the hours would run above 24, and be diminished by 24 at the time indicated by local custom and convenience for a change of day. In Washington, for example, the conventional day might change at 36h., the hours of next day counting on from 12h., or at 39h. and count on from 15h., according as it was preferred to have the change near midnight or about 3h. after midnight. At Greenwich the hour nearest midnight would be 31h. or 7h.

Mr. Farquhar also showed a proposed form of clock-face, in which the hours were numbered from 0 to 42 in two circuits, 24 being opposite 0, and so on.   Such a clock would do for all meridians, but might easily be arranged to have any desired noon-time at the top.

Mr. COFFIN remarked that he had failed to appreciate the importance of standard time to the extent to which it had been frequently advocated.   If we examine the several departments, in which such time is supposed to be needed, we can better determine in what way a requirement of that kind can be best supplied.

In navigation the time of the prime meridian is a necessity; and this is furnished directly by chronometers regulated to that time, while from astronomical observations the corresponding local time may be found; and both are involved in all questions of longitude. No further standard time is needed in this department.

The use of an astronomical ephemeris also requires the time of the meridian for which it is prepared.   A prime meridian common to all nations is a desideratum.   But at present the maritime nations of Great Britain and the United States reckon longitudes from Greenwich, while on some of the nautical charts of Russia, Germany, and Spain, longitudes are given from Greenwich as well as from the prime meridian of each respective country.   Besides this use of the meridian of Greenwich more general than of any other meridian, the meridian of 180° E. or W. from Greenwich passes near Behring Strait and through an extensive unoccupied region of the Pacific Ocean, where it will be most convenient to have the change of day, which is one less on the east side of such meridian than on the west.   Indeed, the change of longitude from east to west, or the reverse, necessarily requires a change of the local day.   *Where* the change is made, is arbitrary.   For instance, the longitude 175° E. is equivalent to 185° W.; but October 7 in the first case is October 6 in the second.   If such noting of the day, which is as much a part of the expression of the local time as are the hours and minutes, is attended to, we have the simple rule, common in navigation and the use of an ephemeris, " To the local time add the longitude if west, subtract it if east, to obtain the corresponding time of the prime meridian; " and this rule includes the day as well as its parts.

Sir John Herschel and others have proposed that longitudes should be reckoned westerly from 0 to 360°.   This would complicate the expression for the local day, and congruity would require that the change of day should be at the prime meridian, which would cause great inconvenience and even confusion.

There are some observations of terrestrial phenomena, which it is desirable to have made simultaneously in the same continent or in all parts of the world. This was notably the case in the magnetic crusade some forty years ago, when certain instants of Göttingen times were specified; but the observers had no difficulty, each for himself, in determining and using his corresponding local time. And in meteorological observations, if times are prescribed in the time of any specific meridian, the observers, if of sufficient intelligence to make valuable observations, can readily convert these times into their local times, or the reverse. The constant difference of longitude, expressed in time, is all that each one requires for the purpose.

The great call for a standard time has been made with regard to railroads. A *uniform* time for each road, or connecting system of roads, is needed for regulating the times of starting and the arrival of trains, which each road can best determine for itself, and the time-tables and clocks at the several stations may be reserved for the employés of such roads only. If the time-tables published for information of the travelling public are given in the local time of each place, or a column of constants for the reduction of the published times to the local times is given, the needs of the traveller seem to be sufficiently provided for. A local time differing but little from local mean-solar time is needed to meet the wants of the social and industrial interests of the country, and if it be exactly the mean-solar time, it varies from place to place directly with the longitude.

An essential is that each time-table for railroads should state distinctly what time is used. A neglect of this has and will produce uncertainty and confusion. In a leading railroad guide I found, at a place which I visited, three time-tables for the same road, without any statement that one of them was in New York time, the others in time of other places.

The suggestion that the dials of clocks should indicate an entire day of twenty-four hours instead of a half day of twelve hours is valuable to a certain extent. This is done in astronomical clocks, and in the astronomical mode of noting time. It would be an improvement in chronometers for nautical use, but sufficient if the dial be marked into the two periods of twelve hours each, into which common, universal use divides the day.

It would seem to be impracticable to change materially the use of local-mean time, now common throughout the country; nor is such change desirable or needed.

It is only within forty years that mean time has been substituted for apparent time in many of our cities, though its advantages had long been recognized by astronomers and time regulators; and within twenty years that the sun's rising and setting have been stated in mean, instead of apparent, time in the popular almanacs of the day.

The subject-matter was further discussed by Messrs. Doolittle, Elliott, Riley, Hilgard, Gilbert, and Mussey.

Mr. G. BROWN GOODE then read a paper

ON THE FISHERIES OF THE WORLD.

This has been essentially printed in the " Cyclopædia of Political Seience, Political Economy," etc., edited by John J. Lawlor, published at Chicago, vol. 2, pp. 211–231, (Art. " Fisheries,") 1883.

222D MEETING.   OCTOBER 21, 1882.

The President in the Chair.

Twenty-two members were present.

The minutes of the last meeting were read and adopted.

Mr. S. C. BUSEY read a paper

ON THE INFLUENCE OF THE CONSTANT USE OF HIGH-HEELED SHOES UPON THE HEALTH AND FORM OF THE FEMALE, AND UPON THE RELATION OF THE PELVIC ORGANS.

(The paper will appear in full in vol. 7, Gynecological Transactions.)

[Abstract.]

The foot and its coverings is not a new subject. Far more attention, however, has been given to the style and display of the covering than to the comfort and physical well-being of the foot. From this point the author gave a historical resumé of the different coverings for the feet which had been used as far back as the ancient Egyptians. The heel at first was designed to make short men look tall, and like other parts had undergone many changes to suit the whims of fashion and taste. During the reign of Louis XVI this objectionable style began to disappear, but has been again revived, and is perhaps more general now than at any previous time. Then followed a brief summary of the causes that produced deviations of form, with special reference to the effect of the constant use of French high-heeled shoes. Diagrams were exhibited showing the distortions of the feet caused by them, and the consequent changes in the joint-flexures and spinal curves. He claimed that the primary deflection took place at the base of the line of gravitation, and above this point there were greater or lesser alterations of the flexures and curves along the bony framework. Special attention was directed to the increased obliquity of the pelvis, and to the probable corresponding change in the position of the womb and other pelvic organs, which might be an important factor in the causation of some of the disorders of the female reproductive organs.

The subject-matter was discussed by various members.

A communication was submitted by Mr. THEODORE GILL

ON THE CLASSIFICATION OF THE INSECTIVOROUS MAMMALS.

In 1875 the author published a "Synopsis of Insectivorous Mammals" in the Bulletin of the United States Geological Survey of the Territories, under Hayden, (vol. 1, No. 2; 2d series, 1875, pp. 91–120,) and proposed several modifications in the classification. The principal of those modifications were (1) the union of the typical Insectivora and Dermoptera (*Galeopithecus*) is one order, as had been long before proposed by Frederic Cuvier and Wagner, but their distinction as two suborders; (2) the distribution of the true insectivores under two groups characterized by their molar dentition, and the complete subordination of the form of the body, and (3) the combination of families into super-families, and (4) the subdivision of several into subfamilies. The scheme thus promulgated has met with gratifying and unexpected favor, and has been essentially adopted by Messrs. Coues, Jordan, Dallas, Trouessart, and Dobson. Surgeon-Major Dobson's opinion is especially weighty, as he has undertaken a monograph of the order, and his opportunities for investigation have been unequalled. Since the publication of the Synopsis, in 1875, several forms have been made or become known which compel the recognition of new subordinate groups in the order; and Major Dobson has also proposed to raise the Solenodontinæ from the rank of a subfamily of Centetidæ to that of a family by the side of the latter. The assessment of the comparative value of different groups is a difficult and delicate task, and much can be said for as well as against any given proposition. The Solenodonts are doubtless as distinct from their nearest of kin as are some of the generally admitted families of mammals, and therefore it will be quite proper to recognize the family value of the type. But there are other groups of Insectivora which have been associated together in the same families which are equally or more entitled to the same distinction. Indeed, the only subfamilies of the "Synopsis of Insectivorous Mammals" which do not contrast more seem to be the Gymnurinæ and Erinaceinæ. If the Solenodontidæ are to be differentiated with family rank from the Centetidæ, so should the others. We would then have the following families:

SUBORDER DERMOPTERA.

1. Galeopithecidæ.

SUBORDER BESTIÆ.

DILAMBDODONTA.—Bestiæ with broad molar teeth surmounted by W-shaped ridges.

TUPAIOIDEA.

2. Tupaiidæ.
3. Macroscelididæ = Macroscelidinæ.
4. Rhynchocyonidæ = Rhynchocyoninæ.

ERINACEOIDEA.

5. Erinaceidæ, with the two subfamilies Gymnurinæ and Erinaceinæ.

SORICOIDEA.

6. Talpidæ = Talpinæ.
7. Myogalidæ = Myogalinæ.
8. Soricidæ.

ZALAMBDODONTA.—Bestiæ with narrow molar teeth having V-shaped ridges.

CENTETOIDA.

9. Centetidæ = Centetinæ.

10. Oryzoryctidæ = Oryzoryctinæ, *Dobson*, Mon. Insect., pp. 2, 71. 1882.

11. Solenodontidæ, *Dobson*, Mon. Insect., pp. 3, 87. 1882.

12. Potamogalidæ.

13. Geogalidæ = Geogalinæ, *Dobson*, Mon. Insect., p. 2. 1882.

CHRYSOCHLOROIDEA.

14. Chrysochloridæ.

The "Monograph of the Insectivora," by Surgeon-Major Dobson, will fill a long-felt want, and exceptionally well represent the present condition of our knowledge respecting the existing representatives of the order.

223D MEETING.   NOVEMBER 4, 1882.

The President in the Chair.

Forty-five members present.

The minutes of the last meeting were read and approved.

A communication was made by Mr. G. K. GILBERT:

ON A GRAPHIC TABLE FOR COMPUTATION.

[Abstract.]

On Nov. 17th, 1881, a new method of barometric hypsometry was presented to the Society, and this has since been published in the Second Annual Report of the Geological Survey. It involves a new formula. In the application of that formula an approximate value of the required altitude is first obtained, to which a correction is then added. For the determination of this correction a table was prepared, to be entered with two arguments. Although this table was spread out on six octavo pages, and although the deduced correction is small, it was nevertheless found impracticable to avoid a double interpolation. To escape this inconvenience the graphic table was afterwards devised.

The graphic table consists of three super-imposed sets of lines. In each of two sets the lines are straight, parallel, and equidistant, and those of one set intersect those of the other at right angles.

These represent values of the two arguments. The lines of the third set are curved, and each one represents a value of the correction. In use, the straight lines representing the values of the two arguments are traced to their intersection, and from the relation of this point of intersection to the curved lines the correction is deduced.

This method is theoretically applicable to the tabulation of any quantity which is the function of two variables, but is practically useful only when the quantity to be determined is either expressible by a small number of digits, or else is subject to only a small range of variation.

A second graphic table was exhibited, having for its object the computation of altitude from horizontal distances and vertical angles as data. On this, successive values of computed altitude are indicated by parallel, equidistant, straight lines. Vertical angles are indicated by the directions of lines radiating from a point, but the intervals of these lines are not equal. Distances are measurable along these radial lines, but are not indicated in the drawing. The scale of distances is identical with that of the map, including the points whose altitudes are to be computed. The lines are drawn on tracing-linen.

For the use of this table it is postulated that the points whose altitudes are to be computed are correctly placed upon a map, and that the same map indicates a point from which the elevation or depression angles of the various points were measured. The transparent linen bearing the table is placed over the map and connected with it by a pin passing through the common origin of the radial lines, and also through the indicated position of the station from which the angles were measured. About this point as a centre the table is then moved until the radial line, indicating the vertical angle of one of the points, is brought immediately over the representation of that point upon the map, The position of that point among the parallel lines then indicates the desired altitude.

The use of this device is limited to a special case, but that case is one of frequent recurrence in the preparation of contour maps, and it is hoped that the device will lead to an economy of time.

The principle involved in the application of a *transparent* graphic table permits of the extension of the graphic table to cases involving three arguments. Two sets of lines could be drawn on a lower sheet, and two other sets on an upper transparent sheet, and these sets could be so constructed that one of them would represent a function of three variables represented by the other three.

The paper was discussed by Mr. HARKNESS and Mr. H. A. HAZEN, Mr. HARKNESS pointed out that the construction of a two-argument computation table by means of curved lines was not novel.

224TH MEETING.   NOVEMBER 18, 1882.

The President in the Chair.

Forty members present.

The minutes of the last meeting were read and adopted.

Mr. E. B. ELLIOTT spoke

ON SURVIVORSHIPS, WITH TABLES AND FORMULAS OF CONSTRUCTION.

(No abstract has been furnished.)

Mr. H. A. HAZEN submitted a paper

ON THE COMING WINTER OF 1882–'83.

The following is an abstract:

It has been a great desideratum, and one which has called out the efforts of many men, to determine in advance the probable character of a season. A prominent meteorologist has inferred that the coming winter is to be a very severe one, because, as he says, "every one knows that a cold and wet summer is invariably followed by a cold and stormy winter." In order to obtain probable sequences in the weather, if we could in any way determine the mean temperature or pressure over an extensive region, it would seem as though results would be far more satisfactory than those from a single station. The following plan has been adopted for ascertaining such mean results:

We may draw isobars or any isometeorologic lines upon a map of a country; then we may rule a large number of squares upon glass or some transparent substance; and after that, by placing these squares upon the map, we may at a glance interpolate the exact pressure or temperature in each square, and a mean of all the squares would give a mean for the whole country.

Such results have been determined for the United States east of the 97th meridian for each month since July, 1873. (These were exhibited graphically before the Society.) We find a singular result on comparing these figures with similar figures for the single station of Providence, R. I., (observations at this station, from 1832 to 1876, were kindly furnished the author by the Smithsonian Institution,) namely, a striking uniformity in the values; and we may conclude that, as far as mean monthly temperatures are concerned, we may consider those at any one station fairly comparable with the same over an extensive region.

In the accompanying table each summer, and the following winter, at Providence, R. I., have been considered as cold, cool, mean, warm, or hot; and an effort has been made to establish the character of the winter that follows a summer having any one of the above characteristics:

Year.	Summer.	Winter following.	Year.	Summer.	Winter following.
1832	cold	warm	1857	cold	hot
1833	cool	warm	1858	cold	hot
1834	warm	cold	1859	mean	hot
1835	mean	cold	1860	cool	hot
1836	cold	cold	1861	cool	warm
1837	cold	mean	1862	cold	warm
1838	hot	cold	1863	cold	hot
1839	mean	cool	1864	cold	warm
1840	warm	mean	1865	mean	hot
1841	mean	hot	1866	warm	warm
1842	mean	mean	1867	mean	mean
1843	mean	mean	1868	mean	cold
1844	mean	warm	1869	cool	warm
1845	cool	cool	1870	hot	hot
1846	cold	hot	1871	mean	cold
1847	mean	hot	1872	hot	cold
1848	warm	cool	1873	mean	mean
1849	mean	hot	1874	mean	cold
1850	mean	hot	1875	cold	mean
1851	mean	cool	1876	warm	cold
1852	warm	warm	1877	warm	hot
1853	warm	cool	1878	warm	cool
1854	warm	cool	1879	mean	hot
1855	hot	cold	1880	hot	cold
1856	hot	cold	1881	warm	hot

On examining this table we find that of the eight cold summers three were followed by a hot winter, three by a warm winter, one by a mean winter, and one by a cold winter, which gives one out of eight cold summers followed by a cold winter, and six by a hot or warm winter. Taking all the cases, in forty-eight per cent. of them any summer was followed by a winter of an opposite character; in forty-two per cent. the summers or winters were mean, and in only ten per cent. of the cases were the summers followed by winters of the same character.

Making a similar comparison at Fort Snelling, Minnesota, we find, out of the sixty-eight summers and winters on record at that station, that fifty-two, or seventy-six per cent., were followed by a season of the opposite character; ten, or fifteen per cent., by a season of the same character; and six, or nine per cent., were doubtful.

We may also infer the character of the coming season for the United States by noting the movement of the permanent winter area of high pressure in respect to the Rocky mountains. It would seem as though these tended to ward off the cold if the high area settles down to the west of the range.

The winter of 1877–'78 was warm, for during every month of that season the high pressure was west of the Rockies, and the cold waves were effectually barred from the Eastern States. In December of 1877 the high pressure was spread over a vast extent of territory west of the range, and the temperature in the east rose to 7.2 degrees above the average.

The winter months of 1880–'81 were cold. During that time the high pressure was well to the east of the Rockies, and the temperature in the east fell below the average from two to six degrees. The winter of 1881–'82 was warm, as the following tabulated form shows, the plus sign indicating so many degrees above the average.

Month.	Temperature.	Position of high pressure.
1881, September	$+4°.6$	Normal.
October	$+3°.8$	Normal.
November	$+2°.2$	Strong west of range.
December	$+7°.7$	Strong west of range.
1882, January	$+2°.7$	Strong west of range.
February	$+5°.6$	Strong west of range.

It is now too early to determine exactly what the weather of the winter of 1882–'83 will be, but the indications are that it will be a medium rather than a severe one, as some have predicted. The past summer having been cold and stormy. a warm winter ought to follow; and the high pressure during last September was slightly west of the Rockies, while during October it was so far to the West and North as to rest over the Cascade range in Oregon. If it continues west of the Rocky-Mountain range a severe winter is not probable.

Mr. HENRY FARQUHAR commenced a communication on

EXPERIMENTS IN BINARY ARITHMETIC.

The meeting was adjourned at the usual hour, (10 o'clock,) with the understanding that the unfinished communication should be taken up at a subsequent meeting.

225TH MEETING.   DECEMBER 2, 1882.

The President in the Chair.

Fifty members present.

The minutes of the last meeting were read and adopted.

In accordance with the by-laws of the Society, the President, Mr. WILLIAM B. TAYLOR, delivered the annual address.

ANNUAL ADDRESS

ON PHYSICS AND OCCULT QUALITIES,

By William B. Taylor.

"Vis abdita quædam."

Lucretius. (*De R. N.*, lib. v. 1232.)

1. *The Dynamic and Kinematic Theories of Force.*

From the remarkable success of scientific investigation in assailing the domain of darkness,—in continually bringing the phenomena of nature more and more under the recognized empire of certain necessary laws and principles, the induction seems natural that outstanding mysteries—the ultimate constitution of matter, the nature and genesis of life and of mind itself—must in time yield to the same persistent siege of searching analysis, and be reduced to subjection under the same government, as simple servitors of an all-embracing mechanical philosophy.

In recent years, a still further induction has been ventured upon by some, to wit, that even the fundamental laws themselves of all physical action must, when properly formulated, be interpreted by simple mechanics ;—all properties of matter resolved into mass or inertia, and finite extension or form,—all potentiality of matter into varying modes of motion. And it has been strongly maintained by this class of physicists, that until such consummation, the mind must still be held in thrall of mysterious unimaginable powers, the helpless devotee of "occult qualities" which science in the past has so laboriously and successfully endeavored to relegate to the shadowy limitary of metaphysics. This form of speculative doctrine, (premonitions of which may be traced back several hundred years,) may now be regarded as having attained the importance and cohesion of a school, numbering in its following a few quite eminent disciples, who agree in denying the real existence of any inherent "forces" in matter, and in holding such a designation to be merely a convenient but provisional ideal abstraction. While on the other hand the large majority of scientific thinkers (perhaps comprising most of those who have reached the conservatism of middle age) still adhere to the older conception of primeval "force" as an essential hypostasis of the operations of nature. And thus the battle so long waged (and so long practically decided) between realism and nominalism in the field of mind, bids fair to be revived (though under quite other auspices) in the field of matter. These two modes of thought may be conveniently designated the *dynamic* and the *kinematic* theories of physics. In the terminology of the *Philosophie Positive*, the dynamic theory still lingers in the shaded vale of "metaphysics," while the kinematic theory has reached the sunny hill of "positivism."* An attempt to examine and compare these divergent lines of interpretation may be a not unprofitable exercise.

The Cohesion of Matter.—Among the earliest of our experiences is the perception that the bodies around us possess in varying degrees a quality of "hardness;" and the child who gathers a rounded pebble on the beach, (if perchance inspired by its inquisitive instinct to see what the interior looks like,) discovers that to break the pebble requires the heavy and repeated strokes of a stone much larger than itself. Whence this remarkable tenacity of coherence? Whence the striking physical difference between the pebble and an equivalent mass of very fine sand?

From a large variety of facts observed in the actions of solution, of fusion, of evaporation, of the very existence of a kinetic temperature in bodies, in the phenomena of crystallization, of isomorphism, of definite and unvarying numerical mass-ratios in chemical combinations, of polymerism or serial groupings in multiple proportion, of isomerism, of allotropy, and of other more recondite habitudes of matter, the general conviction has been reached (by what has been called "a consilience of inductions") that all substance is a collection of constituent molecules of probably uniform magnitudes held together by some powerful agency. A few it is true have asserted their superiority to such popular weakness as the admission of the atomic theory; but as their vague suggestion of some continuous or colloidal form of substance has not even pretended to interpret any of the classes of phenomena just alluded to, such dis-

---

* AUGUSTE COMTE, in his *Positive Philosophy*, maintains that "Forces are only motions produced or tending to be produced. - - - We hear too much still of the old metaphysical language about *forces* and the like ; and it would be wise to suit our terms to our positive philosophy." (Harriet Martineau's Translation. London, 1853: book I, chap. 4.) Even *inertia* is treated as a metaphysical fiction.

sent may be summarily dismissed as the mere exhibition of an unprofitable mental captiousness.*

The kinematist repudiating any attractive force in nature would explain the strong cohesion of matter by the hypothetical external pressure of a hypothetical surrounding fluid. The Plumian professor of astronomy and physics in the University of Cambridge— James Challis—(a successor of Roger Cotes and of George B. Airy) has declared " the fundamental and only admissible idea of *force* is that of pressure, exerted either actively by the æther against the surfaces of the atoms, or as re-action of the atoms on the æther by resistance to that pressure."† And the professor of physics in the University of Edinburgh—Peter G. Tait—having also relegated the source of all material energy to the action of the highly attenuated matter diffused through space, thinks it probable that " force " has no existence, excepting as a convenient expression of a mere rate of transference of kinetic energy.‡

---

* " The existence of atoms is itself an hypothesis, and *not* a probable one. - - - All dogmatic assertion upon such points is to be regarded with distrust." (*A Manual of Inorganic Chemistry*, By CHARLES W. ELIOT and FRANK H. STORER. 2d edition, revised, New York, 1868: chap. XXV, p. 605.) And yet these negative dogmatists have not shown themselves capable even of *thinking* of so elementary a fact in their science as " polymerism " apart from the terms of the atomic conception. As Prof. J. CLERK MAXWELL has well observed, " The theory that bodies apparently homogeneous and continuous are so in reality, is in its extreme form a theory incapable of development. To explain the properties of any substance by this theory is impossible." (*Encyclopædia Britannica*. 9th ed., 1875: art. " Atom," vol. III, p. 38.) The objection to atomism sometimes urged—that since magnitude is admitted abstractly or mathematically to be infinitely divisible, therefore any finite particle of matter must also be *physically* so conceived, —betrays so strange a confusion of ideas as to merit no serious answer. Yet so illustrious a mathematician and philosopher as LEONARD EULER was guilty of this gross paralogism. (*Letters to a German Princess.* May 8, 1761: vol. II, let. 9.)

† *Principles of Mathematics and Physics.* By JAMES CHALLIS. 8vo. Cambridge, 1869: hyp. v, p. 358.

‡ In an evening lecture on " Force " delivered September 8, 1876, at Glasgow, (during the session of the British Association,) Prof. TAIT announced that " there is probably no such *thing* as force at all! That it is in fact merely a convenient expression for a certain *rate*." And referring to the corpuscular hypothesis of force, he thought " The most singular thing about it is that if it be true, it will probably lead us to regard all

It is very certain, however, that the hypothetical fluid of cohesion-pressure must be something entirely different in constitution from the luminiferous æther, since any mode of action which could be imagined for compressing together the elements of matter, would necessarily be incompatible with the transmission of solar radiation having the quality and properties of the vibrations actually observed. The fantastic scheme of Le Sage (in which cohesion is effected by the quaquaversal impacts of infinitesimal corpuscles flying swiftly in all directions, and whose various sizes determine the differing collocations of chemical unions,)—notwithstanding the approval of Prof. Tait,*—scarcely requires a "serious consideration."† Nor has any form of impact, of pressure, or of undulation, yet been proffered by the ingenuity of the kinematist—either at all adequate to the maintenance of the known conditions of matter, or indeed in itself at all conformable with any known modes of action.

The dynamist having searched in vain for any plausible co-ordination of the indisputable facts of cohesion with an intelligible mechanical agency, simply acquiesces in the result, and without invoking the unknown or the irrelevant, accepts this established property as ultimate and inexplicable.

---

kinds of energy as ultimately kinetic." (*Nature.* Sept. 21, 1876: vol. XIV, pp. 459, 463.)

The climax of kinematism however has been reached by the inventor and apostle of the "fourth state of matter,"—WILLIAM CROOKES, who is disposed to dismiss matter itself to the same limbo—of changing position: "From this point of view then matter is but *a mode of motion;* at the absolute zero of temperature the inter-molecular movement would stop, and although *something* [?] retaining the properties of inertia and weight would remain, matter—as we know it—would cease to exist." (*Nature.* June 17, 1880: vol. XXII, p. 153.) This seems to touch the sublime "secret" of GEORGE WILLIAM FREDERICK HEGEL, in which "nought is everything, and everything is nought."—*Seyn und Nichts ist dasselbe.*

* *Lectures on some recent advances in Physical Science.* By P. G. TAIT. 12mo. London, 1876: lect. XII, p. 299.

† "The hypothesis of Le Sage - - - is too grotesque to need serious consideration; and besides will render no account of the phenomenon of elasticity." Sir JOHN F. W. HERSCHEL, "On the Origin of Force." (*Fortnightly Review.* July 1, 1865: vol. I, p. 438. Also, *Familiar Lectures on Scientific Subjects.* 12mo. London, 1866: art. XII. pp. 466, 467.)

The Elasticity of Matter.—To select another illustration, the child throwing his rounded marble downward on a stone pavement finds te his surprise that it rebounds like his play-ball, and that he may, without stooping, catch it in his hand. What explanation is to be given of this direct and sudden reversal of movement? To this familiar quality of matter, we give the name of " elasticity." But by what more simple formula of mechanics shall we represent to ourselves this property *elasticity?* Kinematists abjuring alike objective " qualities " and subjective " abstractions " have been severely taxed in their attempts either to ignore the attribute or to reduce the phenomenon to some phase of molecular vibration.

Some few—consistent in their rejection of all quality from material substance—have boldly denied the existence of elasticity ; or rather have ventured to affirm that perfectly hard or inelastic atoms or masses would on collision alike rebound, precisely as though they were elastic.* This startling conclusion—apparently necessitated by their fundamental assumption " the conservation of motion "—requires for the intelligent student of rational mechanics, no discussion.

Other kinematists have resolutely endeavored to explain the resilience of colliding bodies as the special resultant of composite motions. One of the most earnest of these has been the Italian astronomer and physicist Angelo Secchi, who in an elaborate essay on the ultimate identity of all the physical forces as simple modes of motion, remarks: " It is evident that this ' elastic force' can be admitted only as a secondary force derived from another antecedent in an aggregate of atoms, that is in a compound molecule; and that it cannot be admitted as pertaining to the elementary atoms. Indeed, elasticity in its ordinary acceptation requires a void space within the molecule to allow the form to be changed by compression and afterward restored ; while on the contrary it is the necessary condition of real atoms—by conception—to be impenetrable [in-

---

* This thesis was maintained by JOHN HERAPATH, in his work on *Mathematical Physics.* 8vo. 2 vols. London, 1847: (vol. I, pp. 106–137.) As stated by NEWTON however, " Bodies which are either absolutely hard, or so soft as to be void of elasticity will not rebound from one another. Impenetrability makes them only stop. If two equal bodies meet directly *in vacuo,* they will by the laws of motion stop where they meet, and lose all their motion and remain in rest, unless they be elastic and receive new motion from their spring." (*Optics.* 2d edition, 1717: book III, Qu. 31.)

compressible] and not an aggregation of other solid particles. Hence they cannot be supposed to have any internal voids in which their parts could be contracted or dilated. - - - We believe we are able to show that it is by no means a necessary position to accept this elastic property as a primitive force, but that the apparent repulsion of these atoms and their rebound originates solely from their proper motion, and for this it is sufficient simply to suppose them to be *in rotation*."* He then proceeds to develop his theory of mechanical elasticity from the co-operation of the projectile motion of bodies with the internal rotations of their constituent molecules; citing in support of his assumption, the mathematical researches of Poinsot.† In this important foundation of his system however, the zealous physicist has built upon an entirely mistaken apprehension of true mechanical principles, and hence of course upon a strange misapprehension of the actual discussion by Poinsot. This eminent mathematician who has investigated so thoroughly the theory of rotatory movements has shown that in the collision of inelastic bodies, endowed with rotation, the velocity of deflection may in special cases exceed the velocity of incidence, in other special cases may be just equal to it, and lastly in general will fall short of it, being in many cases entirely destroyed. Thus a rotating inelastic body has two points between the center of inertia and that of percussion, which on impact with a fixed resistance in the line of their direction will produce a resilience of higher velocity than that of collision,—of course by the conversion and absorption of so much of the rotary motion. There are other two points from the direction of whose impact will result a velocity just equal to that of the original motion of the body;—in the one case absorbing one-third of the rotary motion, in the other case absorbing two-thirds of it. If the impact be in the line of the center of inertia, the whole of the translatory motion is arrested without affecting the rotary motion. [In the case of two equal inelastic spheres rotating with equal and opposite velocities on parallel transverse axes and meeting at a point on their equators, the bodies

---

* *L'Unitá delle Forze Fisiche;* Saggio de filosofia naturale. Del P. ANGELO SECCHI. 12mo. Rome, 1864: chap. I, sect. 6, pp. 36, 37.

† Father SECCHI's reference in a foot-note is to "*Questions dynamiques sur la percussion des corps:* pag. 21 e 29, dell' edizione a parte, ed anche il Giornale di Liouville, - - - a pag. 36."

would lose entirely their travelling motion, still retaining their rotations. So also if their axes were equally inclined so as to bring the points of impact on corresponding circles of latitude; the limiting case of which would be an impact on their poles of motion in the line of their common axes of rotation.] Lastly if a rotating inelastic body should meet a fixed resistance in the line of the center of percussion, not only the translatory—but the rotary velocity as well—would be entirely destroyed.* If we conceive a molecule as consisting of a congeries of atoms having an orbital revolution (analogous to a solar system), a very similar analysis will apply to the cases of collision.

It is very clear then that the device of storing up additional kinetic energy in the form of internal rotation (or revolution) fails utterly to reproduce the phenomena of motion exhibited by elasticity. The resulting effects cannot be admitted as at all analogous; since the internal kinetic energy assumed is either wholly or largely absorbed and exhausted by a single collision, and a second impact can never reproduce the effects of a first one; while *elastic* force remains perpetual and unimpaired by constant action.

Elasticity accordingly, equally with cohesion, is a fact of nature, a property of matter, which can neither be interpreted by any form of motion, nor resolved into any mechanical concept.† Those therefore who would formulate the elements of things devoid of

---

* LOUIS POINSOT. The latter portion of a series of mathematical discussions under the general title—*Questions dynamiques sur la Percussion des Corps;* published in Liouville's *Journal de Mathematiques* for 1857: vol. II, pp. 281-308.

† "Elasticity without an action *e distanti*—even between the adjoining particles— is inconceivable. What is meant by elasticity? Surely such a constitution of the assemblage of particles as makes them recede from each other." Prof. JOHN ROBISON. (*A System of Mechanical Philosophy.* 8vo. 4 vols. Edinburgh, 1882: vol. III, p. 139.)
"An alteration of the form of a solid body is called a *strain.* In solid bodies strain is accompanied with an internal force or *stress;* those bodies in which the stress depends simply on the strain are called 'elastic,' and the property of exerting stress when strained is called elasticity. - - - The general fact that strains or changes of configuration are accompanied by stresses or internal forces, and that thereby energy is stored up in the system so strained, remains an ultimate fact which has not yet been explained as the result of any more fundamental principle." Prof. J. CLERK MAXWELL. (*Matter and Motion.* 1876: chap. V, arts. 83, 84; pp. 70, 71.

quality, have on their own declaration no right to the use of either term in considering any physical problem.

Were the examination to stop here, it might appear that the only difference between the dynamist and the kinematist is that the former—failing to find any satisfactory explanation of certain habitudes of matter, despairs of deeper insight and accordingly seeking no further, accepts the conclusion that these are insoluble; while the kinematist more hopeful, has an abiding faith that the same processes which have so successfully (or at least so largely) deciphered the riddles of light, of heat, of gaseous constitution, may be expected in time to resolve these other enigmas though they be not yet expounded. It is necessary therefore to go back still further and examine the character of this induction, by a cursory review of the postulates of the mechanical theory of light, of heat, and of the kinetics of discrete molecules.

---

2. *The Theory of Molecular Kinetics.*

In the last century both light and heat were generally regarded as material emanations; the former, of radiant corpuscles, the latter, of a peculiarly rare and penetrating fluid. Earlier kinetic hypotheses of these so-called "imponderables"—however ingenious—were not supported by a sufficient induction from observed facts to justly entitle them to unqualified acceptance. And the doubts and difficulties suggested by the speculations of Newton were a striking illustration of his recognized sagacity; notwithstanding the occasional censures of modern popular lecturers, trumpeting their own superior wisdom.

The Vibratory Theory of Heat.—The fluid or "caloric" theory of heat (though often questioned or opposed) was first decisively overthrown at the close of the century by Benjamin Thompson, an expatriated American, better known as Count Rumford, whose experiments unescapably demonstrated the resolution of heat into an intestine motion, by the fact of its interminable generation in friction through the agency of continued motion.* It was not how-

---

* *Phil. Trans. Roy. Soc.* 1798: vol. LXXXIII, pp. 80–102. This admirable memoir read before the Royal Society of London, January 25, 1798, (in which RUMFORD—from the fact " that the source of heat generated

ever until about the middle of the present century that the conception attained a scientific definiteness and currency through the accurate determination of the kinetic or dynamic value of heat.

The Undulatory Theory of Light.—Nearly simultaneously with the work of Rumford in the field of heat, the investigations of Dr. Thomas Young, at the beginning of this century, relative especially to the interference of two luminous rays in particular cases, in like manner overthrew the theory of corpuscular emission in the field of light, by demonstrating a destruction or obliteration—quite intelligible as a conflict of wave motion, but entirely inadmissable and unthinkable as a mutual extermination of conflicting substance.* Through the refined labors of Young,—admirably assisted and re-enforced by the able efforts of his skillful and worthy rival Fresnel,—the varied and complex phenomena of dioptrics were more and more fully brought under the dominion of a rational kinetics. And thus it resulted that the new doctrine of insensible motion obtained from the scientific world a much more rapid and general acceptance in its application to light than in its application to heat. So that it was not unusual some forty or fifty

---

by friction in these experiments appeared evidently to be inexhaustible," argued that this product " cannot possibly be a material substance : ") may be said to furnish the first rough approximation to the mechanical equivalent of heat. The author estimated the heat produced by a one-horse power as equivalent to that obtained from the burning of nine wax candles, each three-quarters of an inch in diameter ; or to the combustion of a little more than one-third of a pound of wax in two and a half hours. This essay also presents the first suggestion of the mechanical correlation of animal power with heat motion.

Dr. YOUNG held that Rumford's experiments " appear to afford an unanswerable confutation of the whole of this doctrine :—[that of a ' caloric ' fluid.] - - - If heat is not a substance, it must be a quality ; and this quality can only be motion." (*Lectures on Natural Philosophy.* 1807 : lect. 52 : vol. I, pp. 653, 654.)

" The hypothesis of caloric " says Prof. J. CLERK MAXWELL " or the theory that heat is a kind of matter is rendered untenable—first by the proof given by Rumford that heat can be *generated* at the expense of mechanical work ; and secondly by the measurements of Hirn, which show that when heat does work in an engine, a portion of the heat *disappears.*" (*Theory of Heat.* 1872 : chap. VIII, p. 147.)

* "*Phil. Trans. Roy. Soc.* A memoir read July 1, 1802 : vol. XCII. p. 387 ; and one read November 24, 1803 : vol. XCIV. pp. 1–16.

years ago, to find our college professors zealously inculcating the undulatory theory of light, while still maintaining the hypothesis of a "caloric" for heat.

William Herschel had found, at the beginning of the century, that the solar spectrum, as produced by an ordinary glass prism, manifested a heating power slight at the violet end, but gradually increasing to the red end, and extending a considerable distance beyond the less refrangible limit of visible rays, near which limit the maximum effect was reached.[*]

Johann Wilhelm Ritter, of Jena, a year later found that the chemical action of the solar spectrum, as exhibited in the darkening of silver chloride, increased toward the violet extremity, attaining a maximum beyond the most refrangible limit of luminous dispersion.[†]   Hence, it came to be generally believed that the solar rays comprise three essentially distinct and independent kinds of energy, representing three different forms of wave-motion.   This appeared the more probable from the entirely dissimilar orders of effect observed (as interpreted by the impressions of our senses), in calorific energy, in optical luminosity, and in chemical agency.

It was shown however by Alexandre Edmond Becquerel that the so-called chemical rays were not distinguishable by their refrangibility, and that photographic effects could be obtained with suitable re-agents from any region of the spectrum.[‡]   And finally, by the researches of Dr. John W. Draper, it was fully established that Herschel's results depended on the great distortion (as well as unequal absorption) inseparable from every prismatic or refractive spectrum, and that Ritter's results depended on a very limited and insufficient induction.   And thus it has slowly come be recognized that in every normal spectrum, freed from distortion or selective absorption, (and equally freed from selective generalization), the three classes of effects, thermal, photic, and actinic, are equably or proportionally distributed; that as these several activities are equally amenable to polarization, to interference, and to spectral irradiation and absorption, there is in fact but a single form of

---

[*] *Phil. Trans. Roy. Soc.*   1800: vol. xc, pp. 291, 318, 439, 440.

[†] Gilbert's *Annalen der Physik.*   1801: vol. vii, p. 527.   Nicholson's *Journal of Natural Philosophy*, [etc.]   August, 1803: vol. v, p. 255.

[‡] *Annales de Chemie et de Physique.*   April, 1849: vol. xxv, pp. 447–474.

ætherial undulation, the differences of whose manifestations depend entirely upon the nature of the body, organic or inorganic, on which it falls.*

Molecular Thermo-dynamics.—Passing from the wave theory of radiation to the related subject of the internal re-actions of bodies, the application of thermo-kinetics to the facts of temperature has taught us that the molecules of all bodies are in a state of very rapid though minute movement, and that this movement, while being constantly transferred and expended, (and thus ever tending to the absolute zero,) is yet incessantly maintained in varying quantity by repeated re-enforcements from natural and artificial sources of heat, and by mutual interchanges. In the case of solid bodies, whose constituent molecules are held together by what we must call (in default of any names as yet invented by the kinematist) the qualities of *cohesion* and *adhesion*,—their mutual contact being resisted and prevented by what we must for the present call a repellant quality, the temperature motion is in the nature of an oscillation or rather irregular reverberation within the narrow limits of opposite resistances, by which the relative mean position of the particles and the stability of the body are preserved. By the term "cohesion" is designated simply the observed fact of a resistance to divellent or tensile stress; by the term "adhesion" is designated the observed fact of resistance to torsional or shearing stress.

When the energy of the molecular movements is increased until the modulus of "adhesion" is equalled, the point of melting is reached, and the molecules instead of being restored to their antecedent positions are carried irregularly from the influence of neighbor to neighbor, and thus become fluent by being deflected among each other in all possible directions. In this "liquid" condition of

---

Am. Jour. Sci. Jan. and Feb., 1873: vol. v, pp. 25-38, and 91-98. Dr. DRAPER's results (so far as the refrangibility of radiant heat is concerned) have recently been confirmed by the refined investigations of Prof. S. P. LANGLEY, by means of his "actinic balance." (*Proceed. Am. Acad.* Jan., 1881: vol. XVI, p. 342; *Am. Jour. Sci.* March, 1881: vol. XXI, p. 187; *Nature.* Oct. 12, 1882: vol. XXVI, p. 588.)

"A ray of specified wave-length and specified plane of polarization, cannot be a combination of several different things, such as a light-ray, a heat-ray, and an actinic ray. It must be one and the same thing, which has luminous, thermal, and actinic effects." J. CLERK MAXWELL. (*Theory of Heat.* 1872: chap. XVI, p. 218.)

the mass, adjacent molecules although entirely freed from the adhesion which constitutes rigidity, yet (as has been shown by Joseph Henry) preserve their mutual cohesion practically unimpaired : * and hence devious as may be their wanderings, no portion of their excursions can be called a free path.

If the rapidity of the mean internal motion be still further accelerated until the momentum of the molecules is equal to their modulus of " cohesion," the temperature of evaporation is reached, and the molecules are impelled from their restraining bonds into a free flight, which so long as undisturbed, continues (by the first law of motion) in an indefinite straight path in the direction of impulse. The strength of these two bonds—*adhesion* and *cohesion*—differing very widely in different substances, is thus measured by the amount of kinetic energy absorbed in overcoming them,—the so-called "latent heat" of fusion and of evaporation. In the case of ice, the strength of the molecular adhesion is considerably less than the sixth part of that of the cohesion.

We thus perceive how the most solid bodies—even at low temperatures—are exposed to surface evaporation without the opportunity of passing through the liquid state; since external molecules from the great irregularity of their short oscillations, must occasionally by the composition of motions from concurrent or immediately successive shocks, acquire a velocity transcending the bonds of cohesion, and thus escape entirely from the mass.

We accordingly learn by the kinetic theory of gases that the discrete or isolated molecules are flying about in all directions in straight lines until by encounters with other molecules (or with material barriers) their course is deflected. During the brief period of encounter (the disturbance of mutual encroachment), the trajectory becomes a minute hyperbola. From the infinite variety of possible impacts we also learn that each molecule must necessarily be constantly changing within very wide limits the direction, the velocity, and the length of its free excursions;—even when a perfect equilibrium of temperature imports that the mean kinetic energy of the entire system is constant and uniform.

It is important for us to bear in mind that this wondrous theater of continual intestine commotion does not present an example of a

---

*Proceed. Am. Phil. Soc. April 5, & May 17, 1844: vol. IV, pp. 56, 57; and 84, 85.

mechanical " perpetual motion :" the average velocity of any appreciable volume of gaseous molecules subsists only so long as no work is effected. By whatever amount any considerable number of flying particles impart motion to slower groups, or to a solid mass, by this amount do they reduce their own speed, and thus represent a diminished temperature. By whatever amount they receive any average increase of velocity from repeated impacts or from compression within a contracted inclosure, by this amount do they represent an elevation of temperature, at the expense of the bodies from which such additional energy is derived.

The Kinetic interpretation of the Laws of Gases.—It has been shown by Clausius that the number of collisions of a molecule in a given time is proportional to the mean velocity of all the molecules, to their number in a given volume, and to the square of the distance between the centers of two molecules when at nearest approach,* or at what has been called their dynamic contact. By the mathematical investigations of Krönig, Clausius, Loschmidt, and Maxwell, the foundations of a molecular physics have been successfully established ; and the laws of gaseous action thus far experimentally ascertained, have been found to result deductively as the necessary consequences of the kinetic theory.

Thus the kinetic energy of any volume of molecules (which represents the temperature of the gas) being the product of molecular weight or mass by the mean square of the velocity, it follows that the relative rates of *effusion* and *diffusion* must both be inversely as the square roots of the masses,—that is of the gaseous densities ;— the law of Graham.

It also follows that in the case of diffusion, by reason of the proportional retardations due to more numerous collisions from the presence of other gas, the coefficient must be lower than in the case of effusion.

In any mixture of gases, since from the mutual encounters of molecules of different mass, the average kinetic energy will be the same for all masses, or the mean squares of the velocities will be inversely as the respective masses, it follows that in different in-

---

* " It is to Clausius that we owe the first definite conception of the free path of a molecule and of the mean distance travelled by a molecule between successive encounters." JAMES CLERK MAXWELL. (*Encyclopæd. Brit.* 1875: vol. III, p. 41.)

closures at the same temperature (*i. e.*, the same energy)—for equal pressures there must be the same number of impacts on any given area, or in other words that the same volume must contain the same number of molecules whether light or heavy :—the law of Avogadro and of Ampère.

And conversely, under the same conditions of pressure (or surface impacts) and of temperature (or kinetic energy), the number of molecules being the same, and the masses of the molecules being the only variable,—the densities of different gases must be proportional to their molecular weights or the masses of their individual molecules :—the law of Gay-Lussac.

Since the sum of the moving forces or the expanding power of the molecular excursions is directly proportional to their kinetic energy, it follows that the volume of a true gas under uniform pressure must be proportional to this energy, that is to the absolute temperature :—the law of Charles and of Dalton.

Since the same kinetic energy of the molecules must exert the same impulse, or the temperatures being constant, they must have a definite mean momentum, and each molecule must execute on an average the same number of impacts with the same energy, it follows that the pressure is directly proportional to the number of molecules ; or in other words that the volume of a true gas at any given temperature is inversely proportional to the pressure :—the law of Boyle and Mariotte. Or combining the last two laws, the volume of a gas multiplied by its pressure is directly proportional to the square of the mean molecular velocity, or the absolute temperature. The slight departure from the law of Boyle and Mariotte observed in most gases when compressed (the internal pressure being somewhat in defect,) indicates a small range of attraction between the molecules when brought close together.*

In addition to the external kinetic energy of the molecule due to its velocity of translation, it possesses an internal kinetic energy due to oscillation or rotation of its parts (its constituent atoms) ; and this internal energy according to Clausius—tends to a constant ratio with the external energy. The amount of energy received or

---

* " In the case of carbonic acid and other gases which are easily liquified, this deviation is very great. In all cases, however, except that of hydrogen the pressure is less than that given by Boyle's law, showing that the *virial* is on the whole due to *attractive* forces between the molecules." JAMES CLERK MAXWELL. (*Encyclopœd. Brit.* 1875 : vol. III, p. 39.)

expended by a gas in gaining or losing one degree of temperature (which is known as its " specific heat ") is proportional to this constant ratio ; and hence the specific heat of a gas is inversely proportional to the molecular mass ;—that is to say, to the specific gravity of the gas :—the law of Dulong and Petit.

As the entire kinetic energy—molecular and atomic, is necessarily tending constantly to a dynamic equilibrium both with regard to any connected volume constituting a system, and with regard to any kinetic energy of the circumambient æther as well, there is a continual and mutual transfer of such energy :—the theory of exchanges announced by Prevost.

Mean Length of Molecular Excursions.—By a neat application of the calculus of probabilities, Clausius has determined that of the whole number of free molecular excursions in a given time, (in any large inclosure,) those having less than the mean length will be 0.6321 ; or nearly double the number of those having the mean length or exceeding it. He supposes that under ordinary conditions, the mean length of a free excursion of our air molecules is about sixty times the mean distance between them.

Maxwell has pointed out that three phenomena dependent on the length of the free excursions of gaseous molecules, furnish functions from which the mean length of such paths may be estimated ; first, the rate of gaseous diffusion (or the bodily transfer of matter); second, the rate of diffusion of their momentum, or the degree of gaseous " viscosity " (dependent on the transfer and equalization of motion); and third, the diffusion of their kinetic energy or temperature, (the conduction of heat). In our atmosphere, under ordinary conditions (30 inches and 60° F.) the mean length of the molecular path is thus estimated at about the $1 \div 300,000$ of an inch, or about one-sixth of a wave-length of yellow light.

The average molecular velocity of oxygen has been estimated at 1640 feet per second ;* and of nitrogen (which constitutes about three-fourths of our atmosphere) at 1754 feet per second ; while hydrogen molecules having but one-sixteenth the weight or mass of those of oxygen, would have under the same conditions, four times their average velocity, or 6560 feet per second. And thus while a

---

* A velocity sufficient to carry the molecule vertically about eight miles high, if subjected to no resistance excepting gravitation.

molecule of oxygen would undergo about seven thousand million collisions in one second, a molecule of hydrogen among its fellows would undergo about seventeen thousand million collisions per second. It must be observed that the more violent the collisions of the molecules, the less is their tendency toward the cohesion of the liquid, or the adhesion of the solid form.

Probable Size of Molecules.—From various considerations it has been independently estimated by Joseph Loschmidt (1865), by G. Johnstone Stoney (1868), by William Thomson (1870), and by J. Clerk Maxwell (1873), that the effective size of the molecule is probably not smaller than the thousand-millionth of an inch, nor larger than three or four times this dimension; which is about the twenty-thousandth of a medium wave-length of light. Small as this dimension is, we may reflect that by what may be called the second power of our best microscopes, it would be easily visible,— supposing that light-waves were capable of optical efficiency at this degree of subdivision and amplification.

These estimates of molecular distances and magnitudes are of course but rough approximations; but they indicate at least the order of magnitude of very real things and agencies; and accepting them as probable, we may " compare small things with great " by saying that were the planet Venus brought within a distance from our Earth about one and a half times that of the Moon, this might represent the relative mean distance of two molecules of our atmos-phere; at which separation (about fifty times their own diameters), they would probably count less than twenty million to the inch. In like manner the distance of Venus from our Earth at conjunction (as during the approaching transit of next Wednesday) would be relatively comparable to the length of a mean excursion of the molecules;—some 3,000 times their diameter. While a few of their longest free excursions would be comparable to the flight of the the same planet if carried from the Earth to beyond the orbit of Neptune.

The Relation of Molecular and Atomic Motions.—Returning again from this survey of molecular kinetics to the undulatory theory of light and heat, we may say that the true physical relation of radiation to conduction was first disclosed by the analytic spectrum,— that marvellous instrumentality which physics has presented to her

daughter chemistry, as the most subtile and delicate of all her re-
agents. From this method of observation we have learned that
each of the elements when its molecules are shocked, rings out its
own peculiar series of oscillations, as if by specially adjusted tuning-
forks, each responsive only to the groupings of its own established
periodicities. Newton first taught us that definite refrangibility in
the spectrum signifies simply definite periodicity; and he also computed the data which determine the values of these periodicities.*

The known wave-lengths of different colored light divided by
their known velocity of propagation, give us the inconceivable
rapidity of from 390 to 750 billions per second,† as the number of
atomic impulses transmitted by the æther and appreciated by the
eye. Although this compass is somewhat less than an "octave,"
the entire range of the visible and invisible spectrum comprises
more than three octaves. This extraordinary rate of vibration, no
less than its remrakable uniformity, sufficiently establishes the fact
that the motions of the *molecule* ceaselessly varying in velocity, and
wholly irregular in length and frequency of excursion, take no part
whatever in producing ætherial undulations. It is only to the constituent parts or ultimate *atoms* of the flying molecule that the rhyth-

---

* NEWTON's *Optics.* 1704: book II, part I, obs. 6. When shortly after his
election to the Royal Society, Newton in a letter to the Secretary—Henry
Øldenburg, (dated January 18, 1672,) proposed to offer a communication to
that Society respecting his optical analysis, he spoke of it as "being the
oddest if not the most considerable detection which hath hitherto been made
in the operations of nature." (BIRCH's *History of the Royal Society.* 1757:
vol. III, p. 5.) Although a century and a quarter elapsed before the spectral lines were first detected by W. H. WOLLASTON, (*Phil. Trans. Roy.
Soc.* June 24, 1802: vol. XCII, p. 365;) Newton was fully aware of the
necessity of employing a very small hole or luminous image for obtaining
a pure spectrum, and he pointed out that a narrow slit is still better; "for
if this hole be an inch or two long, and but a tenth or a twentieth part of
an inch broad, or narrower, the light of the image will be as simple as before, or simpler, and the image will become much broader." (*Optics:*
book I, prop. IV.) For delicate observations Newton appears to have been
compelled to rely on the services of an assistant; and thus he missed the
consummation of his "oddest and most considerable detection of nature's
operations"—the spectroscope.

† A *billion* (as is sufficiently indicated by the term itself) is the "second
power of a million;" not (as is commonly taught in school-book numera-
tion) the *third* power of a thousand, or the *second* power of an impossible
number;—a surd

mic motions generating radiant light and heat must be referred
We may thus picture to ourselves the monochromatic lines of the
spectrum as exhibiting a second order of occult or insensible kinetics,
in quality and range as different from and as much below the
kinetics of the molecule, as this differs from and is below the kinetics
of tangible masses.

The Origin of Atomic Motions.—With regard to the nature and
origin of the atomic motions, it appears tolerably clear that they
are primarily derived from the shocks of the molecules or systems
of which they are the components ; and that there is at every
molecular collision a transfer or exchange of energy tending to
equalize the internal momentum of pulsation with the external
momentum of translation.   The *primum mobile* is therefore the
falling together of molecules under the influence either of gravitation, or of chemical affinity.   While it is difficult to realize the
precise manner in which molecular and atomic motions are re-dis-
tributed during the brief instants of impact, it appears in the highest degree probable that the atoms describe *elliptical orbits*, which
may become circular, but never rectilinear.   Were the atomic
motions mere oscillations, it would appear unavoidable that under
the stress of special impacts, some of them must occasionally be
detached,—as in the case of molecular evaporation.   But the *ultimate* molecule is unchangeable and "indivisible : "—held together
in bonds incomparably stronger than those of hardest steel.   And
the loss of an atom may be regarded as an impossible catastrophe. ·
Moreover, from the utter irregularity of direction in molecular
encounters, obliquity of impact on the rapidly changing atoms,
would appear almost a necessity : and hence would result as necessarily—elliptical paths of excursion.

In this constant play of atoms derived from repeated collisions,
we must believe that these atoms are whirled in ever varying *rotations*—simultaneously with their orbital revolutions; but as these
double motions form but parts of their common fund of kinetic
energy, it is not probable that any special phenomena will ever distinctly reveal such axial motions ;—unless indeed it be hereafter
shown that *polarity* is the resultant of concerted directions of rota-
tional or orbital axes, or of both.

The Amplitude of Atomic Orbits.—Of the actual or relative
diameters of these orbits we are as ignorant as we are of the sizes

of the atoms themselves. We may assume the amplitudes of the ætherial waves at their origin, to be a faithful transcript of those of the atomic excursions which generate them : and we must conclude the latter to be—even in the velocities of the highest incandescence, extremely small fractions of the length of the resulting waves. For although the amplitude of the atomic orbit represents but the square root of the brillancy, we may reflect that this latter form of energy presents an enormous range of variation. The light from Sirius—for example, supposing it to be in time twenty years in reaching us,—has but 1 ÷ 1,315,000 part of the amplitude of terrestrial sun-light; the amplitude being inversely as the distance travelled.* And there are among the visible stars doubtless some a thousand times more distant yet than Sirius.

According to the estimates of Wollaston, and of the younger Herschel, lights may vary in brilliancy forty thousand million times, representing a difference of amplitude of two hundred thousand times. To suggest some approximate idea of the form of such ætherial waves, we may liken them to earthquake waves transmitted across the surface of the ocean at the rate of six miles in a minute, which, while leaving on the tide-gage their registered amplitude of 15 inches, have for their length 150 miles : being accurately measurable waves presenting the ratio of one inch to ten miles.†

---

*As the bright sun Sirius is considerably larger that our sun, and probably intrinsically brighter as well, the figure 1,315,000 (representing its distance in units of sun-distance) would be somewhat reduced as a measure of relative wave-amplitude. If the intrinsic splendor of the two suns be the same, the distant one has about 64 times the surface, or eight times the diameter of our own. The probability of greater density in the former—from greater mass,—is offset by the probability of correspondingly higher temperature. Hence assuming the mean densities to be nearly the same, the gravitative pressure of equal gaseous masses on the photosphere of Sirius, would probably be in the neighborhood of eight times that upon our sun, or some 200 times that upon the surface of our earth.

† The earthquake which destroyed the city of Simoda, in Japan, in December, 1854, generated such a system of waves, which crossing the Pacific Ocean, over a distance of 4,500 miles, in the time of 12 hours and 36 minutes, left their record on the tide-gages of the Coast Survey, at San Francisco, as having a maximum amplitude of 18 inches. The height of the ocean wave at its origin was, of course, much greater than this. (*Smithsonian Report* for 1874: pp. 216, 217.—A Lecture " On Tides," by Prof. J. E. HILGARD, (at present Supt. of Coast Survey,) delivered before

Smallness of Atoms.—The extreme minuteness of the atoms is evidenced not alone by the necessary limitations of their orbital excursions under ordinary conditions, and by their inconceivable rapidity of oscillation, but even still more strikingly by the vast number of molecules which may be chemically combined and compacted within the volume of an elementary molecule,—still observing the law of Avogadro.

From such considerations we may infer that the dimensions of the ultimate atoms are probably as much below that of the composite molecule, as this is beneath a visible magnitude: or in other words, that were the molecule an object to be seen, the highest power of our best microscopes would utterly fail to detect its constituent atoms.

The Constancy of the Atomic Periods.—We have learned from the fixity of the spectral lines (whether luminous or dark) that what may be called the tones or pitches of these resonant particles are very accurately maintained through an enormous range of amplitude; that is, that the respective periods of the atomic orbits (infinitesimally brief as they appear to our slow-moving thoughts) are quite unaffected by their radii, or their rates of velocity. The evidence of these uniformities of period in descending temperatures is found in the stability of gaseous absorption lines under all degrees of cold producible; these lines remaining dark when taking up the motion of the incandescent back-ground, simply because the amplitude of the oscillation is not sufficient on the whole to impress our sense of vision. And although at very high temperatures both the number and the distinctness of the spectral lines may be considerably affected, their position (as long as visible) is not at all disturbed. That new lines should appear at increasing temperatures is not surprising, since in every case a certain width of atomic play is required to affect the eye. But that under such circumstances pre-existing lines should disappear,—as has been established by the researches of Dr. J. Plücker and Dr. J. W. Hittorf,*—so

the American Institute, Jan. 27, 1871.) It is instructive to reflect that a wave line of this order (representing an ætherial undulation)—executed by the most skillful draftsman or engraver, on any scale whatever, or with any microscopic appliances, could not be distinguished by any process of direct instrumental measurement or verification from a perfectly straight line.

Phil. Trans. Roy. Soc. Memoir read March 3, 1864: vol. CLV, pp. 1–29.

as to produce an entirely different spectrum, is not so easily explained. The suggestion of a disruption or disassociation of the atomic flight by centrifugal force is negatived by the fact of perfect restoration of the orbit under uniform conditions. Nor does the hypothesis of a resolution of the elementary molecules into still more elementary types, (which seems to have gained some favor,) render the physical conception of the phenomena in any respect more simple. In particular cases a precise equalization of the energies of emission, and of absorption in surrounding heated gas, might effect a neutralization and complete obliteration of one or more of the lines. And it is conceivable that a certain increase of amplitude in the aetherial wave may (as in the case of its length) cease to be recognized by the optic nerves.

The law of Atomic Orbits.—The conception being thus presented to us—of a particle moving in an elliptical or circular orbit of constant period, irrespective of the length of the radius-vector, or of the velocity, (a condition so wholly unlike the gravitative orbits of planets, observing the laws of Kepler,) what is the dynamic interpretation of such a system? This problem has been anticipated by the genius of Newton, who in his Mathematical Principles of Natural Philosophy has demonstrated the *imaginary* case,—" if the periodic times are equal, (and the velocities therefore as the radii,) the *centripetal* forces will also be as the radii." * A law of force *increasing* directly with the distance (as in the extension of an india-rubber, or of a helical steel wire spring,) is undoubtedly a very remarkable one: but whatever its range of action, it will manifestly within that range, secure the atom from all possibility of detachment.

From the perfect uniformity both of chemical and of spectroscopic indications, whether in the smallest or the largest mass of molecules,—from whatever source obtained, we are forced to conclude that the molecules of any simple gas are absolutely similar. Whether we analyze a drop of petroleum or distill an insect or a

---

* *Newton's Principia.* 1687: book I, sect. II, prop. 4, corol. 3. A very beautiful illustration of this orbit is presented by the conical pendulum, when the length of the suspension is very great relatively to the ranges of excursion of the ball, so that an ellipse or different circular orbits shall lie sensibly in the same plane. Another similar example is furnished by the orbits of the balls of a parabolic "governor."

plant, whether we decompose water from the Indian ocean or from Arctic snow-flake, whether we inspect with curious eye the light from sun, or star, or from remotest nebulæ at opposite confines of the heavens, we find in the spectrum of hydrogen the same fixed lines; —assuring us that these are truly the reverberations of periods incessantly repeated alike in every molecule of this particular element.* Taking this—the lightest of all known molecules, (Prout's fundamental unit of chemical equivalency,) we have within the single molecule the widely separated lines of four distinct periodicities, or atomic orbits :—the red line " C " (α) of 456 billion revolutions per second,—the greenish blue line " F " (β) of 615 billion revolutions,—the blue line near " G " (γ) of 689 billion revolutions, and the violet line " h " (δ) of 729 billion revolutions. As no form of either reciprocating or orbital movement could possibly be maintained without an equal and opposite re-action, there must necessarily exist here *at least* eight independent atoms. But it seems wholly improbable that each of these systems of motion should comprise but a single couple of atoms : and it is still more improbable that either these periods, or even the numerous additional ones disclosed in the secondary spectrum of hydrogen, represent all the atomic motions within its molecule, in view of the necessary imperfection of the optical record, and the fact that this embraces less than the third, and possibly not more than one-fourth of the whole actinic spectrum.

Physical Complexity of the Molecule.—We are therefore justified in believing that the most elementary of chemical molecules is a wonderfully complex system, comprising an unknown number of constituent units, held together by dynamic bonds whose nature we can neither guess nor conceive ; and thus the atom of Newton and of Dalton has been carried downward far beyond the horizon of action at which they had imagined it—probably even to a second order of diminished magnitude.

The relations between the translatory motion of the integral gase-

---

* "The same kind of molecule—say that of hydrogen—has the same set of periods of vibration,—whether we procure the hydrogen from water, from coal, or from meteoric iron ; and light having the same set of periods of vibration comes to us from the Sun, from Sirius, and from Arcturus." J. CLERK MAXWELL. (*Encyclopæd. Brit.* 1875: art. "Atom," vol. III, p. 48.)

ous molecule and the internal revolutions about its center of inertia present a new difficulty of conception as to the constitution and action of the ætherial medium. For while the molecule (a mere cluster of atoms) is supposed to be flying freely about without obstruction or retardation, (in order to fulfil the laws of Charles, and of Boyle and Mariotte,) the individual atoms themselves experience a very considerable resistance to their revolutions ;—the precise measure of which resistance is the kinetic energy absorbed and expended by ætherial undulations. And so it results conversely, that if the motion of the æther-waves exceeds that of the molecular atoms exposed to their action, the difference of momentum is taken up by the latter, and through exchanges at molecular encounters is equalized by corresponding increments of velocity in the molecules themselves. Such is the process in all terrestrial heating by solar radiation. And this brings directly to view one important distinction between heat and light,—to wit, that while both are *radiated* in precisely the same manner, " conduction " has no existence in optical action. The only approach to any such effect in light, is found in the obscure and puzzling phenomena of fluorescence and phosphorescence, and of animal luminosity. In the case of *heat* we may have a transfer by radiation—always the result of atomic motion, by conduction—always the result of molecular motion, or by convection—always the result of mass motion.

During the time of a mean free excursion of gaseous molecules at the temperature of incandescence, the atomic periods would permit from ten to twenty thousand revolutions. But from the great amount of energy absorbed by the æther it does not appear probable that any considerable portion of such orbital movement can continue throughout the interval of a mean free path. If then it be true that in a majority of the molecular excursions the whole internal atomic motion is absorbed and destroyed, to be renewed again only by the succeeding collisions, there is a constant drain upon the molecular momentum ; a condition which must alike prevail, however low may be the temperature of the gas. While there is thus a constant tendency to equalization of the orbital atomic momentum and the rectilinear molecular momentum, the total kinetic energy of the former has been estimated at not more than from two-thirds to three-fourths of the kinetic energy of the latter.

It is in the gaseous spectrum alone—that is, in the atomic motions of discrete molecules, that perfect uniformity of period, or as we may call it, perfect purity of optical tone is to be observed. With any considerable compression of a gas, that is, with any great crowding together of the molecules and shortening of their mean free excursions, whereby the increased frequency of collision is constantly disturbing the atomic orbits before their motions can be fully absorbed by the æther, there will result a momentary hastening or retarding of the normal periods, giving to the spectral lines an increased breadth or wider range of refrangibility. And when the condensation reaches that of the "liquid" or "solid" condition, preventing all free excursion, the incessant agitation of the atoms results in a universal clang or optical "noise," in which all uniformity of period seems lost, and perturbations of all possible degrees present us with the discord and confusion of a perfectly continuous spectrum.*

The Chemist has taught us that in numerous cases the normal molecule is divided into sub-molecules. Thus the relations of the compounds of arsenic, as well as of those of phosphorus, indicate the composition by half molecules of these elements; the ratios of the so-called "sesqui-salts" point to the same result; the allotropic condition of oxygen—called ozone—is formulated as having the equivalency of one and a half molecules; one molecule of aqueous vapor (and therefore of water) consists of one molecule of hydrogen and a half molecule of oxygen; two molecules of ammonia are resolved into three equal molecules of hydrogen and one of nitrogen; and a single molecule of hydrogen united with a single one of chlorine will form two molecules of hydrochloric acid,—each containing an equal division of the two constituents. Although this dichotomy of the molecule is suggestive of binary systems in some way specially linked together and at the same time susceptible of various re-arrangements, yet the fact remains that these divided molecules are still extremely complex physical systems,—apparently identical in constitution and construction, and therefore undistinguishable from each other. The Chemist however adhering too literally to the phrase of Dalton, has neglected the obvious import

---

*J. CLERK MAXWELL has felicitously compared the atomic oscillations producing a continuous spectrum, to the clang of a bell "on which innumerable hammers are continually plying their strokes all out of time, [when] the sound will become a mere noise in which no musical note can be distinguished." (*Encyclopæd. Brit.* 1875: art. "Atom:" vol. II, p. 43.)

of the spectral lines, and speaks familiarly of the *diatomic* molecule.*
It is true that the "atom" is properly a physical and not a chemical
unit, since it can never be reached by any possible reactions of
affinity or of decomposition. But if the term is to be still retained
in chemical nomenclature, it should always be understood in its
merely etymological sense of the "undivided," and not in its more
popular sense of the uncompounded.

---

3. *The Fallacy of Kinematic Theories.*

After this rather labored effort to approximate to some definite
conception of the physical nature of the two types of invisible or
elementary motion—displayed in the atomic revolutions or oscillations generating radiant undulations of the æther, and in the molecular flights and encounters generating the thermo-dynamic pressures of gaseous fluids,—let us consider what countenance these
forms of motion may be supposed to lend to a kinematic theory of
universal force.

It is important here to notice that by experiments on the sensible vibrations of bodies,—as of tuning-forks and pneumatic dia-
phragms,—translatory motions of approach and recession have been
produced in light bodies. The "attractions" or "repulsions" have
been shown to depend on the amplitudes of the oscillation, and the
ratio of the wave-lengths to the surfaces of action.; as also on the
symmetrical concurrence or reversal of the phases of vibration in
two confronting systems.†

---

* Prof. GEORGE F. BARKER in his excellent presidential address before
the Chemical Section of the American Association at Buffalo, on the theme—
"The Molecule and the Atom," referring to the constitution of hydrochloric acid, repeats the common view: "hence a molecule of hydrogen is composed of two atoms." (*Proceed. Am. Assoc.* August, 1876 : .p. 95.)

† Dr. JULES GUYOT. *Des Mouvements de l'Air et des Pressions de l'Air
en Mouvement.* 8vo. Paris, 1835.
Prof. FREDERICK GUTHRIE. "On Approach caused by Vibration."
L. E. D. Phil. Mag. Nov. 1870: vol. XL, p. 354. (From his tuning-fork
experiments, the author ventures the bold and startling induction: "In
mechanics—in nature—there is no such thing as a pulling force.")
Prof. C. A. BIERKNES of Christiania, Norway. Hydro-dynamic experi-

Irrelevancy of a Vibratory Hypothesis.—The first remark that occurs to a thoughtful student of these well-known phenomena of hydro-dynamics, (upon which narrow basis some enthusiasts have erected so wide a framework of induction,) is that between these resultant motions and any actions traceable in molecular physics,— (unless possibly in particular habitudes of electricity and magnetism,) there is not even a rough analogy. And the next and most obvious suggestion is that the absolute precedent condition of any reciprocating action whatever is the presence of the very qualities—*cohesion* and *elasticity*—for the production of which such reciprocating action is invoked. The essential powers and characteristics by which alone either atomic revolutions or molecular impacts are for an instant rendered possible, are the inherence of never-slumbering forces of attraction and repulsion. A vibratory particle (assumed by the kinematist for the avoidance of incomprehensible attributes,) is itself the most astounding—the most unrealizable in scientific thought, of all physical concepts. No atom can perform an oscillation or a revolution, or follow any other path than a straight line—excepting under the coercion of other atoms attracting and repelling. The first law of motion is that of perfect continuity both in amount and in direction. A shuttlecock rebounding in the empty air, would not be more conspicuously a dynamic solecism and impossibility than the kinematist's "vibratory particle."

Those therefore who in their backward search of causation would assign the origin of force to some incomprehensible æther action, have no more warrant from experience, induction, or reason, than those less cultured philosophers who taking "the unknown for the wonderful" habitually refer each unfamiliar phenomenon (with easy faith)—to "electricity."*

---

ments on vibration. *Nature.* Aug. 18, 1881: vol. XXIV, p. 360; and Jan. 19, 1882: vol. XXV, pp. 272, 273.

Also a modification of the experiments of Prof. Bierknes, by Mr. AUGUSTUS STROH: (in air instead of in water.) *Nature.* June 8, 1882: vol. XXVI, p. 134.

*"There are not wanting those who appear very much disposed to say that the conception of *force* itself—as part and parcel of the system of the material universe—is superfluous and therefore illogical. - - - Having come to regard heat, light, electricity, as modes of motion, they seem to consider force itself as included in the same category, and think there is

Instability of a Vibratory Hypothesis.—But the kinematic embarrassment is not concluded here. Supposing the marvellous feat accomplished of effecting a rotatory resilience which should simulate in direction and amount the facts of observation, how far would such accordance justify its acceptance as the true and sufficient account of the molecular behavior, in the light of the great established principle of the conservation of energy? As a necessary corollary of this great generalization we know that every system of atomic or molecular oscillation, undulation, and impact, is directly amenable to material disturbance and to the precise mechanical equivalents of kinetic deflection, arrest, and neutralization. But as regards the fundamental qualities of atomic or molecular attractions, repulsions, and elasticities, no such disturbance, or aberration, or interference, is for an instant possible. And these fundamental qualities are persistent, and permanent, as well as unchanging. Hence the countless balls sustained in place by countless fountains, must never be permitted to decline or swerve from their required positions. Every bent spring, every loaded beam, every sustaining rope and chain and cable must therefore have expended upon it a ceaseless rain and battery of impact or of wave propulsion. Nay every solid, every liquid, must be held in its tenacious consistency by the external coercion of a never resting dynamic bombardment. In what manner is the inexhaustible supply of kinetic energy supposed to be obtained? What is its source?—and where is its escape? Why is it that the incessant and violent collisions brought into play

---

'reason to believe that it depends on the diffusion of highly attenuated matter through space.'" Sir JOHN HERSCHEL. ("On the Origin of Force." *Fortnightly Review.* July 1, 1865: vol. I, p. 436. And *Familiar Lectures*, [etc.] 12mo. London, 1866: art. XII, p. 462.)

The learned physical professor in the University of Edinburgh sees "reason to believe that *force* depends upon the immediate action of highly attenuated matter diffused throughout space." (*North British Review.* February, 1864: vol. XL, p. 22,—of Am. edition. And Prof. P. G. TAIT's *Sketch of Thermo-dynamics.* 8vo. Edinburgh, 1868: chap. I, sect. 3, p. 2.)

And the no less learned physical professor in the University of Cambridge, thinking it irrational to ascribe the occult quality of *elasticity* to any sensible molecule, finds no difficulty in relegating this property to the æther. (*L. E. D. Phil. Mag.* June, 1866: vol. XXXI, pp. 468, 469. And Prof. J. CHALLIS's *Principles of Mathematics and Physics.* 8vo. Cambridge, 1869: pp. 316, 358, and 436.)

under this dynasty of percussion, do not speedily raise the temperature of all coherent bodies to a fierce and glowing heat?*

And this brings us face to face with the great radical—incommensurable difference between "force" and *energy*,—that the function of the former is attended with no expenditure, and is capable of no exhaustion. The truth of this bold asseveration has been tested again and again by every expedient which the most skillful and ingenious kinematists have been able to devise for its question, without the suspicion of impeachment; and it remains to-day, one of our strongest and best assured inductions.

On this broad platform rests the issue between kinematism and dynamism,—that the former inevitably contravenes and destroys that bulwark of modern physics—*the conservation of energy*; while the latter is its only support and its necessary foundation. Without the indestructible—unwasting—tensions of molecular attraction and repulsion, it lies beyond the scope of human ingenuity to devise or imagine a conservative system.

The fundamental—the inherent and incurable weakness of every attempt to supersede "force" by motion is betrayed in this,—the inadmissible supposition of a world held together only by the infinite expenditure of *work*, for whose existence no provision is devised, and for whose maintenance no motor can be suggested or conceived.†

---

* Referring to the steady maintenance of material tensions by supposed ætherial motions or vortices, J. CLERK MAXWELL truly remarks: "No theory of the constitution of the ether has yet been invented which will account for such a system of molecular vortices being maintained for an indefinite time without their energy being gradually dissipated into that irregular agitation of the medium which in ordinary media is called heat." (*Encyclopædia Britannica.* 9th ed. 1878: art. "Ether:" vol. VIII, p. 572.)

† "Taking such a system in its entirety (where force exists not), there is no possibility of its reproduction. There is therefore a necessary and unceasing drain on the *vis viva* of such a system. Everything which constitutes an event, whatever its nature, exhausts some portion of the original stock. Such a system has no vitality. It feeds upon itself and has no restorative power." Sir JOHN HERSCHEL, ("On the origin of Force."—*Fortnightly Review.* July 1, 1865: vol. I, p. 437. And *Familiar Lectures*, [etc.] 1866: art. XII, p. 465.)

"It is remarkable" observes J. CLERK MAXWELL, "that of the three hypotheses which go some way toward a physical explanation of gravitation, every one involves a constant expenditure of work." (*Encyclopæd. Brit.* 9th ed. 1875: art. "Attraction:" vol. III, p. 65.)

It is the inversion of the sequence taught us by all sufficiently ob-
servant experience, that motion of any kind or form is ever the
product of force, and can never be its parent.

Inadequacy of a Vibratory Hypothesis.—But after all this lavish
exercise of creative power and ingenuity,—this prodigal expenditure of kinetic energy,—how surprising to find the notable inven-
tion wholly incompetent to produce the observed phenomena.   Cohesive force (for example) apparently incapable of exerting any
attractive power whatever beyond the range of a single layer of
molecules, that is beyond the distance of perhaps the five hundred
millionth of an inch from its center of action, yet exercises for an
exceedingly small space within that distance a holding strength
many thousands of •times greater than the all-pervading power of
gravitation.   By what form of undulation, oscillation, or impulsion,
shall we represent the tenacity of a steel wire sustaining a pull of
300,000 pounds to the square inch beyond the limits of perhaps the
thousand-millionth of an inch between its molecules, yet exerting
within that limit an insuperable repulsion, and again at double the
distance another range of repulsion, so far resisting all human
efforts, that the nicest and closest approximation of the severed ends
of the wire shall fail to develop the attraction of an ounce or single
grain?*   By what form of partial differential equation, shall this
sudden and absolute discontinuity of function be expounded?   Nay
rather, by what hallucination of metaphysical assumption have intelligent men been induced to waste useful time and ink and paper,
on the chase of the *ignis-fatuus* of cohesive undulation or percussion?

The Authority of " Sensible " Impressions.—But it is insisted that
"the principle of deriving fundamental conceptions from the indications of the senses does not admit of regarding any force varying
with distance as an essential quality of matter, because according

---

* Prof. CHALLIS thinks "the ultimate atoms of glass are kept asunder
by the repulsion of ætherial undulations which have their origin at individual atoms," and " it may be presumed that this atomic repulsion is attrib-
utable to undulations incomparably smaller than those which cause the
sensation of light." (*Principles of Mathematics and Physics.* 1869: p. 456.)
But the luminiferous vibrations are themselves *atomic*.   What lower order
of atom is then to be appealed to in support of this fanciful and inept
hypothesis?

to that principle we must in seeking for the simplest idea of physical force have regard to the sense of *touch*."* Let us inquire then what is taught us by tactile experience with regard to the philosophy of physical contact. In the celebrated experiment by which Newton first measured the wave-lengths of light from the colored rings which yet bear his name, he found that on placing a piece of clean plate glass upon the convex surface of a large lens, a very considerable pressure was required to exhaust the series of outcoming interference fringes and to exhibit the central black spot. Professor Robison estimated that a pressure of at least one thousand pounds to the square inch was necessary to effect this approach to a mathematical contact between the two glasses.† And yet even with this very close and perfect physical contact it is shown that at the first appearance of the black spot between the glasses, they are still separated from actual or mathematical contact by the space of the 250,000th of an inch.

Material Contact not Absolute.—Supposing it were desired to directly communicate a push or a pull through the distance of seven miles, a perfectly straight steel bar (properly supported on friction rollers through that space) would probably be as efficient a *mechanical* means for the purpose as could well be suggested. And yet the blow of a suitably heavy hammer struck upon one of its ends would

---

* Prof. JAMES CHALLIS. *Principles of Mathematics and Physics.* 1869: p. 858.

†*A System of Mechanical Philosophy.* By Prof. JOHN ROBISON: vol. I, sect. 241, p. 250. Dr. YOUNG remarks on this: "Hence it is obvious that whenever two pieces of glass strike each other without exerting a pressure equal to a thousand pounds on a square inch, they may effect each other's motion without actually coming into contact. Some persons might perhaps be disposed to attribute this repulsion to the elasticity of particles of air adhering to the glass, but I have found that the experiment succeeds equally well in the vacuum of an air-pump. We must therefore be contented to acknowledge our total ignorance of the intimate nature of forces of every kind." (*Lectures on Natural Philosophy.* 2 vols. 4to. London, 1807: lect. III: vol. I, p. 28.) And Prof. J. CLERK MAXWELL says to the same effect: "We have no evidence that real contact ever takes place between two bodies, and in fact when bodies are pressed against each other and in apparent contact, we may sometimes actually measure the distance between them, as when one piece of glass is laid on another, in which case a considerable pressure must be applied to bring the surfaces near enough

require very nearly two seconds for its transmission and delivery at the opposite end. Or if we reduce our steel punch to the more manageable length of (let us say) one foot, then the blow received by it from a hammer, and the blow given out by it at the other end, will be separated by the interval of the 18,000th part of a second. Assuming the actual approach of the hammer face to the end of the steel punch at the instant of impact to be the millionth of an inch, we may even compute the interval of time elapsing between the delivery of the blow by the hammer and its reception by the steel punch, at the $1 \div 216\,000,000\,000$ of a second; an interval of time real enough and long enough to permit the atoms of the iron molecules to execute from 1800 to 3200 of their normal oscillations or orbital revolutions. By thus considering what is really signified by physical contact and impact, we find it to be something quite different from what the kinematist would suggest by his appeals to "the sense of touch."

The unlucky boy when struck in the face with a ball, or wounded in his finger with his jack-knife, may well refuse to be comforted by the assurance that neither the ball which bruised his face, nor the blade which penetrated and severed the capillary vessels of his finger, ever approached within the millionth of an inch of his flesh, or probably within double that distance from it. But the philosopher who aspires to construct a theory of universal force from the inductions of experience, should at least sufficiently develop his intellectual vision to avoid accepting coarse and external resemblances as evidences of co-ordinated derivation, or adopting the unanalyzed impressions of unobservant consciousness as the revelations of axiomatic truth.

Action at a Distance.—But here our investigation is undermining the very corner-stone of the kinematic system,—the repudiation of all static energy, the alleged fundamental absurdity of any mechanical action at a distance. That "a thing can no more act *where it is not* than *when* it is not," is a plain dictum of common-sense.* Even the provisional admission of such a supposition is

to show the black spot of Newton's rings, which indicates a distance of about a ten-thousandth of a millimeter." (*Encyclopædia Britannica.* 9th ed. 1875: art. "Attraction:" vol. III, p. 63.)

* Prof. JAMES CROLL believes that "No principle will ever be generally received that stands in opposition to the old adage 'A thing cannot act

in violation of the canons of sound thought, and is contradictory of one of the most obvious aphorisms of logical metaphysics.   Whatever our refinements as to the real nature of physical contact (it is said), this action is none the less a fact of constant and familiar occurrence, and is the actual method of kinetic transference manifested to our every-day observation.   If we wish to give a billiard ball a definite motion in a specific direction, we do not whistle to the ball, or attempt to " psychologize " it ; we strike it with a cue. Is it conceivable that " mere brute matter " should be more " spiritual " than man himself?

As these popular and taking propositions involve purely a question of physical fact, their truth can never be decided by any introspections of the consciousness, by any deductions from the " *ego cogito*," or by any disquisitions on " the theory of conception." As a question of fact, the final settlement of the nature of material *action* is to be reached only by the converging inductions of a critical *experience* (aided and enlightened by every expedient of refined investigation), and by the necessary inferences from such experience.   It is very certain that a material body must exert its action—either at *some* distance, or at *no* distance, that is by absolute and perfect contact.   Have we at present the means of intelligently probing this sharply defined issue? *

Action at no Distance.—It is a well-established principle, or rather fact, of dynamics that finite time is required for the production of

---

where it is not.'" (*L. E. D. Phil. Mag.*   December, 1867 : vol. XXXIV, p. 450.)   And GEORGE HENRY LEWES is fully persuaded that " Action at a distance (unless understood in the sense of action through unspecified intermediates) is both logically and physically absurd." (*Problems of Life and Mind.*   1875 : vol. II, appendix C, p. 484.)

* Dr. OLIVER J. LODGE has remarked : " I venture to think that putting metaphysics entirely on one side we may prove in a perfectly simple and physical manner that it is impossible for two bodies *not* in contact to act directly on each other : " and he defends the position by the argument, that since action and re-action are equal and opposite, and since " work " done upon one body is equal to the " energy " so expended by the opposite body, " the distances must be equal but not opposite ; that is, the two bodies must move over precisely the same distance and in the same sense : which practically asserts that they move together and are in contact so long as the action is going on." (*L. E. D. Phil. Mag.*   January, 1881 : vol. XI, pp. 36, 37.)

any finite velocity, or of any finite change in velocity. Only an infinite force could generate motion instantaneously, and this acting for any finite time would produce an infinite velocity. Now the impact of a moving body upon a body at rest, must occur in the absolute instant of contact. No motion could be transmitted *before* contact, for this would be the chimera—*actio in distans*. No motion could be transmitted *after* contact, for then the impinging body could evidently have no more motion than the body impinged upon. And no motion could be transmitted at the *instant* of contact, for this occupies but an infinitesimal of time. But if no motion could be communicated either before, or at, or after contact, it is very clearly established that no motion whatever could possibly be derived from impact pure and simple. This conclusion—applicable alike to an atom or a planet—remains equally unassailable whatever be the magnitudes of the bodies in action.

We are thus strongly reminded of Zeno's celebrated paradox as to the impossibility of motion. For while the kinematist very positively assures us that action at a distance is a metaphysical impossibility, the dynamist assures us no less positively that action at no distance is a demonstrated physical impossibility.* But if mere kinetic energy cannot be transferred excepting through a vacant

---

* This position is so forcibly stated by Prof. JOSEPH BAYMA in his able Treatise on Molecular Physics, that a quotation from that work seems here especially appropriate. " Finite velocity cannot be communicated in an indivisible instant, as we have seen. - - - Nor can the demonstration be evaded by having recourse to the *multitude* of points among which the contact would be supposed to take place. For - - - if each individual point of matter only acquires an infinitesimal velocity (vdt), the whole multitude will acquire only an infinitesimal velocity ; that is, there will be no motion caused at all. Nor can it be said that the motion is communicated by means of a *prolonged* contact. A prolonged contact is impossible unless the velocities have become equal at the very commencement of the contact. Therefore if velocity were communicated by the contact of matter with matter, it would have to be communicated in the very first instant of the contact, not in its prolongation. - - - Therefore *distance* is a necessary condition of the action of matter upon matter. Therefore the contact between the agent and the object acted upon is not material but *virtual*, inasmuch as it is by its active power (*virtus*), not by its matter, that the agent reaches the matter of the object acted upon." (*Molecular Mechanics*. 8vo. London, 1866 : book I, prop. 3, pp. 14, 15.)

space, *à fortiori* must static " force " require distance as the indispensable condition of its action.

So much therefore for the vaunted dictum of " common-sense :" and so much for the antagonistic dictum whose " absurdity is so great that no man who has in philosophical matters a competent faculty of thinking can ever fall into it !" *   And this absurd—this incomprehensible—this inconceivable proposition—that matter is capable of acting *only* where it is not, is proved by the incontestible conviction of reason to be a primary and necessary truth: and the wondrous scholastic dogma resisting it—supposed the sacred oracle of a mysterious intuition,—is but the detected impostor of a crude induction.

True meaning of Contact Action.—To confirm however the explicit deductions of mechanical theory by the verifications of actual experience, let us examine more closely the true character of that transmission of energy by impact which to the kinematist appears to furnish so simple and so obvious an explanation of " force." Taking the most elementary example of the *vis a tergo*, let us suppose two precisely similar billiard-balls—A and B—on the perfectly smooth surface of a frozen lake, B at rest, and A rolled toward it in the direct line joining their centers of inertia.   The familiar result that A is brought to rest by the collision, and B continues the motion in the same direction prolonged, will be fluently explained by the kinematist as a mere case of conservation, or the persistence of motion,—which evidently passes at the instant of contact directly from A to B, like an electric charge.

Overlooking—first, the fallacy of a finite velocity passing into a body instantaneously (already controverted), there is a second difficulty, that *motion*—defined as a change of position in a body, or the occupation of successive portions of space by a body,—cannot exist out of the body, cannot therefore pass through the confines of the body.   But admitting for the moment both these possibilities,—in the third place, how could the ball A part with *all* its motion to

---

* This inconsiderate utterance of NEWTON in his oft-quoted " third Bentley letter," (Feb. 25, 1693,) was wholly repudiated by him a quarter of a century later, when with a graver wisdom he asked the question : " Have not the small particles of bodies certain powers, virtues, or forces, by which they act at a distance ?" (*Optics.* 2d edition. 1717: book III, query 31.) A recantation never cited by the kinematist.

another ball no larger than itself? The two possessing the same inertia, why did not *A* expend just half its motion on collision with *B*, giving the latter its equal share; and thus conserve the original momentum by the double mass moving conjointly with half the velocity? This very simple question—it is safe to affirm—can never be answered by any principles of the science of kinematics.

By the principles of dynamics, these three queries admit of a very satisfactory solution. At the moment of physical contact between the two balls, (there being still an assignable space between them,) their approaching surfaces commence mutually to encroach upon a powerful molecular repulsion crowding back and compressing more closely together vast multitudes of resisting layers of molecules on either side, until their combined pressure gradually absorbs and destroys the momentum of *A*, while simultaneously exerting an equal stress on the inertia of *B*. And thus by the necessary equality of action and re-action, the centers of inertia of the two balls pass successively through the same reversed phases of approach and recession during the brief finite interval of physical contact, attaining a relative velocity of separation precisely equal to that of the encounter: the deformations of the balls, or their compressions, being as the squares of the absorbed velocity, and their energy of recovery being as the square roots of the restored velocity. So far therefore from the original motion of *A* being transferred to *B* (as often loosely stated), it really passes continuously through every stage of decline to actual rest; and a new motion commencing from zero is gradually started in *B*, by the continued application of an elastic pressure, during a finite time.

To take one more example in illustration of the impossibility of action *at no distance*, let us suppose an ivory ball weighing one ounce to be centrally struck while at rest by another ivory ball weighing four ounces, and moving with a velocity of 10 feet per second. If we were to ignore the " occult " force of *elasticity*, and neglect the difficulties already exposed, kinematics would give the simple result of a common velocity of the two balls after impact, of 8 feet per second: 4×10 being equal to 5×8. But this is not what would happen. We should find instead that the four-ounce ball has its velocity reduced to 6 feet per second, while the one-ounce ball takes up a velocity of 16 feet per second ;—just *double* that it should have taken were action at no distance a natural possibility: the latter ball absorbing (so to speak) the whole velocity and three-fifths more, while the former has expended two-fifths of its original velocity.

Here then is presented a new difficulty on the kinematic theory. In what possible manner can a body moving at a definite rate impart to another body *by simple impact* a velocity considerably higher than that possessed by itself? By kinematics, this question also must remain forever unanswered. By the established principles of dynamics—there being no actual or mathematical contact of the two balls,—the static energy of their combined compressions or repulsions acquired during the time of their physical contact precisely equals the kinetic energy of impact; and consequently on resilience refunds a precisely equal kinetic energy of separation ;— to wit, a relative velocity of 10 feet per second.

Impossibility of Action at no Distance.—It turns out therefore when we examine very slightly beneath the surface of " sense information," that *impulsion* (so perfectly obvious and intelligible to the kinematist) is itself a very notable example of the ultra-sensible and recondite : *—that the vaunted philosophy of " the sense of touch " is no more able to escape from the dominion of the unseen, the hidden, the enigmatical, in causation, than is the dynamism which is held to be so superficial, credulous, and undiscerning.

And this mysterious but necessary principle of all dynamics reaches far back of the imagined cases of corporeal contact in collisions,—even to the intimate structure of the densest material ;†

---

*As acutely remarked by the eminent mathematician—JAMES IVORY : "A little reflection is sufficient to show that in reality we have no clearer notion of *impulse* as the cause of motion, than we have of *attraction*. We can as little give a satisfactory reason why motion should pass out of one body into another on their contact, as we can why one body should begin to move, or have its motion increased, when it is placed near another body. - - - If then we are apt to think that impulse is a clearer physical principle than attraction, there is really no good ground for the distinction ; it has its origin in prejudice." (*Encyclopædia Britannica.* 8th ed. 1854 : art. "Attraction : " vol IV, p. 220.)

" When the Newtonians were accused of introducing into philosophy an unknown cause which they termed *attraction*, they justly replied that they knew as much respecting attraction as their opponents did about impulse." Dr. WILLIAM WHEWELL. (*History of Scientific Ideas.* 1858 : book III, chap. IX, sect. 8 : vol. I, p. 278.)

† There is good reason to think that absolute contact never takes place in the component parts of the hardest and most compact solid bodies." JAMES

for it is demonstrable that the component molecules and atoms of the hardest steel are far from being in contact; that carbon molecules have room enough—even when crystal-bound in diamond—to freely execute the oscillations constituting its varying temperature by constant exchanges, and to so alter their relative excursions as to represent the changed specific gravity due to varying temperature.

The conclusion reached, we would wish to express in the most emphatic and unequivocal terms:—that in all nature we have as yet been furnished with no example of absolute contact action;—that "action at no distance" is sheer physical *impossibility;*—that in utter scorn of venerable scholastic axioms, matter is forever incapable of influencing other matter in any manner whatever or in any degree whatever—*excepting* "where it is not!" And thus the paradox of Zeno receives its solution by the thorough confutation of kinematism at every point—inductive or deductive,—theoretical or experimental.

"*Occult Qualities.*"—And now we are fully prepared to encounter the portentous arraignment of having recourse to the witch-craft of magical virtues and to the mystery of "occult qualities." What then is the precise import of this supposed obnoxious epithet *occult* as applied to material property or quality? A property whose existence is once clearly demonstrated, can scarcely with propriety be characterized as hidden, unknown, or undiscovered.* Rather are

---

IVORY. (*Encyclopæd. Brit.* 8th ed: vol. IV, p. 220.) The case of simple traction by a "solid" metallic rod can be explained *only*—(as J. CLERK MAXWELL has well stated)—"by the existence of internal forces in its substance" or "between the particles of which the rod is composed, that is between bodies at distances which though small must be finite," and for these tensions acting through small distances—"we are as little able to account as for the action at any distance, however great." (*A Treatise on Electricity and Magnetism.* 8vo. 2 vols. 1873: part I, chap. V, sect. 105: vol. I, p. 123.)

*LEIBNITZ in his memorable controversy with NEWTON regarding the authorship of the infinitesimal calculus, took occasion—with a somewhat amusing though ill-tempered irrelevancy, to assail his rival's *mechanical* philosophy. In a published letter he says: "His philosophy appears to me somewhat strange, and I do not believe that it can ever be established. If all bodies possess gravity, it necessarily follows (however the defenders of the system may speak, and whatever heat they may display), that gravity

these terms applicable to pretended explanations—having no basis in fact or in reason—proffered in the vain hope of avoiding unexpected or undesired inductions.   But if the phrase be designed to stigmatize either the absolute cause of original properties or their mode of operation, as obscure, hidden, inexplicable, then the epithet is but the expression of a necessary and universal truth, which may be accepted with entire satisfaction.

On contemplating the backward steps of efficient causation, we find them not only finite in number, but in any case even surprisingly few,—if we neglect the complications of perturbation, and the successions of iteration in time.   When we arrive at the primitive efficient cause, (if we accept it as ultimate,) this is by admission and very definition—inexplicable; since any attempt to explain it, necessarily refers it to an antecedent cause, and thus denies it to be ultimate.*   Or if this denial be insisted on, then the series of

---

must be a scholastic *occult quality*, or the effect of a miracle. - - - Nor do I find a vacuum established by the reasons of Mr. Newton, or of his partizans, any more than his pretended 'universal gravitation,' or than his 'atoms.' No one—unless with very contracted views—can believe either in the vacuum, or in the atoms."

With equal dignity and cogency, NEWTON replied to this tirade, in a letter dated February 26, 1716, that he was not to be drawn by M. Leibnitz into a dispute which was nothing to the question in hand. "As for philosophy, he colludes in the significations of words, calling those things 'miracles' which create no wonder; and those things 'occult qualities' whose *causes* are occult, though the qualities themselves be manifest." (Raphson's *History of Fluxions*. Also the *Works of Isaac Newton*, edited by Samuel Horsley. 5 vols. quarto. London, 1779–1785: where both letters are given: vol. IV, pp. 596, 598.)

*Says ROGER COTES in his admirable Préface to the *Principia*: "Since causes naturally recede in a continued chain from the more compounded to the more simple, when the most simple is reached no further backward step is possible. Hence an ultimate cause cannot admit of any mechanical explanation; for if it could, it would by that very fact cease to be ultimate. Will you therefore banish ultimate causes by calling them 'occult?' Then those immediately depending on such must next alike be banished, and straightway those next following; until relieved from every vestige of a cause, philosophy shall indeed stand purged!" (Newton's *Principia*. Second edition. 1713. *Preface*.)

Says Sir WILLIAM HAMILTON, "As every effect is only produced by the concurrence of at least two causes, and as these concurrent or co-efficient causes in fact constitute the effect, it follows that the lower we descend in the series of causes, the more complex will be the product; and that the

explanations is necessarily illimitable, and as necessarily beyond the grasp of human comprehension. Do what we will we cannot escape the inexorable logic of fact,—the certainty of conviction that the ultimate must in the nature of things be forever the unintelligible, the inexplicable, the inscrutable;—that (paradoxical as it may sound) no explanation can be accounted final until it has been pursued backward to the unexplainable.

And this furnishes an additional objection to the kinematic scheme,—that it leaves a vast domain—a phantasmagoria of inconsequent motions—still to be explained;—that however irrational or inexplicable its last postulate, it does not attain to that simplicity of inherent, inscrutable, attribute of power, which must ever be the test of final resolution.

He who supposes, therefore, " that the information of the senses is adequate (with the aid of mathematical reasoning) to explain phenomena of *all kinds*," who refuses to admit " that there are physical operations which are—and ever will be incomprehensible by us," betrays a very imperfect idea—no less of the impassable limitations of finite intellect, than of the fathomless profundity of nature's system.* He who thinks that by formally repudiating the mysterious, and confidently discarding the unknown, he thereby

---

higher we ascend, it will be the more simple. - - - And as each step in the procedure carries us from the more complex to the more simple, and consequently nearer to unity, we at last arrive at that unity itself,—at that ultimate cause, which as ultimate cannot again be conceived as an effect." (*Lectures on Metaphysics:* lect. III, p. 42, of Am. edition. 8vo. Boston, 1859.)

Says HERBERT SPENCER, " It obviously follows that the most general truth not admitting of inclusion in any other, does not admit of interpretation. Of necessity therefore, explanation must eventually bring us down to the inexplicable. The deepest truth which we can get at must be unaccountable." (*First Principles.* 2d edition, 1869: part I, chap. 4, p. 73.)

* Prof. JAMES CHALLIS, in an essay " On the Fundamental Ideas of Matter and Force in Theoretical Physics," maintains that when there is no apparent contact between bodies, " it must still be concluded that the pressing body although invisible, exists,—unless we are prepared to admit that there are physical operations which are and ever will be incomprehensible by us. This admision is incompatible with the principles of the philosophy I am advocating, which assume that the information of the senses is adequate—with the aid of mathematical reasoning—to explain phenomena of all kinds." *L. E. D. Phil. Mag.* June, 1866: vol. XXXI, p. 467.)

abolishes or in the slightest degree diminishes his insuperable nescience of the ultimate,—but imitates the ostrich, and deludes himself.*

When men not yet emancipated from the realism of mediæval scholasticism began to turn their attention from the dreams of ontology to the actualities of sensible phenomena, it is scarcely to be wondered at that to every abstracted property of things around them, they gave " a local habitation and a name; " until the banished Nereids and Oreads, the Naiads and Dryads, the Sylphs and Gnomes, of poetic fable, were re-habilitated in a very pantheon of " occult qualities." When in a later age a larger observation and a more mathematical logic replaced these entities by more mechanical conceptions, it is perhaps as little surprising—in the momentum of re-action—that the term " occult quality " should become a shibboleth of aversion, of apprehension, and of opprobrium, the imputation of which should disturb the philosophy of even a Newton. But that we of the nineteenth century,—capable of understanding and of estimating at their approximate value the limits of these oscillations of intellectual kinetics, should be equally the timid servitors of a vocabulary—seems less excusable. Whether the intended reproach be applied to the *existence* of demonstrated qualities, or more critically to their *cause* and mode of action, is practically of little consequence. Let it be frankly avowed,—let it be boldly heralded, that in their *essence* all the primal qualities of matter *are* " occult; " and must of necessity forever remain so. Let it be recognized—with a fitting modesty—that this veil of Isis shall never be removed by mortal hands.†

---

*The continental philosophers of the seventeenth century desired not only to abolish the fanciful qualities of bodies invented by their predecessors, but (as has been well said) "they tried also to abolish their own ignorance of the causes of the sensible qualities of matter. They would not have occult *causes*, and Leibnitz plainly confounds occult quality with occult cause. But it is needless to dwell upon the fact that the ultimate causes of all qualities are occult." *English Cyclopædia*—Division of *Arts and Sciences :* art. "Attraction :" vol. I, col. 739.)

† *Τὸν ἐμὸν πέπλον οὐδείς πω θνητὸς ἀπεκάλυψε.*—Inscription in the temple of Athene-Isis, at Sais on the Nile. "My veil no mortal ever withdrew."

" In bodies we see only their figures and colors, [etc.] - - - but their inward *substances* are not to be known either by our senses, or by any reflex

The Import of a " Mechanical" System.—It has been a fond assumption of the kinematist that his all-embracing system of *motion* as the origin and essence of phenomena, is pre-eminently the " mechanical " theory of nature as contrasted with a " mystical " or " transcendental " theory. It may be well therefore to consider what is really signified by the term "mechanical."

Underlying every possible conception of the simplest element of a " machine " are two essential postulates :—first, the necessity of a frame-work invested with the inherent qualities giving it structural consistence and endurance,—and secondly, the necessity of a store of potential energy by which it may be actuated and made operative : since it is an elementary truism that no machine can *originate* energy.

The geometrician who ambitious of placing his science on a more rational basis should announce a new system rejecting all assumptions and establishing its theorems by no propositions ,which had not first been mathematically demonstrated, might possibly receive the applause of the inexpert, but would not be likely to meet with approbation or encouragement from the great jury of his brother geometers. The physicist who proclaims that he undertakes to build up a system of mechanical laws on a foundation exclusively mechanical, acts in no sense and in no degree less irrationally. Probably his first requirement will be—" given a rigid body." But

---

act of our minds." ISAAC NEWTON. (*Principia.* 1687 : book III,—concluding " scholium.")

" In fact the causes of all phenomena are at last occult. There has however obtained a not unnatural presumption against such causes ; and this presumption though often salutary has sometimes operated most disadvantageously to science." Sir WILLIAM HAMILTON. (*Discussions on Philosophy and Literature.* 8vo. London, 1852: appendix I, p. 611.)

" The first causes of phenomena lie beyond the limited scope of our perceptive and reasoning faculties. - - - Their intimate nature and prime origin are for us inscrutable mysteries." Dr. A. W. HOFFMAN. (*Introduction to Modern Chemistry.* 1865: lec. IX, p. 138.)

" Ultimate scientific ideas then are all representative of realities that cannot be comprehended. - - - Alike in the external and the internal worlds, the man of science sees himself in the midst of perpetual changes— of which he can discover neither the beginning nor the end. - - - In all directions his investigations eventually bring him face to face with an insoluble enigma ; and he ever more clearly perceives it to be an insoluble enigma." HERBERT SPENCER. (*First Principles.* 2d ed. 1869: part I, chap. III: sect. 21, pp. 66, 67.)

by no construction, by no combination, by no involution or evolution of any purely "mechanical" process can he possibly obtain, or explain, or even conceive his postulate—a rigid body. The attempt is indeed *more* hopeless than to demonstrate an axiom by mathematical deduction. That which is the necessary basis and starting-point of any intelligible mechanics, can scarcely be supposed to be the product or derivative of such mechanics. A truly mechanical theory cannot dispense with an extraneous foundation. Those who would exclude potential causes from the field of mechanical science, but betray the hopeless—helpless nakedness and imbecility of their hypothetic fictions. "Later philosophers" says Isaac Newton, " banish the consideration of such a cause out of natural philosophy, feigning hypotheses for explaining all things *mechanically*, and referring other causes to ' metaphysics ; ' whereas the main business of natural philosophy is to argue from phenomena without feigning hypotheses, and to deduce causes from effects, till we come to the very first cause,—*which certainly is not mechanical.*" *

Give to the ambitious kinematic artist his cloud of sand,—or if he prefer the outfit, let him be furnished with an indefinite quantity of a perfectly continuous frictionless and incompressible fluid— bound up if you please in a chain of " vortex rings,"—by no motions or composition of motions—continued through the æons of eternity—could he ever manufacture therefrom either a lever, or a rope. The kinematic gospel of a *mechanical* theory of primeval motion is therefore a sophism and illusion. It is founded on a misconception of the very *essence* of a true mechanics. And the system that would proudly aspire to an architecture of a kosmos from the elements of matter disrobed and denuded of every quality but motion, would achieve as its highest triumph and product—a universe of dust and ashes.

Without *inertia* there could be neither transmission of motion, nor even continuity of motion. Without inertia, kinematics itself would be but an empty name. And *with* inertia, kinematics would be a science of purely rectilinear movement ; for by no artifice could any other be producible. No curvature of motion—no resilience of motion—is possible without the domination and constraint of occult forces. Without " dynamics " there could be no such thing as a science of " kinetics." Without the ceaseless presence and action of occult forces there could be no such thing as the

---

* *Optics.* Second edition, 1717 : book III, query 28.

conservation of energy; there could be no such thing as the production of energy.

Force—Real and Indispensable.—" Force " then is not a metaphorical abstraction : it is not a convenient asylum of ignorance. It is the most real,—the most fundamental,—the most inseparable of material attributes. It is the potency and faculty whereby all inorganic—no less than organic—forms are builded, and whereby alone their kaleidoscopic phenomena are revealed to our perceptions. And it is from the never resting antagonisms and reprisals of diverse forces that are made up the activity, the life, and the glory of the world in which we have our being; to whose ever changing—ever becoming—ever nascent pageantry, the poetry of antiquity has given the name—*Natura*.

In spite of every effort made to realize a favorite dream, there is no " unity of force." To the dynamics of even a single molecule, the contestation and constraint of at least two opposite resisting agencies are indispensable: and in the various play of matter, other such agencies are no less clearly manifested. Nor is the certainty of multiplicity, in the slightest degree impaired by our admitted ignorance as to the final number of primeval forces. It may be that chemical affinity, and magnetism, are like heat, and electricity,* merely derivative forms of energy; but at least this

---

* It is not a little remarkable that a tendency seems lately to have arisen to assign *electricity* to the station of a primitive force ; and several physicists have almost simultaneously maintained its indestructibility and inconvertibility.

Dr. O. J. LODGE, in a lecture delivered at the London Institution, December 16, 1880, says: " To the question What is electricity?—We cannot assert that it is a form of matter, neither can we deny it ; on the other hand we certainly cannot assert that it is a form of energy, and I should be disposed to deny it. - - - It is as impossible to generate electricity in the sense I am trying to give the word, as it is to produce matter ! " (*Nature.* January 27, 1881: vol. XXIII, p. 302.)

Mr. G. LIPPMAN, in a memoir presented to the Académie des Sciences of France, May 2, 1881, maintains that all electrical changes have an algebraic sum of zero : or in other words, that electricity can neither be created nor destroyed : the subject of the paper being " The Conservation of Electricity." (*Comptes Rendus.* 1881 : vol. XCII, p. 1049.—Also, *L. E. D. Phil. Mag.* June, 1881 : vol. XI, p. 474.)

Prof. SYLVANUS P. THOMPSON, " in Elementary Lessons in Electricity," (preface,) also maintains as an important hypothesis in the treat-

has not as yet been satisfactorily made out. The craving of the
intellect for unity must therefore pursue its quest beyond and above
the material empire of the physical forces.

The Conception of Natural " Law."—The habitudes of forces
form the ultimate goal and boundary of scientific thought : and as
the ascertainment and assignment of these habitudes (which we
formulate as " laws " of matter) form the *object* of all science, so
are their unerring certainty and uniformity of action at once the
necessary *postulates* and the sole *condition* of all science. But the
formulated " law " is but our mental concept of a habitude and a
constancy whose method forever eludes our widest grasp, while forever challenging our most daring speculation. What *is* a law of
nature ? What is there behind it—to ordain or to enforce it. Do
forces conform to the canons of an implicit prescription ? Or is
the so-called " law " but the summary and explication of autogen-
ous deportment? Whichever be our assumption, the marvel and
the incomprehensibility alike remain.

Sir John Herschel, in a playful colloquy " On Atoms," referring
to their prompt obedience to the laws of their being, pithily asks :
" Do they know them ? Can they remember them ? How else can
they *obey* them ?—conform to a fixed rule ! Then they must be able
to apply the rule as the case arises. - - - Their movements,
their interchanges, their ' hates and loves,' their ' attractions and repulsions,' their ' correlations,' are all determined on the very instant.
There is no hesitation, no blundering, no trial and error. A problem of dynamics which would drive Lagrange mad is solved
instanter. A differential equation which algebraically written out
would belt the earth, is integrated in an eye-twinkle." *

When we ask ourselves what these inflexible and unfailing laws of

---

ment of the subject, "the conservation of electricity ; " holding " that
electricity, whatever it may prove to be, is not matter and is not energy,"
and " that it can neither be created nor destroyed." (*Nature.* May 26,
1881: vol. XXIV, p. 78.—*Elementary Lessons*, [etc.] 12 mo. London, 1881.)

The electric and caloric fluids furnish a very striking and suggestive
parallelism ; and the common rotatory glass cylinder would have furnished
Rumford with as pertinent a theme for his argument as his gun-boring
lathe.

* *Fortnightly Review.* May 15, 1865: pp. 83, 84. Also, *Familiar Lectures on Scientific Subjects.* London, 1866 : pp. 456, 458.

force really mean ?—Why they are thus and not otherwise ?—Why
they are so diverse and irreducible, and each so perfectly auto-
cratic ?—Why for example independent molecules bound in the
cohesion and adhesion of the "liquid" or the "solid" condition,
should exhibit an attraction for each other a thousand-fold stronger
than their mutual gravitation ?—Why two atoms within a molecule
should cling together with a tenacity only *increasing* with their en-
forced centrifugal separation, while perfectly similar atoms not thus
united attract each other with a strength *decreasing* with the second
power of their distance ?—Why the chemical affinity of dissimilar
molecules shall attach them with a force incomparably greater than
even that of their physical cohesion ?—so that a drop of water may
be shattered and lifted by the sun-beam, precipitated in snow,
ground beneath a glacier, re-melted and dashed to foam in tumb-
ling cataracts, may be combined in the solid substance of a hydrated
crystal or in the complex constitution of an organic being, may be
tortured in the chemist's retort or forced in hissing fury through
the steam-engine, may pass through protean changes more varied
than fable ever fancied, and yet in all these marvellous pilgrimages
shall never loosen its structure as a compounded molecule of hydrogen and oxygen :—Why these same elements—so firmly enchained
that the oxygen will quit its grasp only under the decomposing en-
ticement of a more powerful affinity, or under the dissociative
violence of a molecular velocity and clash representing the temperature of highest incandescence,—are yet so averse to separate condensation that only the combination of extremest cold and pressure
attainable by human artifice has succeeded in bringing the molecules
of either to a momentary liquid or solid cohesion ?—we find such
questionings though irresistibly suggested, as irreversibly removed
outside the pale of oracle or answer.   There is no mystery in the
world of mind, that is not fully parallelled by mysteries as bewilder-
ing in the world of matter.

   Hemmed in by the impassable limitations of a restricted experience and of a no less restricted faculty of reason, we find the finite
radius of our science touching in every direction the shadowy universe of nescience; and where most we seem to know, there most
we encounter the cloud-land of the unknowable.   In our highest
reach and proudest triumph of analytic achievement,—in that
symbolical reasoning upon quantitive relation which we call *par
excellence* the "mathematical,"—we find that our symbols over-step

their appointed purpose, and our equations traversing the mystic region of " imaginary " expressions, transcend alike our interpretation and our comprehension.

Final Unity of Causation.—As every suggestion of an assignable limit to space or time directly impels us to " overleap all bounds," so the very definiteness of the *physical* leads us to spring in imagination beyond its frontiers, and to seek refuge in the transcendental;—not the *supernatural* as replacing or suspending the natural, but as supplementing and completing it—the ultra-natural,—in its best and highest sense the *metaphysical.* Incapable though we be of realizing in thought anything but the finite and the relative, we none the less find ourselves alike incapable of confining our thought to these; and the necessity which inexorably forbids our conception of the infinite and the absolute, no less imperiously compels our unhesitating acceptance of the unknown infinite and absolute as the unavoidable counterparts of the known finite and relative.*

Our visible material universe—to all appearance limited in extent—an islet in the boundless void,—is no less limited in duration,—at least as to any of its aspects now displayed. Nor have the falling leaf or the ageing man, the disappearance of races or the past extinction of species of genera and of orders,—more clearly inscribed upon them, the universal law and lesson of ephemeral birth development and decay, than have the starry heavens themselves. *Under the present system of dynamic law*, it is certain that as radiating and cooling bodies,

> " The stars shall fade away, the sun himself
> Grow dim with age, and nature sink in years."

---

*Sir WILLIAM HAMILTON has well remarked (in his Essay on the " Philosophy of the Unconditioned "): " The *Infinite* and the *Absolute* (properly so called) are thus equally inconceivable to us. - - - We are thus taught the salutary lesson that the capacity of thought is not to be constituted into the measure of existence; and are warned from recognizing the domain of our knowledge as necessarily co-extensive with the horizon of our faith. And by a wonderful revelation we are thus in the very consciousness of our inability to conceive aught above the relative and finite, inspired with a belief in the existence of something unconditional beyond the sphere of all comprehensible reality." (*Discussions on Philosophy and Literature.* 8vo. London, 1852: part I, pp. 13 and 15.) This Essay—a Review of Victor Cousin's *Cours de Philosophie*,—was originally published in the *Edinburgh Review*, October, 1829: vol. I, pp. 194–221.

Nor is there known to science any natural process whereby this cosmic doom may be either averted, or repaired by ulterior reversal.* And when turning backward through precessive geneses of worlds and suns and systems, and recalling in imagination the heat continuously expended and dissipated during millions of millions of years, until all matter is volatilized and re-expanded in the uniform tenuity and diffusion of the primitive nebular chaos, we endeavor to extend our retrograde inspection for another billion of years,—lost in the dizzying retrospect, we find that we have neither scale, nor mechanical principle, nor hydrodynamical theory, whereby to gage or guess the antecedents of this nebular chaos.

And here again—behind the mystery and inconceivability of atomic forces, lies the still greater mystery and inconceivability of primæval nature. And yet majestic as the wondrous march of cosmic evolution—(by purely human standards), it has probably consumed no greater number of our fleeting years, than the revolutions executed by the slowest atoms in a single second of time! Or by whatever number this be multiplied, how brief an interval has it fulfilled in the great infinitude of panoramic time,—in the far-stretching ages of a past eternity.

While an intellectual necessity demands the continuity of causation and of sequence, and holds any cessation of these as positively unthinkable, we thus observe that on every side we are confronted

---

* Of various suggestions (made from a teleological stand-point) for reversing the great law of "dissipation," and supplying to declining systems an *elixir vitæ* for their perpetual regeneration, perhaps the two most notable are those of Rankine and of Siemens.

WILLIAM J. M. RANKINE, in a paper " On the Re-concentration of the Mechanical Energy of the Universe," read before the British Association at its Belfast meeting, in September, 1852,—assuming a boundary to the æthereal medium, argues that the radiations dissipated outward, would at the limiting surface be all reflected inward to foci, at which exhausted suns would be re-kindled into incandescence, or "vaporized and resolved into their elements." (*Report Brit. Assoc.* 1852: part II,—abstracts, p. 12.— Or more fully in *L. E. D. Phil. Mag.* November, 1852: vol. IV, p. 358.)

CHARLES WILLIAM SIEMENS, in a paper " On the Conservation of Solar Energy," read before the Royal Society, March 2, 1882, assuming gaseous products of combustion to be thrown off in a dissociated form from the equatorial regions of the revolving sun, (as from a centrifugal fan,) argues that they would be constantly indrawn at the polar regions, to be reburned and again given off,—in a perpetual circulation. (*Nature.* March 9, 1882: vol. XXV. pp. 440-444.)

and beset by barriers through which no loop-hole of escape appears. The mind thus baffled and bewildered in its backward inquest through illimitable series, in which to its dismay is found at no great distance—whether in atom, or in universe,—the chasm of a strange and incomprehensible discontinuity, the inevitable transition to an entirely different order of links from those made thinkable by experience, seems driven in the last resort to the unifying induction of a single, first, eternal, and all-powerful Cause—from which all other causes are dependent and derived.

This ultimate and highest induction of scientific thought—the Inscrutable made Absolute—is restful and satisfying. This ultimate and highest induction—as highest and ultimate, cannot be manipulated as a " working hypothesis." This ultimate and highest induction—as such—cannot be subjected to the subsequent verification of mathematical deduction. This ultimate and highest induction detracts nothing from the certainty of orderly sequence so irresistibly impressed upon us by every deepening channel of research, but gives us rational ground and guarantee of such unfailing regularity. This ultimate and highest induction accepting to the uttermost the mechanical interpretation of nature's administration,—whose ceaseless evolution seems ever opening up new vistas of an automatic teleology,—gives significance to our imperfect conception of a regulated system, (so necessarily involved in the very existence and operation of a " machine,") and accounts consistently for the unfaltering obedience and instantaneous response of all the countless atoms of the universe to the reign of " law," by positing behind such law—an Infinite LAW-GIVER.

In Richard Hooker's never trite though memorable words: " Of *Law* there can be no less acknowledged than that her seat is the bosom of God, her voice the harmony of the world: all things in heaven and earth do her homage,—the very least as feeling her care, and the greatest as not exempted from her power."

226TH MEETING.   DECEMBER 16, 1882.

TWELFTH ANNUAL MEETING.

The President in the Chair.

About fifty members were present during the evening.

The President announced the usual order of exercises.

The minutes of the last annual meeting were read and approved.

The Secretary, Mr. GILL, read the list of members who had been elected since the last annual meeting.

The Treasurer read his report upon the finances and property of the Society.   (See page 180.)

The Chairman appointed as Auditing Committee, Messrs. Thomas Antisell, Benjamin Alvord, and Otis T. Mason.

The Treasurer read the roll of names of members who were entitled to vote at the election of officers.

The Society then proceeded to ballot for the election of officers, with the following result: (See next page.)

The rough minutes of the meeting were read and approved; and the meeting then adjourned.

OFFICERS

OF THE

PHILOSOPHICAL SOCIETY OF WASHINGTON.

ELECTED DECEMBER 16, 1882.

President _____ _____ J. W. POWELL.

Vice-Presidents _____ _____ J. C. WELLING,　J. E. HILGARD,

　　　　　　　　　C. H. CRANE,　J. S. BILLINGS.

Treasurer _____ _____ CLEVELAND ABBE.

Secretaries _____ _____ G. K. GILBERT,　HENRY FARQUHAR.

MEMBERS AT LARGE OF THE GENERAL COMMITTEE.

W. H. DALL,	C. E. DUTTON,
J. R. EASTMAN,	E. B. ELLIOTT,
R. FLETCHER,	WM. HARKNESS,
D. L. HUNTINGTON,	GARRICK MALLERY,

C. A. SCHOTT.

STANDING COMMITTEES.

On Communications :

J. S. BILLINGS, *Chairman.*　　G. K. GILBERT,　　HENRY FARQUHAR.

On Publications :

G. K. GILBERT, *Chairman.*　　HENRY FARQUHAR,　　CLEVELAND ABBE,
　　　　　　　　　S. F. BAIRD.*

*As Secretary of the Smithsonian Institution.

ANNUAL REPORT OF THE TREASURER.

WASHINGTON, D. C., *December* 17, 1881.

To the Philosophical Society of Washington:

Owing to the change in the time of presentation of the Treasurer's report, I have the honor to present herewith my annual statement as Treasurer for the years 1880 and 1881, showing a cash balance on December 16th, in the treasury, of three hundred and twenty dollars and sixteen cents, ($320.16.)

The investments of the Society consist of—

One United States bond, No. 4569 A, (registered,) of the funded loan 1891, for $1,000, yielding $4\frac{1}{2}$ per cent.;

One United States bond, No. 20031, (registered,) of the funded loan of 1907, for $500, yielding 4 per cent.

The further assets of the Society consist of unpaid dues amounting to about three hundred and thirty dollars, ($330.)

The active membership of the Society is to-day about one hundred and fifty-five, (155.)

The stock on hand of the publications of the Society is about as follows, by actual count:

	No. of copies.	Price to members.
Vol. I of the Bulletin	93	$2 00
II "	92	3 00
III "	182	1 00
IV "	190	1 00
Taylor's Memoir of Prof. Henry—		
1st edition	64	50
2d "	30	1 00
Welling's Memoir of Prof. Henry	4	50

The Library has lately received, by way of exchange, about fifty volumes, but these have not yet been catalogued and arranged.

Special copies of each communication that appears in the Bulletin of the Society are promptly printed for distribution by the author; the annual volumes of the Bulletin are sent usually to about 125 domestic and foreign recipients, selected with special view to the general dissemination of information as to the activity of the Society.

The distribution of stitched annual volumes, instead of individual signatures, gives general satisfaction, and is much more economical in time and labor.   Much attention is given to collecting the scattered signatures of the first volume, and thus the stock in hand of the complete volume is being slowly replenished.

Volumes I, II, and III of the Bulletin have been stereotyped and printed (with some corrections) at the expense of the Smithsonian Institution as Volume XX of the Miscellaneous Collections.   It is certainly a matter of congratulation that the Society has thus assured to it the economical, permanent, and most extensive publication of its proceedings ; and the general effect of this arrangement is to offer stronger inducements to our members to publish through this medium.

The expense to the Society of the publication of the first three volumes of the Bulletin was easily borne by reason of the slow accumulation of the funds in the treasury ; but the cost of publication of Volume IV has been entirely defrayed out of the income of the past year, and has required very nearly the whole of our receipts, so that the balance in the treasury is now only $320.16, as compared with two hundred and fourteen dollars and eighty-two cents, ($214.82) at the beginning of 1881.   The Treasurer has therefore felt himself under the necessity of distributing this volume only to members who are not in arrears.

The actual expense of the editions of 500 copies each of the respective volumes has been very nearly as follows :

Vol.	No. of signatures.	Cost per edition.	Cost per copy.
No. I	10	$386	$0 77
II	18	686	1 37
III	12	333	67
IV	12	391	78

It is therefore probable that the steady increase in the membership and work of the Society is likely soon to so increase the extent and cost of our Bulletin as to absorb our whole income.

In view of the fact that the free use of our present admirable quarters is a privilege granted by the Surgeon-General, liable at any time to be revoked, I think it important that there should always be a very considerable annual surplus to be added to the permanently-invested fund, the income of which will at some future day enable the Society to lease appropriate quarters in some central locality.

I have the honor to remain, very respectfully,

CLEVELAND ABBE, *Treasurer.*

The Philosophical Society of Washington in account with Cleveland Abbe, Treasurer.

DR.

EXPENDITURES.

Date.	Voucher.	Check.	To whom paid.	Amount.
1880.				
Jan. 29	1	36	S. N. Griffin	$8 00
Jan. 23	2	37	E. M. Whitaker	14 25
Apr. 14	3	38	Judd & Detweiler	12 50
June 29	4	39	Judd & Detweiler	43 49
July 22	5	40	C. Abbe	10 30
July 24	6	41	T. K. Collins	194 09
July 31	7	43	M. Joyce	15 50
July 28	}8	42	Judd & Detweiler	50 00
Aug. 4	9	44	C. Abbe	91 33
Aug. 4	10	45	T. K. Collins	20 00
Aug. 13	11	46	Judd & Detweiler	4 00
Aug. 31	12	47	Judd & Detweiler	13 56
Dec. 6		48	T. K. Collins	14 20
1881.				
Jan. 6	13	49	Judd & Detweiler	52 50
Jan. 26			To Balance on hand	543 72
				214 82
			Check	$758 54

CR.

ANNUAL DUES RECEIVED DURING 1880.

Date.	1877.	1878.	1879.	1880.	1881.	Total.
1880.						
Apr. 30			$15 00	$30 00		$45 00
July 24			25 00	325 00		350 00
Aug. 25	$5 00	$5 00	10 00	20 00		40 00
Oct. 27			10 00	40 00		50 00
Nov. 9				70 00	$5 00	75 00
Dec. 22			10 00	20 00	15 00	45 00
Dec. 31		$5 00	5 00	5 00	5 00	20 00
By total dues received						$625 00
By interest on invested funds:						
One $1,000 U. S. bond, yielding 4½ per cent					$45 00	
One $500 U. S. bond, yielding 4 per cent					20 00	
Total from invested bonds						65 00
By Balance carried forward from 1879						690 00
						68 54
By Total from all sources						$758 54

CR.

The Philosophical Society of Washington in account with Cleveland Abbe, Treasurer.

CR.

EXPENDITURES.

Date.	Voucher.	Check.	To whom paid.	Amount.
1881.				
March 3	1	50	Judd & Detweiler	$29 31
March 4	2	51	Judd & Detweiler	10 00
June 6	3	52	Judd & Detweiler	10 00
Oct. 10	4	53	Judd & Detweiler	250 00
Nov. 18	4	55	Judd & Detweiler	156 20
Nov. 4	5	54	C. E. Dutton	20 65
Nov. 22	6	56	C. E. Dutton	20 00
Dec. 14	7	57	C. Abbe	5 00
Dec. 15	8		F. B. Mohun	3 50
				504 66
			To Balance on hand	320 16
				$824 82

ANNUAL DUES RECEIVED DURING 1881.

Date.	1878.	1879.	1880.	1881.	1882.	Total.
Feb. 26		$5 00	$45 00	$15 00		$65 00
May 9			5 00	20 00		25 00
May 19				85 00		85 00
May 28			5 00	25 00		30 00
May 31			5 00	45 00		50 00
Sept. 30		5 00	25 00	105 00		135 00
Nov. 25				55 00		55 00
Dec. 1	$5 00	10 00	15 00	55 00		85 00
Dec. 15				15 00	$5 00	20 00

By total dues received — $550 00

By interest on invested funds:
One $1,000 U. S. bond, 4½ per cent — $45 00
One $500 U. S. bond, 4 per cent — 15 00

Total from invested funds — 60 00

By Balance carried forward from 1880 — 610 00 / 214 82

By total from all sources — $824 82

ANNUAL REPORT OF THE TREASURER.

WASHINGTON CITY, *Dec.* 16, 1882.

To the Philosophical Society of Washington:

I have the honor to present herewith my annual statement as Treasurer, covering the year ending with December 15, 1882, and showing a cash balance deposited with Riggs & Co. of $521.07. This balance is much larger than would have been the case had it not been decided to delay the publication of Volume V of the Bulletin.

The investment of the funds of the Society remains as in my last report, viz.:

One U. S. registered bond, $1,000, at $4\frac{1}{2}$ per cent.

One U. S. registered bond, $500, at 4 per cent.

The further assets of the Society consist of unpaid annual dues to the amount of $300 for 1882, and of about $200 for 1881 and earlier years.

The number of active members is now about 150; the corresponding annual income, about 800 dollars.

The stock in hand of publications remains as about as reported by me a year ago.

An accession catalogue of the library has been recently compiled. The number of volumes at present on hand is 68; these have been presented by way of exchange; and we are especially indebted to the Royal Societies of Edinburgh, of Munich, and of New South Wales, and the Literary and Philosophical Society of Manchester for long series of volumes.

      Very respectfully,

  (Signed)   CLEVELAND ABBE,

                             Treasurer.

PHILOSOPHICAL SOCIETY OF WASHINGTON. 181

DR. *The Philosophical Society of Washington in account with Cleveland Abbe, Treasurer, from Dec. 15, 1881, to Dec. 15, 1882.* CR.

EXPENDITURES.

Date.	Vou'r.	Check.	To whom paid.	Amount.
1881. Dec. —	1	59	Judd & Detweiler	$5 40
1882. Jan. 30	2	60	S. J. Waldo	3 35
Jan. 18	3	61	Marcus Baker	3 50
Feb. 8	4	62	S. F. Bartlett	4 50
March 2	5	63	Marcus Baker	3 00
Feb. 28	6	64	Judd & Detweiler	21 30
June 1	7	65	Marcus Baker	6 00
May 31	8	66	Judd & Detweiler	22 95
June 15	9	67	C. Abbe, Treasurer	7 25
June 30	10	68	Judd & Detweiler	51 53
June 30	11	69	Marcus Baker	2 00
July 14	12	70	Marcus Baker	2 00
Oct. 4	13	71	Judd & Detweiler	2 50
Oct. 11	14	72	Judd & Detweiler	161 81
Oct. 14	15	73	B. F. Brown	2 00
			Total	$379 09
			Bal. on dep't with Riggs & Co.	521 07
			Total	900 16

RECEIPTS.

From what source.	Amount.	Total.
Credit by receipts as follows: Balance carried over from December, 1881		$320 16
Annual dues received:		
and deposited December 19, 1881	$75 00	
and deposited June 30, 1882	190 00	
and deposited July 31, 1882	175 00	
and deposited December 2, 1882	75 00	
	$515 00	
Interest on invested funds, viz.:		
One $1,000 U. S. bond, at 4½ per cent	45 00	
One $500 U. S. bond, at 4 per cent	20 00	
Total receipts		580 00
Total from all sources		$900 16

We have examined this account and find the same correct and properly vouched. December 18, 1882.

Auditors: { THOMAS ANTISELL.
BENJ. ALVORD.
O. T. MASON.

INDEX.

―――

I. NAMES OF PERSONS.

Abbe, Cleveland, 37, 85, 175, 177, 180.
Alvord, Benjamin, 85, 89, 90, 106, 174.
Amici, 59.
Amidon, 83.
Ampère, 139.
Antisell, Thomas, 21, 91, 97, 98, 100, 101, 106, 174.
Arago, 43.
Aristotle, 52.
Arrow, Sir Frederick, 33.
Averani, Joseph, 42.
Avogadro, 139, 145.
Airy, George B., 128.

Baird, Prof. S. F., 175.
Baker, Marcus, 85, 88, 91, 106, 107, 108, 112.
Barker, Geo. F., 80, 82, 83, 84, 150.
Barnes, J. K., 85.
Basch, 77, 83.
Bayma, Prof. Joseph, 158.
Becquerel, A. E., 135.
Bernard, Claude, 82.
Bernstein, 58, 61, 80, 81.
Bert, Paul, 76, 83.
Billings, J. S., 85, 99, 112, 175.
Birch, 142.
Bjerknes, Prof. C. A., 150.
Blankenhorn, 75.
Bouvard, 43.
Boyle, 139.
Broca, Paul, 76, 83.
Brown, George, 34.
Burger, Franz, 47.
Busey, S. C., 117.
Byasson, 75, 82.

Chadwick, F. E., 34.
Challis, Prof. James, 128, 152, 154, 164.
Charles, 139.
Chauvenet, Prof., 88, 89.
Clark, Ezra Westcott, 101.
Clausius, 138, 139, 140.
Christie, A. S., 112.

Coffin, J. H. C., 115.
Comberousse, 89.
Comte, Auguste, 127.
Coues, Elliott, 102, 104, 118.
Crane, Dr. C. H., 175.
Croll, Prof. James, 156.
Crookes, William, 129.
Cotes, Roger, 128, 163.

Daboll, 32.
Dall, William H., 90, 98, 100, 175.
Dallas, 118.
Dalton, 139.
Daniell, 57, 61.
Darwin, Charles, 70.
Derham, Dr. W., 41, 42, 43.
Des Cartes, 64.
Diaconow, 75.
Dobson, Surgeon Major, 118, 119, 120.
Donders, 78, 84.
Doolittle, M. H., 88, 105, 107, 117.
Draper, Dr. J. W., 135.
Duane, Gen., 32, 33, 43.
Du Bois-Reymond, Emil, 57, 58, 59, 60, 61, 62, 80, 81.
Dulong, 91, 93, 140.
Dutton, C. E., 85, 100, 175.

Eastman, J. R., 85, 175.
Eliot, Charles W., 128.
Elliott, E. B., 21, 85, 91, 100, 102, 106, 107, 112, 117, 175.
Engelmann, 58, 81.
Epicurus, 52, 72.
Euler, Leonard, 128.

Farquhar, E. J., 100.
Farquhar, Henry, 97, 106, 113, 114, 125, 175.
Faure, 46, 47.
Ferrel, William, 90, 91, 101.
Fletcher, Robert, 84, 89, 175.
Foster, Michael, 60, 62, 80, 81, 82.
Frank, Francois, 76, 83.
French, Henry Flagg, 101.

Fresnel, 134.

Galen, 51, 52, 80.
Gamgee, Arthur, 59, 60, 75, 81, 82.
Gay-Lussac, 43, 139.
Gilbert, G. K., 21, 48, 84, 89, 91, 101, 108, 117, 120, 175.
Gill, Theodore N., 84, 85, 90, 98, 102, 104, 106, 117, 174.
Gley, Eugene, 78, 83.
Goode, G. B., 117.
Graham, 138.
Gray, L. C., 76, 83.
Guthrie, Prof. Fred., 150.
Guyot, Dr. Jules, 150.

Haller, A. von, 56, 61, 81.
Hahn, O., 66, 82.
Hamilton, Sir William, 163, 166, 171.
Harkness, William, 39, 85, 88, 90, 97, 98, 105, 122, 175.
Hansen, C. A., 60, 81.
Hazen, Henry Allen, 101, 108, 122.
Hegel, G. W. F., 129.
Henry, Mrs. Joseph, 97.
Henry, Joseph, 29, 32, 33, 35, 37, 39, 40, 41, 43, 44, 46, 49, 137.
Herman, L., 56, 58, 59, 61, 80, 81.
Herapath, John, 130.
Herschel, J. F. W., 94, 115, 129, 144, 152, 153, 169.
Herschel, William, 135.
Hilgard, J. E., 49, 85, 100, 117, 144, 175.
Hirn, 134.
Hirsch, 78, 84.
Hittorf, Dr. J. W., 145.
Hoffman, Dr. A. W., 166.
Hooker, Richard, 94, 173.
Hoppe-Seyler, 75.
Humboldt, 41, 43, 46.
Huntington, Dr. D. L., 112, 175.
Huxley, T. H., 78, 84.

Ivory, James, 162.

Jenkins, T. A., 32, 84.
Johnson, A. B., 23, 37, 98.
Jones, H. Bence, 75, 82.
Jordan, 118.

Kepler, 86, 146.
Knox, John J., 84, 89.
Koyl, C. H., 46.
Krönig, 138.
Kummel, Chas. Hugo, 101, 106.

Landois, L., 80.
Langley, Prof. S. P., 136.

LaPlace, 55.
LaVoisier, 55.
LeCat, 81.
LeSage, 129.
Lewes, G. H., 157.
Leibnitz, 162, 165.
Liebreich, 75.
Linnaeus, 67, 82.
Lippmann, Prof. G., 168.
Lodge, Dr. O. J., 157, 168.
Lombard, 75, 83.
Loschmidt, Joseph, 138, 141.
Lucretius, 52, 72, 126.
Ludwig, 77.

Mallery, Garrick, 85, 175.
Maloney, J. A., 47.
Mansel, 73.
Maragliano, 83.
Mariotte, 139.
Mason, O. T., 91, 174.
Mathieus, 43.
Matteucci, 59, 81.
Mayer, J. R., 59, 80, 81.
Maxwell, Prof. J. C., 128, 132, 134, 136, 138, 140, 141, 147, 149, 153, 155, 162.
Mills, C. K., 83.
Mivart, St. George, 80.
Mosler, 75, 82.
Mosso, Angelo, 77, 83.
Mussey, R. D., 100, 101, 117.

Newcomb, Simon, 85, 88.
Newton, Isaac, 86, 87, 130, 142, 146, 159, 162, 163, 164, 166, 167.
Nichol, J. P., 93, 94.

Oldenburg, Henry, 142.

Pagliani, 77.
Petit, 91, 93, 140.
Plato, 51, 52.
Plücker, Dr. J., 145.
Poinsot, Louis, 132.
Poisson, 87.
Pouillet, 91, 93, 94, 95.
Powell, J. W., 85, 100, 104, 106, 175.
Prévost, 140.
Prony, 43.
Prout, 147.

Radcliffe, C. B., 61, 81.
Rankine, W. J. M., 172.
Reynolds, Osborn, 39, 40, 44, 46.
Riggs & Co., 89.
Riley, C. V., 112, 117.
Ritter, J. W., 135.

Robison, Prof. John, 132, 155.
Rodgers, Admiral John, 102, 105.
Rollet, 83.
Rouché, 88.
Rumford, Count, 133.
Russell, Israel Cook, 101.

Savart, 100.
Schiff, Moritz, 76, 83.
Schott, C. A., 85, 175.
Schwann, 59, 81.
Secchi, Angelo, 130, 131.
Senator, H., 80.
Seppelli, 83.
Shields, Chas. W., 105, 106.
Siemens, C. W., 172.
Spencer, Herbert, 51, 62, 64, 67, 72, 73, 82, 164, 166.
Stokes, Professor, 35, 40, 41, 44, 46.
Stoney, G. J., 141.
Storer, Frank H., 128.
Stroh, August, 151.
Struebling, 75, 83.

Tait, Prof. P. G., 128, 129, 152.
Taylor, Wm. B., 21, 37, 38, 39, 85, 90, 91, 97, 100, 102, 106, 107, 112, 125, 126.

Thanhoffer, 77, 83.
Thompson, Benjamin, 133.
Thompson, Prof. Sylvanus P., 168.
Thompson, Sir William, 141.
Thudicum, 75.
Toner, J. M., 22.
Townley, Richard, 42.
Trouesart, 118.
Twining, Wm. J., 102.
Tyndal, 29, 31, 33, 41, 44, 94, 96.

Upton, Wm. Wirt, 101.

Ward, L. F., 91, 102, 105, 106.
Webb, Captain, 33.
Webster, Albert Lowry, 101.
Weinland, 66.
Welling, J. C., 39, 85, 175.
Whewell, Dr. William, 161.
White, C. A., 99, 101.
Woodward, J. J., 21, 49, 85, 102, 112.
Wollaston, W. H., 142, 144.
Workman, 83.

Young, Thomas, 134, 155.

Zeno, 158.
Zuelzer, 75, 82.

II. SUBJECTS.

Page.

Annual address of the President 49, 126
Annual Meeting of the Society 84, 174
Anomalies of sound from fog-signals, recent investigations by the Light-
House Board 23
Anomalies of sound signals 39
Artesian wells on the great plains 101
Audibility, relation of fog and snow storms to 38
Auditing Committee appointed 84, 174
         report of 89, 181

Barometric hypsometry 48
Barometric observations produced by winds, errors of 91
Beaver Tail fog-signals, November 16, 1880 24
Binary arithmetic, experiments in 125

Carré's ice machine 100
Circle equally distant from four points, geometrical problem to determine a 88
Climate, Quaternary, of the Great Basin 21
Coins and medals of national historic interest exhibited 22
Committee, general 14
         general, standing rules of 10
         standing 14
         fills vacancies 115
Compass plant 106
Constitution 6
Credit of the United States, past, present, and prospective 102

Eclipse, lunar, of June 11, 1881 90
Electric energy, storage of 46
Error from single causes of error, composition of 106

Fallacy, curious, as to the theory of gravitation 85
Fisheries of the world 117
Fog, relation of, to audibility 38
Fog-signals, anomalies of sound from 23
Fog-signals, Beaver Tail 24
Fog-signal tests at Little Gull Island, July 11 26

Geometrical problem to determine a circle equally distant from four points 88
Geometrical question relating to spheres 107
Government securities, accrued interest on 21
         some formulæ relating to 106
Graphic table for computation 120-122
Gravitation, a curious fallacy as to the theory of 85
Great Basin, Quaternary climate of 21
Great Plains, artesian wells on the 101

                                                                      Page.
Halo, remarkable, witnessed at Washington, June 15 _____   112
High wind as a probable cause of the retardation of storm-centres at
     elevated stations _____   108
House of Representatives, ventilation of _____   99
Hypsometry, barometric_____   48

Ice machine, Carré's _____   100
Interest, accrued, on government securities _____   21

Library of the Society _____ 176, 180
Life, organic compounds in their relation to_____   91
Life, modern philosophical conceptions of _____   46
Little Gull Island, July 11, fog-signal tests _____   26
              July 15, 1881, observations at_____   28
              August 9, 1881, observations at_____   30
              August 10, 1881, observations at _____   32
Lunar Eclipse of June 11, 1881 _____   90

Mammals, on the classification of insectivorous_____ 118–120
Members, list of_____   15
Mollusks, some peculiar features of, found at great depths_____   90

Officers of the Society _____ 14, 85, 176
Order, philosophical, of sciences_____   105
Organic compounds in their relations to life_____   91
Organic matter, building up of _____   97

Panorama, exhibition of a photographic print including 140 degrees of___   21
Power Circle, some of the properties of Steiner's_____   89
Protoplasm, possibilities of_____   102
Publication of the Bulletin, rules for the_____   13

Quaternary climate of the Great Basin _____   21

Ravages, peculiar, of Teredo navalis_____   98

Sciences, philosophical order of_____   105
Sherman, Wyoming, solar radiation at_____   101
Shoes, influence of high-heeled _____   117
Siemen's deep-sea thermometer_____   100
Snow-storms, relation of, to audibility _____   38
Solar radiation_____   101
Solar parallax, relative accuracy of different methods of determining____   39
Sound, anomalies of, from fog-signals_____   23
Sound signals, anomalies of _____   39
Spheres, geometrical, question relating to _____   107
Storage of electric energy _____   46

Page.

Storm-centres, retardation of, at elevated stations_____ 108

Standard time, a system of _____112–117

Standing rules, constitution, list of officers and members_____ 5

       for the government of the Philosophical Society of Wash-

          ington_____ 7

       of the General Committee_____ 10

Steiner's Power-Circle, some of the properties of_____ 89

Survivorships on_____ 122

Temperature, conditions determining_____ 90, 91

Teredo navalis, peculiar ravages of_____ 98

Thermometer, Siemen's deep-sea_____ 100

Treasurer of the society, annual report of _____ 176, 180

United States, credit of, past, present, and prospective_____ 102

Ventilation of the House of Representatives _____ 99

Washington, remarkable halo witnessed at _____ 112

Wind, errors of barometric observations, produced by _____ 91

Winter weather, on the prediction of_____122–125